ONLY THE BEST IS GOOD ENOUGH

ONLY THE BEST IS GOOD ENOUGH

The Howard Kendall Story

HOWARD KENDALL and IAN ROSS

MAINSTREAM
PUBLISHING

EDINBURGH AND LONDON

Dedicated to the memory of my late father, Jack, without whose encouragement and guidance very little would have been possible.

Acknowledgements: Thanks to Colin Wood, Phil McNulty, Terry Mealey, Marj Hesk, *Liverpool Daily Post* and *Echo* picture library.

First published in Great Britain 1991 by
MAINSTREAM PUBLISHING COMPANY (EDINBURGH) LTD
7 Albany Street
Edinburgh EH1 3UG

ISBN 1 85158 486 2

A catalogue record for this book is available from the British Library

Typeset in 11/13pt Plantin by Blackpool Typesetting Services Ltd, Blackpool
Printed in Great Britain by Butler & Tanner Ltd, Frome and London

CONTENTS

CHAPTER ONE

The Long and Winding Road

It is difficult to recount tales of my childhood without painting the wholly predictable picture of a young boy with his badly worn football boots anchored to the ground while his mind bathed in the lavish fantasy of a fanciful world of success, fame and fortune.

It is, of course, quite wrong to believe that every male under the age of ten years is possessed by the desire to become a professional footballer, but I would venture to suggest that a very high percentage of adolescents do, at one time or another, actively flirt with the idea of pursuing a career within a game which manages to retain a compelling appeal despite a deserved reputation for ruthlessness and lack of sentiment.

Even now, I cannot agree with those people—and there are many—who say that footballers are born, not made. There are those hugely talented schoolboy players who fall by the wayside and look on in disbelief as the sport's honest journeymen emerge from positions of relative obscurity to sweep up the big prizes.

The vital ingredient has always been, and will always be, sheer hard work. If endeavour is allied to a sense of purpose and a basic talent, however raw, much can be achieved. This is not to say that players with an instinctive, almost God-given, gift for football do not occasionally make the grade because they do, but so often latent talent is wasted and potential unfulfilled.

There have been many celebrated English players who have fallen into this category over the past 25 years but listing them here would be a futile exercise for they know who they are and they do not need me to remind them that life is short and that a failure to seize, with both hands, a gilt-edged opportunity ultimately leads to a sense of deep regret.

At the risk of introducing an early cliché, I must say that I felt I was born to be a football player. I cannot remember one stage during my formative years when the target was not to secure a full contract with one of the country's leading clubs. The idea of growing up to be a train driver, or running away to join a travelling circus, never entered my mind, but in all honesty I can place hand on heart and say that I have never met anyone who envisaged his future either behind the controls of the *Flying Scotsman* or beneath the canvas of the big top. That is a quite ridiculous notion which should be treated with the suspicion and disrespect it deserves.

I was born on 22 May 1946, in Ryton-on-Tyne, not that my entry into the world dramatically affected the lives of anyone outside of my immediate family. It would be trite to say that "times were hard", because, while life in the North-east was far from being a bed of roses, I was blessed with a caring, affectionate family, one which closed ranks in times of trouble and which provided assistance and support upon request.

A love of football was prevalent within my family but it was not until my cousin, Harry Taylor, signed for Newcastle United that we could boast a professional player within the clan. My father, Jack, who died in 1978, was an enthusiast and played for Crawcrook Albion in one of the local leagues. From my earliest days as a promising youngster he did everything he could to assist me. His advice, his help was invaluable. It is doubtful that I would have achieved what I have within football had he not been at my side when I most needed him.

Like most young men in the area at that time, my father was a miner but, after being advised to curtail an uneasy relationship with life at the pit-face on health grounds, he became the caretaker at Mowden Hall, Newton, a private boarding school near Hexham in Northumberland. The familes of those who worked at the school lived in nearby lodges but we were only allowed to mix freely with those in the "posh" blazers once a year, on sports day.

Like most boys, I picked up the basics of football at a tender age, aided, inevitably, by my father who spent hours teaching me how to control and trap a ball. If I arrived home from school with my right shoe noticeably more dirty than my left, he would take me to task. He wasn't concerned about the condition of my footwear, he simply believed that footballers should be proficient with both feet.

The sense of discipline which I always tried to display as a professional was drilled into me at an early age for as soon as I started to fool about, my father would call a halt to his impromptu training sessions and head back indoors. He took things seriously and, after a time, so did I. On Sundays one of my uncles, who ran a junior team, would come over and the three of us would spend hours just kicking a ball around. Their enthusiasm was such that they could have been my own age.

The relocation of our family home to Washington did nothing to disrupt my learning process; indeed, my father continued to coach me until the day I left to join Preston North End as a 15-year-old.

Although he never said as much, I know that my father would have given almost anything to play the game at the highest level. It is nice to think that, perhaps, through me, he was able to realise at least some of his dreams and aspirations.

My mother was also a major influence if in a quieter, more restrained way. She did not want me to leave grammar school to join Preston but when she saw the look of determination on my face she withdrew her objections and gave me all the support I needed. My mother even went to London for the first FA Cup final I ever attended, the game between Bolton Wanderers and Manchester United in 1958. I say went to London rather than went to Wembley because as I sat entranced watching Nat Lofthouse score the two goals which took the Cup back to Burnden Park, my mother was in the city centre, shopping.

After passing my 11-plus, I attended Washington Grammar School where, I am reliably informed, I was a contemporary of Bryan Ferry, the former Roxy Music singer. To be honest I don't remember him and it is highly unlikely that he has any recollection of me.

On my 13th birthday, I was selected to play for the Chester-le-Street district team and while that was to be my only appearance for the side that season, I was a regular only a few months later. Things began to move quickly for me and after working my way into the county team, I was selected to take part in the first of the inter-national trials—the North against the North Midlands at Stockton. We lost the game 5-0 but I had obviously impressed someone and I was chosen for the next round in the schoolboy elimination process—the North v South trial.

We won 2-0 and I moved on to the England team with, among others, Peter Storey (Arsenal), Glyn Pardoe (Manchester City), John Sissons (West Ham United and Sheffield Wednesday) and Alan Ogley (Manchester City).

The final trial match was against the Rest, probables against possibles, I suppose you could call it, and we won 4-2. I was unsure whether I had done enough to win a place in the team for the season's first international against Wales but, thankfully, I had. I became something of a celebrity back home, even appearing on Tyne Tees Television shortly before leaving for the game which was held in Swansea.

We defeated Wales 7–3 but I was unhappy in the dressing-room afterwards. If that one game did nothing else, it brought home to me just how competitive a sport football can be when the element of desperation is introduced. I was not an aggressive, go-ahead type of a person at the time. Unfortunately, practically everybody else out on the pitch that night seemed hell-bent on impressing the watching selectors. They succeeded where I failed and I was never to win another schoolboy cap.

*   *   *   *

The first football jersey I ever owned was red and white, the colours of Sunderland, but because my cousin, Harry, was on the books of rivals Newcastle United, it was they who became my team; my passion.

Harry was a talented, unselfish player but I don't feel that he was ever given the chance to make a name for himself at St James Park and it was no real surprise to me when eventually he moved down south, joining Fulham before dropping down into non-league football.

I don't think I have ever enjoyed watching football as much as I did through the eyes of a child. Saturday afternoons were always something so very special: an event which was eagerly anticipated all week long. Although I attended matches to laud praise on my own sporting heroes, my father was insistent that I should also study carefully the performances of those players in opposition. He said that much could be learned from observation and he was, as usual, correct.

At that time, Newcastle had what I firmly believe to have been one of the greatest inside-forward trios of all time in George Eastham, Ivor Allchurch and Len White. I marvelled at their ability to blend together in a way which suggested that telepathy was not so much an unfounded rumour as an exact science. The way in which those three men played football elevated the game to new levels as far as I was concerned. Those were great days to watch Newcastle even if they did fail to win the trophies which their occasional brilliance deserved.

10

Although United was my first love, I often flirted with Sunderland, travelling to Roker Park with my friends if only to marvel at Charlie Hurley who was one of the finest centre-backs ever to grace a football field.

Reflecting on those boyhood heroes now, it is interesting to note that not one of them was a Geordie. That is not to suggest that the region has not exported its fair share of quality players down the years because it has. Football is still in the blood up there and these days there is scarcely a dressing-room in the Football League which is not illuminated by a raucous North-east accent.

It is no reflection on the school I was attending, or the teachers therein, but I simply couldn't wait to bid a fond farewell to my studies. At the time, leaving school as a 15-year-old constituted something of a gamble but I thought it to be the right decision then and I know it to have been the right decision now. As soon as the scouts began to turn up at the Kendall household I knew my school days were numbered. My world was football-shaped and nothing was going to stand in my way—come hell or high water.

Several clubs showed a keen interest in me, including Arsenal, Birmingham City and Middlesbrough. My two local sides, Newcastle and Sunderland, were also anxious to see my name upon apprentice professional forms but both had the habit of signing up a number of local lads, a policy which severely restricted a youngster's chances of making progress through often overcrowded ranks.

One club, which I shall not name, even went so far as to offer my father a financial inducement to encourage my signing. They were immediately placed on an unofficial blacklist. My father's attitude was that I could not be bought. He said that we would take our time, look around and then decide. That is exactly what we did.

Preston North End had a scout in the area called Reg Keating who had monitored my progress carefully over a considerable length of time and who had become something of a family friend. We had promised him that before we agreed anything with anybody, we would visit Deepdale and take a look around the place.

We travelled down to Preston to run the rule over the club while still suspecting that my immediate future would lie elsewhere. The week after I had returned home from Preston, Arsenal invited me down to Highbury for a trial but they were too late—my mind was made up. After Jimmy Milne, the Preston manager, had come up to discuss things with my father, and allay my mother's fears about

11

the life I would be leading away from parental control, I agreed to join the club as an apprentice.

After moving to North Lancashire I was lonely, which was hardly surprising bearing in mind my tender years. I used to write home three or four times a week, always enclosing the local football paper for my father to scrutinise. The club provided me with free travel vouchers so that I could return to Tyneside once a month and even now I can vividly remember Carlisle station and those seemingly interminable waits for my connection.

It wasn't all football at this stage for Preston was rightly proud of its reputation for training the minds, as well as the bodies, of its apprentices. I attended night school where I studied English, mathematics and book-keeping, the latter interesting me a good deal more than I thought it would.

The main problem encountered by all the young players was the boredom of having little or nothing to do on the afternoons when there was not a scheduled training session. I spent some time hanging around various snooker halls before taking a course in ladies' hairdressing in Manchester. I was quite useful with a pair of scissors but hardly proficient enough to quit football and open a salon. I filled my spare time in any way I could, often visiting the cinema two or three times a week, irrespective of what was being screened.

My first wage packet at Preston contained the princely sum of around £7 and although £3.50 had to be handed over to cover the cost of my digs, I still had enough left over to enjoy myself *AND* buy some Post Office savings certificates.

When I joined Preston, they had promised that if I was offered, and accepted, full-time professional terms on turning 17, they would bring my family down to the area to live with me. This was something of an unusual arrangement for most clubs did this only for married players. The club was as good as its word and shortly after turning pro, my parents moved down to join me. It must have been a terrible wrench for them to leave behind family and friends but it was a typical display of loyalty and unity, one which I greatly appreciated.

Apprentices did not get the same holiday entitlement as the seasoned professionals and as the seniors departed for the beaches of Spain and Italy, we were kept on at Deepdale to help with essential ground maintenance. Even so, I still managed to get back to the North-east for six weeks where I would spend as much time as possible playing cricket for Philadelphia, who were in the Durham Senior League. I turned out for them at junior, third team, second team and first team level and at one point it was suggested that I should consider channelling all my efforts into cricket and not football.

Philadelphia was a good, solid breeding ground for young talent with a reputation for producing players of county standard. Indeed, several of my contemporaries went on to play at a higher level—Peter Graham, Ronnie Miller and Kenny Miller joined Warwickshire and Stephen Greensword went to Leicestershire. I retain my fondness for the game to this day and I still don the pads occasionally for charity games.

CHAPTER TWO

From Deepdale to Goodison (via Wembley)

Preston's relegation from the First Division shortly before I joined the club in August 1961 had not been well-received by supporters who, quite rightly, felt that a slump in fortune was totally inexcusable. There was no great feeling of depression within the club itself—certainly not in the dressing-room—but there was dismay and apprehension out on the terraces and I think everyone was fully aware of the importance of launching a sustained assault on promotion during the following season.

I started that season in the B team which is not quite as glamorous as it may sound as it was in fact the fourth team. I spent most of that term playing in the Lancashire League but I was a member of the youth side which defeated Blackburn Rovers 4–1 in an important cup-tie. I remember the encouragement which I took from a local newspaper report which said: "Right-half, Howard Kendall, an England schoolboy international from Durham played the Blanchflower type of attacking game in constantly prodding the right wing." It seemed strange to read those words because Danny Blanchflower was one of the players I had studied so closely as a child in a bid to improve my basic technique.

There was a great deal of enthusiasm for youth football in the Preston area at the time and that particular match attracted 3,441 spectators—a figure which most Fourth Division clubs, and many Third Division clubs, would regard as more than satisfactory today.

In the first round proper of the competition we were paired with Crewe Alexandra and I was to learn that in football, particularly in cup football, nothing at all can be taken for granted. Complacency was the big enemy then in much the same way as it is today. We had beaten Crewe 5–1 in the previous season but they surprised us by holding out for a goalless draw at Deepdale. We applied ourselves with more gusto in the replay at Gresty Road and won 2–1.

15

Sadly, we went out to Blackpool in the next round, losing 2–1 in a replay at Deepdale after drawing 3–3 at Bloomfield Road.

Later that season, I made a few appearances for the A team before reaching a landmark on 2 April 1962, when I made my first appearance for the reserve team in a Central League fixture against Stoke City. There were more reserve games towards the end of the season and I played against a Leeds United side which included a very young Norman Hunter. He wore the number 11 shirt but he did not look cut out to be a delicate left-winger.

I was still confined to the reserves at the start of the following season but at least this life in the shadows—a process of natural progression which I was more than content to accept—did give the opportunity to play at Goodison Park for the first time. Even though it was practically deserted, it was a wonderful place to play football. I marvelled at the superb playing surface and the expansive stands. I still do so today.

The 1962–63 season will always be remembered for the big freeze which threw the Football League programme into absolute chaos. The inevitable backlog of fixtures proved to be to my benefit.

As we entered May there were still several outstanding fixtures to be fulfilled and with the recovery period between matches drastically reduced, senior players began to pick up injuries. I was unexpectedly called into the first-team squad for a game against Newcastle United at St James Park.

I had been away with the seniors on several occasions to gain experience so I was not unduly excited even if the prospect of a trip back to my native North-east was warming. After arriving in Newcastle the manager announced his starting line-up and astonishingly I was in it. There it was, number six, H. Kendall. It seemed inconceivable that I should be making my League debut against the team I had supported for so long.

I rushed around like a man possessed, collecting as many tickets for the match as I could find. I was determined that anyone who knew me from the old days who wanted to be there, would be there. I was delirious with joy, before, during and after the game even if the critics were slightly less enthusiastic about my contribution to a game which was, in truth, a typical end-of-season encounter.

My manager was obviously as pleased as I was with my performance because he kept me in the first team for our next game, against Middlesborough. I was injured at Ayresome Park and was still on the casualty list when the season drew its last breath.

It is often said that footballers and managers are like women in so much as they have a tendency to lie about their age. I could never attempt this particular ploy with any measure of success for it is in the record books that on 2 May 1964, at the age of 17 years and 345 days I became the youngest player ever to appear in an FA Cup final when I played against West Ham United.

A season which was to end in such dramatic fashion for me started quietly, in the reserve team to be precise. Although I had accepted full professional terms on my 17th birthday, a settled

Three days before the 1964 FA Cup final against West Ham and not a sign of nerves . . . (with Preston North End as a 17-year-old)

17

Preston side was enjoying welcome success, so restricting my chances of senior football.

Our progress in the League was steady rather than spectacular but we were given little hope of progressing beyond the third round of the FA Cup after being drawn against Nottingham Forest at the City ground. However, knock-out football back in the Sixties was every bit as unpredictable as it is today and we secured a goalless draw with a display of resolute defending.

Not having figured in the first game, I was not expecting to be involved at Deepdale so I was surprised to be withdrawn from the youth team squad which was preparing for a game against Manchester City at Maine Road and told to link up with the first team. Jimmy Smith had failed to recover from injury and I was the one selected to take his place.

Despite a fierce snowstorm a crowd of around 30,000 gathered to watch two evenly matched sides fail to score during the opening 90 minutes. Three minutes into a period of extra-time, I moved forward to support an attack and found the ball at my feet some 25 yards from goal. I just hit it, as they say, and in it went. It was the only goal of the game and we were through to a fourth-round meeting with Bolton Wanderers, our near-neighbours.

I awoke the next morning to find that the popular press had christened me the "KO Kid". I felt so happy that they could have called me whatever they wanted.

I retained my place for the Bolton tie which we won 2-1 in a replay at Deepdale after drawing 2-2 at Burnden Park. A goal by Alan Spavin was sufficient to dispose of Carlisle United in the next round and although I didn't figure in our quarter-final tie against Oxford United at the Manor Ground because of injury, my absence was hardly noticeable and we won 2-1.

The other clubs through to the semi-finals that year were Swansea City, Manchester United and West Ham United. Swansea, although they had managed to knock out Liverpool, at Anfield, in the sixth round were struggling near to the foot of the Second Division. They were the ones we wanted and they were the ones we got. The draw served to strengthen the belief that this just could be Preston's year.

I still wasn't fit enough to be considered but I shared the jubilation of each and every Preston supporter at Villa Park when Tony Singleton scored the only goal with a spectacular, long-range shot.

Even when I was recalled to the first team for a game against Northampton the week before the final, I did not give much

Howard Kendall pictured at the organ prior to the Preston–West Ham Cup final

The price of fame! After my appearance in the 1964 Cup final I'm something of a celebrity and am invited to judge a beauty competition in Blackpool

Face to face with an idol. Watched by Preston manager, Jimmy Milne, I listen intently to Danny Blanchflower

thought to my chances of playing at Wembley. It was inconceivable that a somewhat naïve 17-year-old would achieve something which so many seasoned players had failed to achieve during the course of long, illustrious careers. Naturally, I lived in hope, but that is all it was—hope.

As the town became enveloped in what is popularly referred to as Cup fever, I made my way to the ground on the Wednesday before the final. The team sheet was pinned up in the dressing-room and astonishingly my name was included.

We were taken up to the club gymnasium for a team photograph which, for publicity purposes, was to feature each member of the team sitting astride a rocking horse. I instinctively went up to Ian Davidson, the regular first-team player whom I had replaced in the game against Northampton, and said: "Go on, sit down. It's your place."

He replied: "No, it's yours." We stared at each other for a split-second before both of us burst into floods of tears. My joy, unconfined though it was, had been tempered by the disappointment I could see etched across Ian's face.

20

It was not until the following morning that the full reasons behind my unexpected selection became clear. Ian had dropped out of the team to play Northampton on compassionate grounds after claiming that he had to return to his native Scotland to attend a funeral.

Deepdale was besieged by the media who sensed a scandal just three days before English football's most prestigious occasion. It fell to Alan Harrison, the Preston Chairman, to explain the circumstances behind Ian's non-appearance on the team sheet.

"Davidson was chosen to play in the home game with Northampton last Saturday but was given leave of absence after informing the manager of a bereavement and asking to be allowed to attend the funeral in Edinburgh. The reasons Davidson had given were found to be untrue. The manager reported the facts to the board and he agreed that they had no option but to suspend the player," he said.

Even after learning the facts, I was not sure that I felt any better about taking Ian's place at Wembley but my mind was slightly more settled as we set off for our pre-final headquarters in Weybridge.

Twenty-four hours before the game itself, we visited Wembley to try and get the feel of this country's most imposing stadium. It was the first time I had ever set foot on the famous turf and I was impressed. It resembled a billiard table.

I was never a player who had to resort to sleeping pills before important matches and I slept well that night, blissfully unaware of the nervous anxiety which would hold me firmly in its grip the following afternoon.

The journey to the ground was pleasant but the tension within our dressing-room was more than a little apparent. I busied myself during these anxious moments by reading some of the dozens of telegrams which were set out in neat piles before us. One of them was from Cliff Bastin who, until that day, was the youngest-ever FA Cup final player after appearing for Arsenal against Huddersfield Town in 1930. It was a nice touch.

The silence was eventually pierced by the shrill of a bell which was designed not to frighten us, but to inform us that we should prepare ourselves for the grand entrance.

In the tunnel, I looked across to the West Ham team and saw John Sissons with whom I had played schoolboy and youth team football not so very long ago.

We were the obvious underdogs but I felt we played very well against one of England's more accomplished sides. We certainly

21

I can only look on as Ronnie Boyce scores the winning goal for West Ham United in the 1964 FA Cup final against Preston

Howard Kendall, Alex Dawson and Brian Godfrey relaxing the night before the FA Cup final Preston v West Ham

settled quicker and fully deserved a lead given to us by Dougie Holden, the left-winger I had watched help Bolton win the Cup six years earlier. Sissons, a man I had long appreciated as both a friend and as a footballer, levelled the scores with a goal which I did not appreciate at all before Alex Dawson ensured that we would lead at the interval with a firm header. Geoff Hurst restored the status quo shortly after half-time and as the game drifted into injury time, two tired teams began to conserve energy in readiness for an extra 30 minutes.

That was the way I read the situation but sadly my judgement was faulty. Peter Brabrook, one of West Ham's better players, crossed the ball and Ronnie Boyce lunged forward to knock the ball beyond our goalkeeper, Alan Kelly, who had been carrying an injury for much of the afternoon. The final whistle sounded shortly afterwards to curtail any thoughts of a recovery.

Traditionally, losers' banquets are about as lively as are wakes but, I must admit, I had a wonderful time and even managed to enjoy the cabaret which was provided by Des O'Connor, the Vernon Girls and The Batchelors. Inebriated by the events of the day, I was content to drink nothing stronger than orange squash all night long.

The scenes which greeted us on our return home were remarkable as thousands upon thousands assembled to mark what was in truth a fine achievement. One paper said it was akin to Beatlemania. I enjoyed myself so much I considered selling my boots and buying a guitar.

Although defeat at Wembley was a bitter pill to swallow, the 1963–64 season was one of the most memorable of my entire career because I managed to realise the dream of every youngster by captaining my country. After forcing my way into the England Youth side, I was made skipper as we prepared for the defence of the so-called "Little World Cup", the 24-nation European youth tournament which England had won the previous year.

The tournament was staged in Holland that year and after qualifying from our group at the expense of Poland and the Republic of Ireland, we defeated Czechoslovakia and Portugal to set up a showdown in the final against Spain. On 5 April 1964, I proudly led out the England team in Amsterdam's Olympic Stadium. We won convincingly, 4–0, and returned home in triumph to find ourselves labelled as the "Young masters of Europe".

After a relaxing summer break during which I learned a great

Howard Kendall as a newcomer to the Under-23 England squad

deal about how to handle the media, I returned to Deepdale, grimly determined to play my part in restoring Preston's First Division status.

After finishing third the previous season, behind Leeds United and Sunderland, we were reasonably confident of laying claim to a promotion place but, after a promising start, results began to fall away, our confidence subsided and we could only finish the season in mid-table.

The FA Cup, which had proved to be such a source of joy a few months earlier, was an equally inhospitable environment and we were eliminated in the fourth round by Bolton Wanderers.

Consolation, from a personal viewpoint, came when I was selected to go with a Football Association party to Gibraltar. Under the watchful eye of Alf Ramsey, we won the two games we played and I managed a goal in each.

Our disappointment made us all the more determined to impress during the 1965–66 season but while I felt the side to be well-balanced, we continued to struggle despite playing some attractive football. We finished the season closer to the foot of the table than to its summit and that was instrumental in my questioning whether

24

I would ever realise my dream of playing First Division football with Preston North End.

My affection for a club which had been gracious enough to grant me entry into an envious profession had not waned in the slightest but I was young, ambitious and worried by the club's apparent fascination with taking two steps forward and three steps back.

At the start of the 1966–67 season, my thoughts were once again exclusively centred on Preston. I worked hard and I don't think that anyone could have faulted my attitude, or questioned my commitment, during the months which were to follow—months which were filled with transfer requests and incessant media speculation about my long-term future.

Everton was one of the first clubs to be linked with me although Harry Catterick would never confirm, nor deny, his interest. As I discovered later, that was very much Harry's way.

I didn't quite know what to make of it all but if the press reports were to be believed Liverpool and Tottenham Hotspur were the favourites to lure me away from Deepdale eventually with Stoke City and Southampton both fancied outsiders.

I finally decided to act and, after a family conference, it was agreed that I should submit an official transfer request. My father and I drafted a letter which outlined not only my limitless ambition but also my deep affection for Preston. My manager, Jimmy Milne, called me into his office and informed me that the board had rejected my request and that I would be staying.

Undeterred, I drew up a second letter. It was delivered and promptly rejected on the grounds that Preston would need me to help sustain an assault on promotion.

What should have been a relatively straightforward process was developing into a thoroughly unpleasant saga although I do believe that the Preston supporters fully understood my reasons for wanting to leave Deepdale.

Obviously, I was keen on joining Liverpool but while I was in Newcastle with the England Under-23 squad, I learned that Bill Shankly had bought Emlyn Hughes from Blackpool. I was disappointed because I knew that it was highly unlikely that even a club of Liverpool's considerable wealth would sign two young midfield players in one season.

My situation at Preston changed swiftly after an off-the-record conversation with a journalist I had previously trusted was splashed across the pages of a national newspaper. The Chairman was upset by my comments and said that he would "look into" the question of my two failed transfer requests.

That same night Jimmy Milne turned up on our doorstep and announced that a club had come in for me and were willing to back up their interest with a firm bid. I thought it must be Liverpool but it wasn't—it was Everton. Whether or not Harry Catterick was worried about another club coming in with a more substantial eleventh-hour bid, I don't know, but he was waiting for us at Deepdale when we arrived.

The two of us were left alone to discuss personal terms, signing-on fees and exactly what position I would fill, if selected. Harry was anxious to wrap up the deal there and then but my father said there was no real need to rush things as Everton's weekend fixture was an FA Cup tie and I was ineligible, having already played in the competition for Preston.

I travelled down to Merseyside the following day to take a look at what Everton had to offer, arriving at Goodison Park in my car, an MGB GT which unfortunately was red in colour. I was quickly to learn my first lesson about the fanaticism of the local people as regards football. Harry took one look at my pride and joy and said: "Either get it resprayed or prepare for the worst. You've no idea what they are like down here." I heeded his sound advice and within a week I had swapped it for a blue model. I'm not sure what the exact shade was but I think it was called Diplomatic Blue.

I didn't have much hesitation in agreeing to join Everton and I was not slow to complete an £80,000 deal just in time to beat the transfer deadline. The timing of the transfer was significant, although I didn't fully appreciate it at the time, for it was completed on the eve of one of football's great occasions—an all-Mersey FA Cup tie.

The interest in the game was such that the kick-off was moved back until 7.30 p.m. to accommodate a live TV screening at Anfield. More than 100,000 paying spectators at the two grounds witnessed a memorable spectacle.

My parents and I were given the full VIP treatment in the directors' box at Goodison Park that night and mercifully a 48-hour period which had its roots in sheer fantasy was not soured at the death. Alan Ball, the stranger who was to become a firm friend, saw to that by scoring the only goal of the game to guarantee my new club's passage through into the quarter-finals.

I found the Everton players to be a friendly, humourous bunch and I settled in quickly, thanks in no small part to Jimmy Gabriel, the man who returned to the club shortly before I started my second spell as manager in 1990.

Ironically, it was Jimmy's place I took in the side when I made my debut in an Everton shirt on 18 March 1967, against Southampton at Goodison. It is difficult to imagine that my new career could have had a less auspicious beginning. I missed an open goal from about two yards out, made numerous mistakes and, on the whole, contributed very little during the course of a 1–0 defeat. Someone, quite possibly me, had not read the script properly.

On the way back home, I stopped at a nearby garage to get some petrol and was recognised by two supporters who made their way towards my car. Mindful of my totally inadequate performance, I was a little concerned as to what exactly it was they wanted. I was staggered when they went down on their hands and knees in the middle of a large, muddy puddle as if to pay homage. I was an Everton player and that meant everything to them. In true scouse style, I received a letter from one of those lads just a few days later cheekily asking for a couple of free tickets for our next home game.

It took me quite a while to adapt to life at a big city club. I found the training difficult and the switch from defence, where I had played for Preston, to midfield a good deal more demanding than I had anticipated. Gradually, the extra work I was putting in out on the training pitch began to pay dividends and I began to feel that, at last, I was justifying my transfer fee.

Football has a nasty habit of turning around and slapping you in the face when you are at your most buoyant and I sustained a bad hamstring injury during a game at Chelsea which all but ended my season. I didn't take a holiday during that first summer at Everton, preferring instead to work my way back to peak fitness in readiness for a new season. I still had much to prove and I was determined that any shortcomings could not be attributed to lack of general fitness.

CHAPTER THREE

Giving the People What They Want

I know all too well what it is like to be a two-time loser as a player in an FA Cup final. To suggest that the experience is unpleasant would be a gross understatement. Losing once at Wembley is bad enough; losing a second time is, if anything, even worse. Having been beaten as a 17-year-old with Preston, I was then beaten as a 21-year-old when West Bromwich Albion overcame Everton at the end of the 1967–68 season. That I never made it back a third time to collect a winners' medal is one of my great regrets in football.

Of course, I was fortunate enough to lead Everton to just such a triumph as manager in 1984 but by the summer of 1986 I had become a two-time loser as a manager as well, thanks, if that is an appropriate word, to Manchester United and Liverpool.

Many players who have been fortunate enough to be members of a Cup-winning side will tell you they felt as if they were fated to achieve success in the most unpredictable of competitions; they suspected their club's name was on the famous old trophy many months before the engraver was called upon to undertake his annual ritual.

I know for a fact that several of those who played in the Everton side which defeated Sheffield Wednesday in 1966 felt that way and I was similarly convinced that we would enjoy a prolonged and successful run in August of 1967. I suppose this feeling of confidence was only to be expected because I knew that we had a more than useful side, something which was confirmed on the opening day of the season when we defeated Manchester United, the defending League champions, 3–1 at Goodison Park.

That particular road to Wembley actually began on my own doorstep as we were drawn away to Southport, then of the Third Division. At the time, I lived far closer to their Haig Avenue ground than I did to Goodison Park.

The tie proved to be something of a grand reunion, for Southport boasted several former Everton players in a senior squad which was particularly strong for a club which was outside of the top two divisions. Alex Parker, Arthur Pleat, Alex Russell, Amby Clarke, Stuart Shaw, Eric Curwen and Dave Pearson had all been on Everton's books at one time or another. Oh yes, their manager was one Billy Bingham who was later to prove that it was not all one-way traffic between the two clubs.

The build-up to a game which was eagerly anticipated on a parochial level but virtually ignored by the rest of the footballing world, was so intense that you would have thought a place in the final itself was at stake. We anticipated a tough game and we were not to be disappointed. In some respects, Southport could be said to be tactical pioneers for on that afternoon they used the long-ball game to telling effect. They simply pumped the ball high into the midst of our defence in the hope of forcing an error. We held firm and booked our passage through into the next round when Joe Royle scored, late on, with a fine header.

The fourth-round draw was no kinder—Carlisle United at Brunton Park. Another tricky game. Again it was difficult and again we were indebted to big Joe who scored a stunning goal after Jimmy Husband had given us the lead.

In the fifth round we were paired with either Coventry City or Tranmere Rovers at Goodison. Rovers, our neighbours from Birkenhead, had done remarkably well to hold First Division City to a draw at Highfield Road. The entire Everton squad was in attendance when they won the replay 2-0 at Prenton Park.

Sadly for Rovers, George Yardley, the country's leading goal-scorer at the time, was injured shortly before the tie and as a result of his absence, opponents who, on paper at least, were potentially dangerous posed only a limited threat. Even so, we struggled to underline our superiority and, but for the precise finishing of Royle and Johnny Morrissey, we could easily have found ourselves embroiled in a replay.

We were sent on our travels once again in the sixth round, this time to Filbert Street, the home of a Leicester City side which had a justifiable reputation for attractive football. What a fine game that one was. We survived several very uncomfortable moments before running out deserved 3-1 winners.

With Liverpool being involved in the draw for the semi-finals after holding West Bromwich Albion to a goalless draw in their quarter-final at The Hawthorns, the talk began to turn to the possibility of a first-ever all-Mersey FA Cup final. The city was ablaze with anticipation.

The other two teams definitely through to the last four were Leeds United and Birmingham City. We desperately wanted to avoid Leeds but that was the team we got.

As the game at Old Trafford drew nearer, we suffered one body-blow after another. Alan Ball was ruled out through suspension, John Hurst was laid low by a jaundice complaint and several other experienced players were complaining of minor injury problems. Despite our self-belief, the omens were not good.

We discussed a variety of tactical ploys in the days leading up to the game and it was somewhat fitting that one of our manager's more subtle schemes should ultimately have decided the outcome. The instruction was that either Joe Royle or Jimmy Husband should stand directly in front of Gary Sprake, the Leeds goalkeeper, whenever he had possession of the ball, simply to stop him clearing with his right foot. Harry Catterick felt that Sprake's left foot was weak and that if he was denied the use of his powerful right boot, anything could happen.

Just before the interval, Joe stood right in front of Sprake who, in his haste to clear, decided to use his less-favoured left foot. Sprake's kick was under-hit and poorly directed. It fell at the feet of Husband who directed it straight back towards goal. Jack Charlton had only one option open to him and he did not hesitate to stick out a hand to prevent the ball crossing the line. The scam had reaped a handsome reward and we had a penalty.

In the absence of Ball, our regular spot-kick expert, Johnny Morrissey took on the responsibility and scored with a sweet drive. Leeds rallied bravely in the second half but we held on; we had made it.

West Brom, who had finally disposed of our neighbours from Anfield in a second replay at Maine Road, were to be our opponents at Wembley after defeating Second Division Birmingham City at Villa Park. Having beaten Albion 6–2 at The Hawthorns earlier in the season, we fancied our chances and the bookmakers concurred, installing us as the firm favourites to lift the Cup for the first time in more than a decade.

I was now experiencing the build-up to an FA Cup final for the second time in a career which was still very much in its infancy. The only real pressure I felt was attempting to ensure that all my family and friends would be at Wembley to see me play. I could comfortably have disposed of my allocation five times over.

31

Our last match before the final was against West Ham United at Upton Park and although we were well below strength, we emerged with a highly creditable 1–1 draw. No-one could have accused us of slackening off as Wembley approached. We didn't lose many matches at all during the build-up and eventually finished in fifth place, just two places below Liverpool and a Fairs Cup berth.

After settling in at our headquarters at Selsdon Park in Surrey, and with the final only a matter of 18 hours away, the first-team squad went to the cinema. I don't remember what the film was. It didn't really matter because the object of the exercise was for the players to sever all ties which existed between themselves and reality, if only for 90 minutes.

I shared a room with Colin Harvey that night, a man who, to this day, remains one of my closest friends.

We had dispensed with the traditional viewing of the stadium in preference for a series of team talks at which we discussed the strengths and weaknesses of our opponents. The nerves began to mount as we made our way down Wembley Way but I was still in a confident frame of mind.

All the expectations were of a free-scoring classic which would be laden with exhilarating, open football of the very highest order. Nothing could have been further from the truth as both teams laboured through an unproductive, and unappealing, opening 90 minutes.

Everyone was tired during the period of extra-time and with both sides fully aware that the first goal would almost certainly prove to be the winner, the standard of football did not improve appreciably.

We were the better side but we missed our chances. Unfortunately, Jeff Astle, Albion's prolific striker, didn't miss his and after picking up a highly fortuitous rebound, he swept in a wonderful shot from the edge of the penalty area. As was the case in 1964 with Preston, there was just no way back.

Having been the favourites, we were totally despondent afterwards. We used the reception at the Grosvenor Hotel as an excuse to drown our collective sorrow.

A few days later we had our final League game of the season against Fulham at Goodison. We couldn't finish any higher, they couldn't finish any lower, having already been relegated, so the pressure was off. We played as we should have done at Wembley and won 5–1. The supporters eased the pain of another season of unfulfilled dreams by refusing to go home until after we had taken a bow from the directors' box. Remarkable people, those Everton fans.

By practically anyone else's standards, the following season would have been recognised as a success. But the only people who are more difficult to satisfy than those who take their places at Goodison Park every fortnight are the players of Everton Football Club themselves.

Our level of consistency was reasonably good throughout the entire League campaign but the gap which separated ourselves and the leading two, Leeds United and Liverpool, always had an unbridgeable quality about it. We did actually top the First Division for seven precious days in early November after defeating Sunderland at home but we slipped back the following week and by the end of term the points difference between ourselves and the champions, Leeds, had grown to ten.

Once again the FA Cup seemed likely to be our salvation but after defeating Manchester United in the sixth round, we fell at the semi-final stage to their neighbours, City, losing 1–0 at Villa Park.

Although I was conscious of the fact that after two-and-a-half years at Everton I had still to help the club win a major trophy, I remembered the words of Tommy Eggleston, our trainer who had left the club at the start of the 1967–68 season to take over as manager at Mansfield Town. After announcing that he was severing his ties with the club, he had stood in front of the first team and said: "This is going to be a great side; a really great side." I had carried with me those words of rich encouragement through two hard seasons of bitter disappointment and was determined to prove correct a man I respected a great deal.

I was in pristine condition when the new season opened against Arsenal at Highbury. Although we were lacking the inspirational qualities of Alan Ball, who was suspended, we won that game 1–0 but I was reduced to a watching brief after only 30 minutes after falling heavily and turning an ankle.

I missed the next six games but the team was on such a high that it didn't really matter a great deal. Manchester United were beaten, both at Goodison and Old Trafford, and Crystal Palace, Sheffield Wednesday and Leeds United were also accounted for. The only disappointment was a 1–1 draw against Manchester City at Maine Road but 13 points out of 14 was a solid foundation upon which to build.

I returned in a League Cup tie at Darlington, a game which we won but which hardly fell into the memorable category. My first

League game for almost a month was against Derby County at the Baseball Ground and although I marked my comeback with a goal, we lost our unbeaten run.

However, the sense of destiny within our dressing-room was such that we looked upon that result as a mere blemish rather than a possible turning point. We took 19 points from our next ten League games to put us eight points clear of our nearest challengers, Leeds United.

It was only early November but already many of the newspapers had decided that the title was ours and that we only had to go through the motions for the remainder of the season to finish well ahead of the chasing pack. Such talk was unlikely to prompt complacency on our part because Leeds had two games in hand and, at that time, they were one of the most accomplished, resilient sides ever to have graced English football.

Inevitably, things began to go wrong for us. Most Championship-winning teams hit a sticky patch at one time or another and ours came in the shape of a defeat by West Brom at The Hawthorns and a draw against Chelsea at Stamford Bridge. Leeds, as we had feared, were winning their games in hand and beginning to close a gap which so many people had assured us was unbreachable.

Injuries to Colin Harvey and Jimmy Husband disrupted our sense of rhythm and the growing feeling that the tide had turned against us was underlined when Liverpool defeated us 3–0 at Goodison.

The signing of Keith Newton from Blackburn Rovers helped to restore a measure of stability and we were still top of the table at the turn of the year despite losing 2–1 to Leeds at Elland Road.

A week later we were back in Yorkshire to face Sheffield United in the third round of the FA Cup. We were beaten 2–1 and the rollicking which Harry Catterick served up in the dressing-room afterwards was fully deserved for we were all acutely aware of having let down not only ourselves but the many thousands of supporters who had crossed the Pennines. I remember Brian Labone stood up and said that we simply *HAD* to go on and win the League title to make amends. It was almost a threat.

These days it is almost fashionable for managers, players and fans to complain about the severity of punishments handed out by football's governing body but to my mind they are a good deal more lenient than they were 20 years ago. In early January of 1970, Alan Ball was called before the Football Association to explain why it was he had collected three bookings. It was hardly an outrageous total

The 1969–70 Championship-winning team completes a lap of honour

for a player whose game placed such a heavy reliance on physical contact but his appeal for clemency fell on deaf ears and he was banned, not for one or two games, but for *FIVE* weeks.

On 17 January we surrendered not only two points against Southampton at The Dell but also the leadership of the First Division which we had enjoyed since mid-September. Leeds were now the clear favourites to successfully defend the title they had won in such style 12 months earlier. We picked up just six points from our next five games and although Leeds had failed to take full advantage of our dip in form, we knew that a monumental effort would be required if the League Championship pennant was to be returned to Goodison Park.

Our luck began to change for the better against Burnley at Turf Moor during a match which was in jeopardy right up until the last minute because of a heavy snowfall. We mastered an atrocious pitch to win 2–1 while Leeds were dropping a crucial point at Anfield.

The following week we travelled down to White Hart Lane for the third time that season. The first time the game was called off because of a water-logged pitch; the second time we got started only for the floodlights to fail, but, at the third time of asking, we won 1–0 to return to the top of the Division.

1970—Cynthia and I marry

The game against the old enemy, Liverpool, at Anfield was even more significant during the course of the run-in. We needed to win to maintain our challenge and we needed to win to erase the bitter memory of that crushing defeat at Goodison. Goals by Joe Royle and Alan Whittle ensured that revenge was ours.

Leeds' massive fixture congestion (they were still in both the FA Cup and the European Cup) finally began to take its toll and, as a result of having to field below-strength teams in important League fixtures, they began to lose ground.

The key game for us was possibly the one against Chelsea at Goodison for although the London side had reached the FA Cup final, Dave Sexton, their manager, was adamant that they could still achieve an unlikely success in the League—if they could take two points away from Merseyside. More than 58,000 people squeezed into Goodison Park on 28 March to watch us record a magnificent 5-2 victory. After the match, we heard the delightful news that Leeds had unexpectedly been beaten at home by Southampton. We would have to try very hard to lose the title now.

A week later we played badly at Stoke but still won, a result which lent credence to the old adage which suggests that when you are riding high the luck goes with you. With Leeds having been beaten by Derby County at the Baseball Ground, we only had to beat West Brom at home to be certain of the Championship.

Once again the famous old stadium was full to overflowing. We won 2-0 and the scenes of delirium which followed the final whistle will live forever in my memory.

As it turned out, a season which had promised so much for our great rivals, Leeds, fell apart in the latter stages. They finished poorly in the League, were knocked out of the European Cup by Celtic and lost the FA Cup final to Chelsea in a replay. They received a lot of sympathy and they deserved it.

The season was over but I had one final fixture to fulfil. A few weeks later, at Fulwood Methodist Church, I married Cynthia Halliwell, a girl I had met during my time with Preston.

*1 April 1970. We defeat West Brom 2–0 at Goodison Park to clinch the League title.
Harry Catterick congratulates Joe Royle as I head for the dressing-room*

CHAPTER FOUR

Shades of Blue

Having returned the League Championship to Goodison Park after an absence of seven years, the 1970–71 season was eagerly anticipated by everyone connected with the club, no more so than by the players who had been told by everyone from opposing managers to self-styled television pundits that the immediate future firmly belonged to us. Revelling in the fact that the famed School of Science had once again been declared open for business, we prepared to defend the title and prove correct those who had been bold enough to suggest that in sport success will inevitably breed success.

I don't know whether it was down to complacency or ill-fortune but we started the season like a team which had designs on claiming a relegation place rather than the top spot which we had grown so accustomed to occupying just a few months earlier. Of our opening six League fixtures we lost three and drew three, a dismal, almost incomprehensible, record which left us stranded in 18th place after less than a month of what was expected to be another memorable campaign.

After defeating West Ham United at Upton Park on 5 September, our form improved signficantly but the impetus was again lost in the following month and we found ourselves hopelessly adrift of the leaders, struggling to impose our will on lesser teams in the wasteland of mid-table.

There were mitigating circumstances in so much as the injury problems which we had fortuitously avoided in the previous season began to materialise on an almost weekly basis. Brian Labone, whose commitment and leadership underpinned a defence which was as enterprising as it was reliable, was missing for several weeks and other influential members of the side, like Johnny Morrissey, were also unavailable for matches of great significance.

By Christmas the realisation that the title had been prematurely surrendered, almost without a fight, began to envelop the dressing-room.

Our immense disappointment at letting down supporters who demanded, and deserved, far better was tempered by our steady progress in the FA Cup and in the European Cup. If Lady Luck had been notably absent during our League programme, she was very much in evidence when the draw for successive rounds of the FA Cup was made. We were drawn at home in rounds three, four, five and six, defeating Blackburn Rovers, Middlesborough, Derby County and Colchester United respectively, without conceding a solitary goal. In the semi-final we were paired with Liverpool, something which became a common occurrence during the Eighties but which was a rarity at the time.

Our entire season was to hinge on the outcome of two games during the course of just three days at the end of March. The prospect of facing Liverpool at Old Trafford was enticing enough but on the Wednesday before that tie we had to steel ourselves for a trip to Athens and a European Cup semi-final, second leg against Panathinaikos, the uncompromising champions of Greece. Having drawn 1–1 at Goodison Park a fortnight earlier (a match which we should have won with some considerable ease) we were up against it.

We planned very carefully for the game but, in truth, nothing could have adequately prepared us for what we encountered during the course of that particular trip. The night before the game the Panathinaikos supporters, dozens and dozens of them, actively set about ensuring that not one member of the playing squad was allowed a moment's peace. They drove around and around our hotel on their motorcycles, screaming, shouting and blaring their horns and sirens. The police would move them on but as soon as the squad cars disappeared they would be back, even more determined to shatter the calm which invariably shrouds the headquarters of a football team in the hours before a crucial game.

There were only about 20,000 people in the stadium the next day but I have never experienced anything quite like it in all my years in the game. We were spat at as we walked towards the crowd to take throw-ins and some of the things which occurred out on the field of play were simply unbelievable. In the first couple of minutes we won a corner and John Hurst ran forward to take up his usual position in the penalty area. As he moved towards the far post, one of the Greek players ran at him and stabbed him in both eyes with two outstretched fingers. It was ridiculous, really.

We ended up drawing 0-0 which, if taken in isolation, was a tremendous result. It wasn't enough, however, and our shortcomings during the first leg saw us knocked out on the away goals rule.

It was a tragic waste in so many respects because the final that year was staged at Wembley and had we defeated Panathinaikos, I honestly believe that we could have taken the most coveted of trophies back home to Merseyside many, many years before Liverpool succeeded in doing so.

I was not at all surprised when Ajax of Amsterdam defeated Panathinaikos 2-0 in the final. It would have been a damn sight closer, and a damn sight more entertaining, had Everton been there on that night. Of that I am certain.

We returned home disappointed but not totally despondent for there is nothing quite like a game against Liverpool to renew the appetite.

It was possibly during the course of that one week that I began to fully appreciate the real demands of playing football at the highest level, for at a club like Everton credence is lent to the old adage which suggests that *EVERY* game is a big one; *EVERY* game is as significant as was the one which has only recently been confined to the pages of history.

Harry Catterick kept us away from Merseyside, and the inevitable pressures, in the 48 hours before the FA Cup semi-final but if the relative solitude of a pleasant Cheshire hotel was designed to help us rediscover the killer touch which had been sorely absent in Athens, it did not work.

We took the lead at Old Trafford courtesy of an Alan Ball goal but after Brian Labone was forced to withdraw because of injury, Liverpool assumed control of a typically frenetic derby and won through to the final with second-half goals by Alun Evans and Brian Hall.

For the best part of two decades people have been seeking to explain why it was that a team which just 12 months earlier was poised to dominate English football should capitulate so swiftly. In my opinion that disastrous week in March 1971 was largely instrumental for, had we won those two games, who knows what we might have achieved in the following years?

The following season was equally unpalatable. There was no consistency, no fluency and, as we entered a new year in the wrong half of the table, no Alan Ball.

41

Alan was one of the two greatest players I ever played alongside, the other being Trevor Francis who became a team-mate of mine after my transfer to Birmingham City in 1974. With all due respect to Mick Bernard, who eventually took his place in the Everton team, Alan was simply the best. I don't think anyone could have replaced him at that time, such was the massive influence he had exerted on the team.

In the years before his disenchantment with the club began to set in, Alan was quite possibly the finest midfield player Everton has ever had—or is likely to have. We had a marvellous situation where Colin Harvey was working the left with Johnny Morrissey, I was working the right and Jimmy Husband was making his runs across the park in support of Joe Royle. Alan was what managers like to call a "half-and-half" player, insomuch as he would nick in, pinch possession and start attacks with one instinctively driven pass.

Things started to go wrong for him at Everton when his goals-per-game ratio began to fall quite dramatically. I think that perhaps he realised that he could no longer cover the enormous amount of ground which he used to and, instead of pushing forward, he began to drop back to take on the mantle of a more orthodox midfield player.

He was still a tremendous player but although his influence could still be felt by those around him, the team suffered as a direct consequence of his subtle change in role.

It was around this time, in late 1971, that I became aware of his increasing unease with life and I knew it would only be a matter of time before he left a club he had served so well.

Harry Catterick sold Alan to Arsenal in December of that year for £220,000, a diminutive sum by today's standards, but a transfer record at the time.

Obviously, it wasn't what you could describe as a popular decision but there is always going to be a problem when footballing folk-heroes are allowed to leave, especially when they still have so much to offer. The transfer made a great impact on the Everton public who, perhaps not too surprisingly, felt a sense of betrayal.

I distinctly remember a friend of mine ringing me up a couple of days after Alan had left and saying: "What the hell is going on? Bally's gone and the kids can't sleep." I think that places into clear perspective the esteem in which Alan Ball was held by one of British football's most knowledgeable audiences.

Thankfully, the leaving of Everton did not signal a premature end to Alan's career. He went on to serve both Arsenal and Southampton splendidly and I'm just a little sad that he has not enjoyed greater success in the field of management because I know all too well just how passionate he is about the game. There is a great deal of luck involved in managing a football team, irrespective of its status, and perhaps Alan was unfortunate to select the wrong clubs at the wrong time.

I don't believe that Alan's decision to leave Goodison Park can be totally attributed to his increasingly strained relationship with Harry Catterick because there was not one player in the first-team squad of that time who did not have the occasional run-in with a manager for whom the tag enigma was admirably suited.

To be honest, the players very rarely saw Harry during the week. He would come into work and go straight into his office, only appearing out on the training ground when the television cameras were present. He used to have a tracksuit hanging in his office but he only ever put it on when the film crews gathered—or when he knew a director was going to call in.

It amused us all but we sniggered rather than roared with laughter because Harry was an unpredictable man and you could never gauge what his reaction was going to be. He spent a great deal of time sitting alone in his office but while there was precious little contact between players and manager, there was tremendous respect in the dressing-room for the man. He had an indefinable presence about him and I never really looked forward to knocking on his door and talking to him.

A brave attempt to take the ball around the Southampton goalkeeper, Eric Martin, in a League game at Goodison Park in 1969

A meeting of great minds. Harry Catterick and Bill Shankly

He was not a man to trifle with, something which I had learned to my cost as early as 1969. We had reached the semi-final of the FA Cup that season and had been paired with Manchester City at Villa Park. I had been suffering from a hairline fracture of the leg but I had resumed training and was desperate to play in a reserve team game a few days before the tie to press my claims for a recall to the senior side. I was asked by a journalist if I thought I would be given the all-clear to play at least part of the Central League fixture and I said it was highly likely.

The next day the headline on a story I felt to be inoffensive and of very little importance read: "Kendall Demands Reserve Team Spot." Harry, refusing to take into account my naïvety, called me into his office and said, "Who are you to demand that you play for this club?" As I struggled to come up with a reply which would pacify my clearly annoyed manager he looked me straight in the eye and said, "Well, you're not playing." Three days later he promptly turned logic on its head by selecting me for the semi-final.

Harry was fully aware that all his players felt intimidated when in his company and he would use this feeling of insecurity on our part to best advantage.

I remember an international player sitting in the dining-room at the training ground, moaning that he hadn't had a pay rise for three or four years. We told him he was right to complain and that he should immediately confront the manager and demand more money. He was reluctant to do so, so one of the other players quite literally lifted him up, carried him to Harry's office and knocked on the door. We waited patiently for his return.

About five minutes later, he was back and being pressed to give full details of both the conversation and of the outcome. The player, who will remain nameless to spare his embarrassment, said, ''I ended up apologising profusely for disturbing him.''

The changing climate of football in general, and the workings of the transfer market in particular, were instrumental in lessening Harry's effectiveness in a managerial sense as Everton moved towards the mid-Seventies with a collective attitude which embraced apprehension, trepidation and, of course, the more traditional optimism.

A sport which had remained untouched for so long began to change quite dramatically as clubs which had previously been more than content simply to exist and survive sought to challenge the authority of their more glamorous contemporaries by altering, significantly, the infrastructure of the game.

For so many years, the leading clubs—Everton, Liverpool, Manchester United, Arsenal, Tottenham Hotspur, Leeds United and Manchester City—had it all their own way. They enjoyed an almost complete monopoly of the best players simply because they had healthier bank balances. It was a very simple equation; the club which could afford the transfer fee got the player. It was possibly unfair but it was simple and at least under a system which guaranteed the survival of the fittest, everyone knew exactly where they stood.

Almost overnight the term ''hire-purchase'' was introduced into football and things would never be quite the same again. It no longer mattered that, in a strict financial sense, a club didn't really have two coins to rub together; the monopoly had been smashed and those players who had made themselves available for transfer were suddenly the subject of offers, quite substantial offers, from all over the place.

The big clubs were now battling against the rest and the loss of what could be described as the exclusive rights to football's brightest talent hit many leading clubs very, very hard. It certainly had a significant effect at Goodison Park, for as the mood of the game altered, it became apparent that the players being bought by Everton were not of the same quality as those who were leaving.

Many clubs used the HP scheme very unwisely, for, in their desperation to assemble a squad which would make an impact in the major competitions, they saddled themselves with enormous debts. Because clubs were allowed, if not positively encouraged, to enter into deals with only a very small downpayment, transfer fees began to spiral out of control and people ended up paying ridiculously inflated prices, often for players of little experience and rather dubious quality. As a direct result of this unprecedented elevation in price, it was decided that clubs must lodge half the transfer fee with the game's governing body before a deal could be ratified. This measure did help to stabilise an unhealthy situation but perhaps it was introduced too late to stop many clubs maso-chistically inflicting wounds which took many years to heal.

It became increasingly hard for Harry to entice the best players to Everton during this spell, which said more about the changing face of football rather than about his own personal abilities, for his business acumen had never been in any doubt.

The idea of HP deals was hardly revolutionary because in 1967, when I was poised to join Everton from Preston North End, Stoke City made an 11th hour bid to sign me by utilising just such a system. Because they would be making only a small downpayment, Stoke were actually able to offer me a far better deal than did Everton.

The late Alan Ball, father of Everton's Alan, was working for Stoke at the time and my late father and myself met him to discuss exactly what was on offer at the Victoria Ground. My father, who always attempted to look after my best interests, asked him why it was he was trying to get me to sign for Stoke while his own son was enjoying success at Everton, the club which I had all but agreed to join. Ball senior, who was one of football's great enthusiasts, smiled and replied that Alan Ball junior would definitely be playing for Stoke within the next two years. It was a light-hearted, cheeky manoeuvre but it didn't work and I joined Everton shortly afterwards.

46

The 1972–73 season brought little relief for a team which had lost its direction. We finished 17th in the table and went out of the FA and League Cups in the early rounds. It was depressing to say the very least.

The Championship-winning side broke up very quickly and it was inevitable that the club's board of directors would start to consider the possibility of a new manager. Harry, who had suffered a heart attack in 1972, was troubled by health problems and in April 1973, with four years of his ten-year contract still left to run, he was moved sideways into a senior executive role.

Harry was only rarely seen at Everton after stepping down as team manager, and his death, during an FA Cup quarter-final tie against Ipswich Town at Goodison Park in March 1985, deeply saddened me. He was a difficult man to work with sometimes but his love of Everton, and his dedication to the cause, was unquestionable.

Billy Bingham took over in May 1973 and, to be fair to him, he inherited a team which was badly in need of major reconstruction. He was anxious to make changes and get things moving in the right direction, which was perfectly understandable because at a club like Everton success is something which is not so much desired as expected.

I think Billy realised that while the board had not issued him with an ultimatum, or a set deadline, he had to achieve at least a measure of success, however relative, very swiftly. The Everton public was growing impatient.

I suffered an injury early on in the season and while I was out of the first team, newspaper reports linking me with a possible move to Sunderland began to appear at regular intervals. Apparently the idea was that I would move to Roker Park in an exchange deal which would have brought Dennis Tueart to Goodison. As I have always believed that it is better to be among people who want you rather than among those who are indifferent to your presence, I would probably have agreed to the deal and accepted the challenge had it been offered. I realised that my days at Everton were numbered and I actually thought I was on my way back to the North-east in March 1974 when I was asked to report to Goodison. It was my day off so I knew something was in the offing.

Billy took me into his office and said that a club had come in for me. I asked who it was, expecting the reply to be Sunderland, but he surprised me totally by informing me it was Birmingham City.

City were struggling near the foot of the table at the time but I decided to meet up with Freddie Goodwin, the manager, for a chat.

The deal was a highly complicated affair which involved Bob Latchford moving from St Andrews to Everton and myself and Archie Styles moving in the opposite direction. I was told that everything hinged on my decision because Bob had agreed terms and was more than happy to put pen to paper.

I thought about the move very carefully before coming to the conclusion that I may as well sever my ties with Everton if only because it was clear that my manager no longer wanted me. I felt a little sad because I was certain that Everton could have afforded to pay hard cash for Latchford without using me as a peculiar form of bait. However, it quickly became clear to me that it was players, and not cash, which Birmingham required and that they would not have sanctioned a straight deal involving Latchford.

Having signed for a club which had fallen on hard times, it was just a case of rolling up my sleeves and working hard to prove right Freddie's decision. It was hard to leave Everton because the unshakeable bond which still exists between myself and the club was established during my days there as a player. It became an integral part of my life; it was in my blood. The fascination for the club never wavered, which explains why it was I decided to leave Manchester City and return to Goodison Park as manager in 1990.

Shortly after joining Birmingham, I returned to Everton for a League game and the reception I received from the supporters was overwhelming. Young fans ran on to the pitch before the kick-off just to say "Thank you". It was very touching.

Our fight against relegation went right to the last game, which was somewhat surprising bearing in mind the quality and experience within the squad. The obvious star player was Trevor Francis. Had he not suffered so badly with injuries, I have no doubts that Trevor would have established himself as one of the greatest English players of all time. He managed to combine electrifying pace and close control. He was a very special player indeed.

It was during my time at St Andrews that I first began to show an interest in other facets of football, coaching and, to a lesser degree, management. Freddie proved himself to be far more accessible than had been Harry Catterick and he took me into his confidence, constantly asking my opinions on a variety of subjects.

There is a veil of secrecy and suspicion which divides players and managers. Freddie allowed me to cross the dividing line between dressing-room and manager's office and I was not only grateful but intrigued by what I encountered. Having been allowed to study what went on behind the scenes, I thought that perhaps my future lay in that area of the game. If I had stayed at Everton maybe it wouldn't have happened. It is conceivable that had I not moved to City, I would have drifted out of football when my playing days were at an end.

I was still unsure about my long-term future plans but I followed my natural instincts and won my coaching badges. I was not sure that I would ever need them but it was comforting to know that I would have something to fall back on if all else failed.

We won our last game of the season to avoid relegation and as we were relaxing in the bath afterwards, someone came in to tell us that supporters were steadfastly refusing to go home. They were demanding that we go back out on to the pitch and do a lap of honour. We dried off, got dressed and ran around the pitch amid scenes of wild celebration. It was a strange feeling because four years earlier I had done exactly the same thing at Everton to celebrate the winning of the League Championship. It didn't matter though. Avoiding the drop was success in the eyes of those supporters and they wanted to express their happiness. The sense of relief was almost tangible.

The highlight of my brief, but enjoyable, stay at City came in 1975 when we reached the semi-final of the FA Cup. We were drawn against Fulham, then a Second Division club, at Hillsborough. Although they had players like Bobby Moore and Alan Mullery in their line-up, we were the clear favourites to reach Wembley.

We drew 1–1 but lost the replay at Maine Road in the last seconds of injury-time at the end of extra-time. It was just one of those days when the ball simply would not go into the opponents' net. The pain I felt at losing was intensified because I was captain.

Even though I had joined City in a deal which had cost them their hero, Bob Latchford, I think the supporters appreciated my efforts in attempting to transform the club's fortunes.

Willie Bell, City's assistant manager, took over from Freddie in 1975 and he dropped me for the first time in my career. He also left out Terry Hibbitt, Freddie's other big-name signing, and unfortunately the game in question was against Liverpool at Anfield.

I suppose that I still had the Everton mentality because it just didn't matter that I was no longer a part of the Goodison Park set-up, it was still Liverpool and it was still the big one; possibly the greatest challenge a player could have in those days. Not much has changed really because going to Anfield still constitutes the acid test both on an individual and a team level.

Perhaps Willie realised that he had made a mistake because we were comprehensively beaten by Liverpool and I was recalled the following week.

Naturally, I was pleased to be back in the side but the damage had been done. My confidence had been undermined to a certain extent and although I continued to channel all my energies into helping City, I was fully aware that my long-term future was suddenly shrouded in doubt. I think I appreciated that it would not be too long before there was a parting of the ways and in 1977 the chance to start afresh came along.

CHAPTER FIVE

So Near, Yet So Far

There is hardly a season which goes by without someone reminding me, as if I needed reminding, that I was never fortunate enough to win a full England cap.

This particular topic is usually raised either by those Everton supporters who felt me worthy of such an honour during the early Seventies, when I was arguably at the peak of my playing career, or by journalists who foolishly assume that the passing of so many years has done nothing to lessen my obvious sense of disappointment.

If the media hopes that any sense of injustice which I may feel is going to manifest itself in some form of attack, veiled or otherwise, on those chosen to represent their country today, they are barking up the wrong tree for I would not begrudge any player this very special moment of personal satisfaction, irrespective of his calibre or pedigree.

Simply because I was playing alongside Alan Ball and Colin Harvey at the heart of a Championship-winning side, people assumed that my promotion to the full England team was something of a formality. Sadly, football is a sport which is built upon a bed-rock of uncertainty and I was never to win that elusive cap.

It is somewhat ironic that despite our effectiveness as a unit within the Everton side, Alan, Colin and myself were to enjoy sharply contrasting fortunes with regard to international football. Alan finished his career with 72 caps, Colin with just one and I was left empty-handed.

I think that I probably came as close as any uncapped player to making a senior appearance.

In October 1972, England were playing Yugoslavia in a friendly international at Wembley and because Sir Alf Ramsey's initial squad had been reduced because of injuries and withdrawals, I was draughted in as one of a number of replacements. After we had finished a training session at the Bank of England ground in

Roehampton on the day before the game, Sir Alf stood up at the front of the players' coach and said that he was going to name his 12 players for the following night. Although he was allowed a full compliment of substitutes, Sir Alf was in the habit of naming his 12th man—the player who would automatically be called upon if someone was injured during the course of the game.

I sat there nervously as he began to rattle off the names and mine was about the fifth he read out. I thought that was it; I'd made it. I think the other players did so too because Bobby Moore, who was seated opposite me, gave me the nod as if to say, "Well done."

Sir Alf then sat down but two or three minutes later when he climbed back to his feet and said: "Rodney Marsh, have I named you?" Rodney shouted back: "No, you haven't, Sir Alf."

"Oh, you're my 12th man," said Sir Alf. I was even more convinced that I was going to start the game.

I went back to the hotel and phoned my father and my wife and told them to get ready to come down to London. However, I woke up in the morning to read in the papers that I would only play if Colin Bell failed a fitness test.

My excitement began to drain away because I knew that Colin had trained the previous day and was fully fit. Sir Alf's conversation on the coach had left me confused and uncertain as to what exactly was going to happen.

He was obviously a good deal less confused than I was and he put me on the bench while telling me that I would definitely be the one to go on should any outfield player sustain an injury. The game ended in a 1–1 draw, no-one was injured, and I spent 90 frustrating minutes scouring Wembley in a forlorn search for a limping colleague.

To be honest, I think that I blew my chances of playing for England some time before that fixture. I had played for the Football League against the Scottish League at Hampden Park, and I think that it is fair to say that my performance that day was instrumental in setting Danny McGrain on the road forward to a long and distinguished international career with Scotland. He played left-side and I was on the right and he just kept bombing past me as if I wasn't there. I tightened up, lost my confidence and my rhythm and didn't do myself justice at all.

I was bitterly disappointed never to represent England at senior level, having done so at schoolboy, youth and under-21 level but, to be fair to Sir Alf, I think he had a settled squad and he was going to stick with it. With the benefit of hindsight, I believe that he was right to do so because those players in whom he had placed his faith had beeen successful.

It is difficult to say whether or not I would have made a good international player because, over the years, several exceptional League players have failed to make the transition to the bigger arena where so much more is demanded, and expected, of you. It took Colin Bell eight or ten internationals before he began to produce what everybody knew him to be capable of and I suspect that I would have required a similar bedding-in period.

It is still nice to read that some people regard me as one of the best players never to have won a full cap but there is no great sense of injustice because I fully understood the reasons behind Sir Alf's decision.

My heavy commitments at Everton did not exactly help my cause because I remember being selected for another Football League game and being withdrawn, even though I was fully fit. The decision was taken by Harry Catterick and I was so disappointed that I went behind his back and contacted Sir Alf to explain the situation. I was so desperate to ensure that my future prospects were not harmed that I even considered just turning up at the team's headquarters to underline my enthusiasm.

I spoke to Harry about it but he simply said that we had several important games on the horizon and that he did not want to run the risk of my getting injured. Harry's list of priorities was rather short; it had just the one entry and that was Everton Football Club.

Funnily enough, a few years later, when I was playing for Birmingham City, Sir Alf came up to me after a game against Arsenal at Highbury and said that he had never seen me play better. Unfortunately, he was no longer the manager of England. It was a classic example of the so-near-yet-so-far syndrome which all footballers experience at one time or another.

CHAPTER SIX

A Change of Emphasis

Having reached the inescapable conclusion that it was time to leave St Andrews, I bided my time until the right offer came in. I was not going to be hurried into a decision which I knew was of paramount importance and which could conceivably shape my entire future. My next move not only had to be beneficial to Howard Kendall, the footballer, but to Howard Kendall, the family man, because, by this point, I had the dual responsibility of bringing up two youngsters, Simon, who was born in December 1974, and Hayley, who had arrived in July 1976.

I have always been grateful to my wife, Cynthia, for the unstinting support which she has provided throughout my career. It can't be easy for the wives of footballers and managers, for no sooner have they put down roots in one place than they find themselves packing up to relocate.

When a player arrives at a new club, he will generally find that he already knows several of his new team-mates; settling in is easy. Sadly, that does not apply to wives who must start the process of making new friends all over again. Whenever I have needed Cynthia she has been there, at my side. I can't thank her enough for that.

Thankfully, when a club did come in for me, all my fears were allayed. Stoke City had been relegated from the First Division the previous season but they were openly ambitious and I had little, or no, hesitation in agreeing to a £40,000 transfer. It was just nice to feel that I was wanted once again for I knew that I still had much to offer as a player, not least my experience and enthusiasm. If players can maintain a love for the game, there is no reason at all why they should be apprehensive about going anywhere because, irrespective of what level you are involved at, football is football.

The fact that George Eastham, one of my boyhood idols, was in charge at Stoke when I negotiated the deal may have proved to be the decisive factor, but I somehow felt the move to be right. Over the years, I have learned that you must sometimes rely on your instincts, that gut feeling, whether you are changing clubs as a player or investing in new talent as a manager. Of course, everyone makes errors of judgement which he or she ultimately regrets, but things do tend to level themselves out over the course of a working life.

George was looking to rebuild the Stoke side swiftly with a view to climbing out of the Second Division at the earliest opportunity. He had a relatively youthful senior squad at the time and he felt that the arrival of someone who had played in the big games, the FA Cup finals, would help those inexperienced players mature at a faster rate than was normal.

George, and his assistant, Alan A'Court, treated me in much the same way as had Freddie Goodwin at Birmingham. I think that they recognised my desire to learn, my appetite for knowledge. They took me into their confidence and asked my opinions about certain things which I really appreciated. I was forever asking questions about tactics, preparation and coaching technique as I subconciously began to ready myself for a change in role. If they ever tired of my constant search for information, they never showed it and I shall always be grateful to the pair of them, not only for their help but for their astonishing patience.

Rather sadly, George's reign as manager at the Victoria Ground did not last very long and after Alan had been in charge of first-team affairs for a short period in 1978, Alan Durban, who was in charge at Shrewsbury Town, was appointed.

Alan offered the job of coach to Ritchie Barker, who had been his assistant at Gay Meadow, but he decided to stay where he was after being offered the manager's job. Although I think Alan was a little disappointed when informed of Ritchie's decision, he was not slow to offer me the post of player-coach. I promptly accepted.

Once again, a combination of circumstances had set me on the way down a road which I might otherwise have bypassed. Had Ritchie taken up Alan's offer at Stoke, things might have been so very different for me. For the second time in my career, the distinct possibility of my drifting out of football at the end of my playing career was averted.

I was very impressed with Alan in the weeks immediately after his appointment. He seemed to know exactly what he wanted and he quickly laid down a set of rules and principles, something which the club had possibly lacked in its recent past.

He was a tactically sound manager and under his guidance we embarked on a useful run which kept us near the top of the table. I enjoyed the extra responsibility and the gamble of having a player-coach seemed to be paying dividends because I was able to carry forward his instructions to the field of play itself. I was his mouthpiece out on the pitch, where it really mattered.

Having settled himself in, Alan tried to sign three players to help sustain a push for promotion which was beginning to gather momentum. He missed out on signing David Moss, Swindon Town's wide player who went to Luton Town, but he did manage to get Mike Doyle from Manchester City and Sammy Irvine, whom he knew very well from his days at Shrewsbury. The injection of new blood had a telling effect and, as our basic football began to improve, so too did our level of consistency.

We entered the last League game of the season, against Notts County at Meadow Lane, assuming that we would only require a draw to go up. Certainly that appeared to be the scenario before we kicked off.

We were level with about ten minutes to go when Alan raced to the touchline, desperately trying to attract my attention. He had been listening to the progress of our nearest rivals on a small radio and those other crucial games were not going the way we had planned. He shouted to me: "We need a goal; we have to win the game." Our reaction was: "OK, you can have one." Paul Richardson promptly scored and we were back in the First Division. Those last few minutes were unbelievably tense but the best things in life are always worth waiting for. Steering Stoke back into the top flight was the near-perfect way in which to celebrate the birth of my third child, Lisa, on 1 April 1979.

The partnership of Durban and Kendall had proved to be a winner and it was soon to become clear that our success had not gone unnoticed outside of the Potteries. As the club began to wind down in readiness for a well-deserved summer break, newspaper reports began to appear linking Alan with a move to Derby County and myself with a move to Blackburn Rovers. For the first time, I was actually being talked about as a manager.

For obvious reasons, the Stoke board did not want to see the partnership which Alan and I had forged broken up. The club was back where it belonged, in the First Division, and yet it seemed highly likely that both the manager and the coach were going to leave. Their distress was perfectly understandable but throughout what must have been a very traumatic period, they behaved like gentlemen.

I had talks with Blackburn and decided that I wanted to join them. It was quite obviously a major gamble from a personal point of view because I was turning my back on the prospect of playing First Division football again in preferring a drop into the Third Division for the first time in my career.

I thought very carefully before agreeing to move to Ewood Park but the club had such a fantastic tradition that I was anxious to give it a go. I could not think of a better place to start my managerial career and, after working as Stoke's unofficial assistant manager, I felt I was ready. My time working alongside Alan Durban had taught me what the job of football manager entailed, so I did not feel as though I was stumbling blindly into a profession of which I had no experience. A lot of former players have fallen into the trap of assuming that there is only a negligible difference between playing and managing. Both jobs are exceedingly difficult but both jobs are different.

Shortly after I had announced my intention of leaving, Alan announced that he was to stay at the Victoria Ground, a decision which possibly surprised the Stoke board, but one which was warmly welcomed by everyone connected with the club. I was so pleased for Stoke because I think it would have been dreadful, even morally wrong, had we both departed and left them facing the prospect of a return to the First Division without a management team.

One of the reasons behind my decision was that I felt Alan was preparing to replace me as a player. I believe that he thought I was possibly a little too long in the tooth to cope with the very special demands of football at the very highest level. I didn't want to curtail my playing career so the prospect of moving forward into management *AND* still being able to pull on a shirt every Saturday was doubly appealing. Had Blackburn insisted that I concentrate solely on coaching and administration, I doubt very much that I would have accepted their offer.

I knew that it was going to be difficult at Ewood Park but I also knew that dedicated support for the club was not confined to the terraces. When they had visited Stoke for a League fixture the previous season, the enthusiasm shown by the club's directors was exceptional to say the very least. They beat us on that day and I distinctly remember David Brown, who was to become Chairman shortly after I had joined the club, standing in the tunnel, punching the air with delight as he congratulated each and every one of his players. Rather sadly, my working relationship with Derek Keighley, the Blackburn Chairman who had convinced me that my relationship with the club would prove to be of a fruitful nature, was very short because he died within a matter of a few weeks of my arrival. He was a good, enthusiastic man whom I respected greatly.

Obviously, I was anxious that my new career should be launched with a bang rather than a whimper, but we did not start particularly well. I had inherited a squad which contained several experienced players, including Duncan McKenzie, but it was obvious to me that things needed balancing out. It is amazing how many times a new manager finds himself faced by this particular problem within a matter of days of taking up the reins.

I found that I had three left-wingers at my disposal. How on earth can you justify that? I solved the problem by not selecting any of

Howard Kendall at Blackburn

Moving in at Ewood Park for my first taste of managerial life

them. It was a luxury which a club in Blackburn's position simply could not afford.

I didn't have a great deal of money to spend but I did manage to buy Andy Crawford from Derby County. He was a player with flair but one who also had an exceptionally good goal-scoring record. Thankfully, he did the job for us and was a key player during the second half of the season when we enjoyed a really tremendous run in the League.

My first season as the manager of a football club ended in promotion. The sense of satisfaction was immense because a difficult job had been assessed, tackled and completed with a high degree of professionalism. Perhaps more importantly, Blackburn, as a town, was appreciative of our efforts and had awoken to the potential of its local club.

I never once thought about managing a "bigger" club during this period in my life because things were going well for me and I was a more than contented man. Despite moving back into the Second Division, things were still very tight in a financial sense. I remember attending board meetings where we were all asked to do our little bit to help cut costs. Unusual measures were called for, like

Kendall of the Rovers

cutting down on milk in our tea and using only second-class stamps, but we all understood the problems and were happy to oblige. It was that sort of a club. The term "family atmosphere" is probably over-used these days but that is what prevailed at Blackburn; we all pulled together because we all shared the same objectives.

1974 and it's back to Goodison Park for the first time as a Birmingham City player

I think it was actually good for me that Blackburn was not a wealthy club because having to be prudent, having to work within the confines of a strict financial framework, taught me a lot and it made me appreciate the real meaning of money later on, after I had joined the likes of Everton, Athletic Bilbao and Manchester City.

After winning promotion, the Chairman asked me to sign a new contract. I said that there was no problem at all with that because I was very happy at the club.

Because Blackburn had encountered problems in the past, when Jim Smith had left to take over at Birmingham City and when Gordon Lee had moved to Newcastle United, I was asked to agree to a clause which would guarantee my employers compensation if I was to leave Ewood Park before the end of my contract. I said that was fine but then asked what would happen if they sacked me. I pointed out that perhaps this arrangement should work both ways and that I should also have a clause giving me compensation if I was dismissed before my contract expired. They agreed.

We had another good season and as we prepared for our final League game, the dream of promotion to the First Division was still very much alive.

We needed Swansea City to slip up against Preston at Deepdale while we were winning at Bristol Rovers. We had thousands of supporters at Eastville that afternoon but they were powerless to help us. At half-time we were drawing 0-0 but Swansea were two goals to the good.

I just told my players to forget all about Swansea and concentrate on scoring the goals which would beat Bristol. I could do no more; our destiny was in the hands of others.

During the second half, Mick Heaton, my assistant, sat on the touchline with a radio pressed to his ear, in just the same way as Alan Durban had done in identical circumstances at Stoke a couple of years earlier. About ten minutes after the restart our supporters went wild, cheering and singing. They were trying to give us a psychological lift by pretending that Preston had scored. For a few seconds I was almost convinced but one look at Mick dashed my hopes. Sadly, Swansea beat Preston and we missed out on goal difference.

Even before our fate was sealed, I was aware that Everton had made an approach to Blackburn enquiring about my availability. There was a gentlemen's agreement that managers would not be approached, lured, tapped, call it what you will, during the course of a League season but, typically, Everton had gone about things in a right and proper manner and expressed their interest on a Chairman to Chairman level. My Chairman had kept me fully informed about the situation but, at the time, promotion was still my only priority and I told him to forget all about it.

There was never really a decision to be taken because I would have walked barefoot from Blackburn to Liverpool to get the job of Everton manager. It might sound harsh, even cruel, but I would still have left Rovers even if results had gone right for us on that final Saturday and we had won promotion. I would have been proud to have left Blackburn Rovers as a First Division club; that is what I really wanted to do more than anything.

I had thoroughly enjoyed my time at Blackburn, as I had at Birmingham and Stoke, but I still felt myself to be a part of Everton Football Club. It was where I had been at my happiest and I wanted to go back to a place I regarded as a home from home.

CHAPTER SEVEN

Looking for Clues

If the Blackburn public was surprised by my decision to leave
Ewood Park, the directors of Crystal Palace must have been
astonished upon learning of my move to Everton because a few
months earlier I had turned down the chance to manage them,
insisting that I was happy where I was.

Palace, who had just parted company with Terry Venables, came
in for me halfway through the season and made it clear that they
were willing to meet any demand for compensation. I discussed the
matter with my Chairman and although he said that he did not wish
me to leave, I felt it only fair that I travel down to London to talk
to representatives of the Palace board of directors.

After returning from Selhurst Park, I saw my Chairman and told
him that I needed time to think about the offer but that I would
ring him immediately I reached a decision. The following morning
at about 1.30 a.m., I was sitting in bed with my wife, drinking a
glass of champagne, when I turned to her and said: ''No. It's not
right for me.'' She didn't particularly want to move down to
London and was so happy at the news that she insisted I ring David
Brown straight away. It was a ridiculous time to discuss business
but he didn't seem to mind at all.

My refusal of Palace's offer had nothing at all to do with my
feelings for Everton. I wasn't sitting around waiting for a phone call
from Philip Carter or anything like that, the move just didn't seem
right somehow. It was probably a case of that instinctive feeling
surfacing once again.

Most people, no matter what walk of life they find themselves in,
want to better themselves in terms of career and finance, but while
Palace were offering more money than Blackburn could ever have
afforded, I was not convinced that I would ultimately have benefited.
Had I gone, my chances of managing Everton may possibly have
disappeared altogether.

65

When I left Everton to join Birmingham City in 1974, I had always hoped to return to the club one day, not necessarily as manager but in some capacity. Gordon Lee was sacked by Everton on 6 May and I was genuinely upset for him, because, like myself, he has a real affection for the club. I know how much the decision

29 August 1981 and I face the Everton public for the first time as manager

must have hurt him. His dismissal sparked a bout of predictable speculation—speculation which was ended just 48 hours later when my appointment was announced.

Perhaps it was the wrong time to go back to Goodison Park. Certainly David Brown thought so because he urged me to stay at Blackburn for another 12 months. However, I knew that it was not every day the Everton job became vacant. Had I turned down the chance, it certainly wouldn't have been open the following season, even if absolute disaster had befallen Gordon's successor. It was a case of grabbing the opportunity while it was there.

Strange though it may seem, assuming control of a football club at the end of a season is particularly difficult. I believe that the best time to go in as a manager is just after the turn of the year—ideally in either January or February.

The logic behind this is that you can then have a close look at your playing staff in a competitive setting and quickly assess the strengths and weaknesses of your squad. Also, provided that your board is willing to make money available, you can do some wheeling and dealing before the transfer deadline. If all goes well, by the end of the season you know exactly where you stand and so do your players.

If you join a club during the summer, one of the first tasks you have to undertake is the negotiating of players' contracts. On top of that you will have unsettled players knocking on your door demanding away and there will be protracted negotiations with those members of the squad who think they want away but who are open to persuasion.

If you haven't been in a position to analyse what each individual has to offer his club, then how on earth can you decide whether you want him to stay or not? I am sure that many new managers have fought strenuously to hang on to players, talked them into signing new deals and then realised, within a matter of a few weeks of the following season, that they are either not really good enough or are surplus to requirements. It is a peculiar Catch 22 situation which is avoided if the timing of your appointment is just right.

So from that point of view, I most definitely returned to Goodison Park at the wrong time.

After completing the formalities of my move, I immediately travelled to Japan to link up with the senior squad which was midway through a brief, end-of-season tour.

Just as I had done after taking over at Blackburn, I came to the conclusion that the whole staff was unbalanced. We didn't have three left-wingers but there seemed to be an unbelievable number of centre-backs and midfield players.

I knew very well that my first signing was going to be crucially important. As a new manager you have to try and get off on the right foot, not so much with the players, but with the supporters. If you buy the wrong player and he fails to produce the goods, those people who hand over their hard-earned cash to watch football are going to be immediately suspicious of you. In a way, they need to be reassured; they need to believe that the new man in charge knows what he is doing. All signings are important to a manager because he is placing his judgement firmly on the line but that first one is the big one, the acid test.

The first player I tried to bring to Everton was Bryan Robson, who was then playing for West Brom. The board had made £750,000 available to me for transfer market activity and I had no hesitation at all in offering Albion the lot.

Ron Atkinson was in charge at The Hawthorns and he refused, point-blank, even to discuss the offer. I think he had other plans for Bryan. Who knows, perhaps he had an inkling that he would one day be placed in charge of Manchester United and was keeping him in cold storage until such a time as he could take him to Old Trafford?

I was bitterly disappointed because, even at that stage, I had recognised Bryan as a natural leader; someone who could motivate those around him. He had suffered badly with injuries but he was a top-class player. The important thing was that there was no doubt at all about his ability, he was good enough and he would have been a tremendous asset to Everton. His signing would have been the perfect way of lifting the curtain on my new career.

Bryan would have been an enormous success irrespective of which major club he decided to join. All he needed was the big stage upon which to display his talent. I offered him that stage but unfortunately he was not in a position to accept my invitation.

In Gordon Lee's last two seasons in charge, Everton had finished 19th and 15th in the First Division and that was simply not good enough. If it had been good enough then Gordon would never have been dismissed in the first place.

I was fully aware of the level of expectation and while the money available to me did not, in any way, constitute a fortune, I was not prepared to sit around and let things carry on as they had done in the recent past. Having failed to prise Bryan Robson away from West Brom, I decided to buy Alan Biley from Derby County. As it turned out, he was hardly the monumental first purchase I had hoped for but he was young, enthusiastic, available and he had a very good track record. I had played against him and although he hadn't figured in too many First Division games, his scoring record was superb and he really did look to be top-class. Ironically, Ron Atkinson had moved to Manchester United by this point and he was also trying to sign him.

Alan started at Everton like the proverbial house on fire, scoring in his first two games and looking every inch a quality footballer. The problem is that you don't really know players until you work with them on a regular basis. Alan was a very good penalty-area player but there is far more to the game at the top level insomuch as you have to work a lot harder and prove your worth, not just as an individual, but as a team member. His contribution to the team was very disappointing after a promising start. Things just didn't work out for him at Goodison and it was not too long before he was confined to the reserve team.

I have always believed that all good sides are built from the back so my next job was to sort out the goalkeeping situation. When I joined Everton, Jim McDonagh was the first-choice as Martin Hodge was sidelined because of injury. Both were highly competent but I felt we needed that little bit extra.

Neville Southall had first been brought to my attention when I was at Blackburn. He was playing non-league football for Winsford in the Cheshire League and the reports about his performances were so glowing that I took the trouble to go and watch him in action. I really did fancy taking him to Ewood Park but I already had Jim Arnold and a lad called John Butcher so I couldn't really afford the luxury of a third goalkeeper. Consequently Neville remained very much in the shadows until Bury moved in and offered him full professional terms. Ridiculous though it may seem now, they paid just £6,000 for a man who is now widely regarded as one of the finest, if not the finest, goalkeeper in the world.

I checked on his progress at regular intervals and then decided that his potential was such that I had to bring him in. I paid £150,000 for Neville and, although I say it myself, it was a damn fine piece of business for Everton.

Neville was highly promising but too raw to throw straight into the first team so, having decided that Jim McDonagh was not suitable, I went for Jim Arnold, the man who had served me so well at Blackburn. Although he was 29 years old, I didn't think there were many better goalkeepers around. He wasn't the strongest of goalkeepers in a physical sense but he was safe, reliable and a good shot-stopper. It was a question of buying an experienced man, and using him, until Neville was ready to take over. I wasn't even sure that Neville would make the grade but I was confident that he had a fair chance.

I sold Jim McDonagh to Bolton Wanderers in a deal which saw Micky Walsh move in the opposite direction, to Goodison. He was always going to be a squad player but when he did turn out for the first team, he worked hard. He was a good pro, his only problem being that he lacked pace and mobility, characteristics which the Everton public naturally assume all their club's players should possess.

I wanted to keep Bob Latchford at the club but it soon became clear to me that he was determined to leave. John Toshack, the manager of Swansea City, had made him an attractive offer—an offer he couldn't refuse—so to avoid the unpleasantness of a tribunal, we agreed on a fee of £125,000.

I was disappointed because I really did want to work with him, having been a part of the deal which had taken him to Everton in the first place. I didn't want him to feel that I somehow resented the way in which I had had to leave Goodison Park in 1974 to pave the way for his arrival. That wasn't the case at all because I respected greatly what he had achieved in his seven years on Merseyside.

If public unrest was anticipated when the news of Bob's departure was announced, it did not materialise because I think the supporters knew that I had nothing at all to do with it. He was something of a folk-hero and I was anxious for him to remain and use his vast experience to help educate our younger players.

Having lost my leading striker, I looked around for a suitable replacement and again was swayed by a player's goal-scoring record. This time it was Mike Ferguson whom I bought from Coventry City in August 1981. Like Biley he had the instinct for scoring but this time the problem was not application but getting him out on to the pitch. Mike always seemed to be injured.

It might sound totally ridiculous but the root cause of many of his troubles was the size of his feet! He was about six foot three inches tall but wore only size six-and-a-half boots. It meant that when he was landing it was like coming down on stilts or high-heeled shoes. As a result, he was forever twisting his ankles.

Mike had enjoyed a tremendous partnership at Coventry with

Ian Wallace and I was looking for him to forge a similar relationship with Biley at Everton. On paper it should have worked, but it didn't. Mike made only ten full senior appearances for the club before leaving to join Birmingham City in 1983 but he scored six goals which proved my point that he was a talented player when fit.

Another problem area was out on the flanks because, although I had Joe McBride, I felt that we needed more width to our play. My philosophy has always been to use wide midfield players rather than orthodox wingers. I don't like out-and-out wingers unless they are very, very special.

If someone is working the flank for me, he has to be able to do something more than hug the line and provide the occasional good cross into the penalty area. He has to be able to move inside when required and also fall back to bolster the defence. Few players meet the requirements.

So, in an attempt to give my midfield an extra dimension, I bought Alan Ainscow from Birmingham City and brought in Mickey Thomas from Manchester United in a deal which saw John Gidman move to Old Trafford. John was a very solid and reliable player but I felt that I had sufficient cover in the right-back area to let him go.

The left-back position wasn't too much of a problem because I had John Bailey and Kevin Ratcliffe vying for the position. Bailey was in fact the first player I ever sold after moving into management at Blackburn. It was an historic transfer in many respects because it was the first time ever that a tribunal was called upon to decide a fee. The deal went through in July 1979 with Everton ordered to pay £300,000 for one of modern football's great characters.

Some things had worked out for me that season, some had not, including the purchase of Thomas, whose Everton career encompassed 11 senior games in four months. Mickey is one of those players which football spawns every so often who is unable to harness an enviable natural talent. He was skilful and lively but also somewhat undisciplined.

He had started every game until he picked up an injury shortly before a League Cup tie against Coventry City at Highfield Road. His replacement, Paul Lodge, played so well in a 1-0 win that I decided I would keep him in the side for our next game against Manchester City at Goodison.

To help Mickey's recovery, I included him in the reserve team squad for a Central League fixture at Newcastle. Unfortunately,

71

that was the only reserve team game that season which necessitated an overnight stay. The squad assembled on the Friday afternoon in readiness for the journey to the North-east but as the coach was about to leave, Mickey announced that he was not going. He told me that he had signed for Everton to play first-team football and that he had no intention of turning out for the second team.

It's funny, a lot of players have expressed the same sentiment down the years but they are quite definitely out of order because they don't sign a contract which guarantees first-team football, they sign a contract which does nothing more than bind them to a particular club. I told him that he was being plain silly and that one run-out for the reserves did not signal the end of his senior career. He was having none of it and was adamant that he would not travel.

Mike Bailey, the manager of Brighton, had tried to sign Mickey shortly before he joined us, so I rang him and asked if he was still interested. I explained the problem and he agreed to meet my asking price.

I am sure that Mickey will now look back on his career and admit that he was a little bit too single-minded on occasions, but the main thing is that he still has a career and that is only because of his great enthusiasm and ability.

Shortly after selling Mickey, I was to lose another experienced midfield player when Asa Hartford asked me to confirm newspaper reports linking him with a move to one of his former clubs, Manchester City. It was with some reluctance that I allowed him to move to Maine Road.

CHAPTER EIGHT

A Question of Balance

Having to tell people that their services are no longer required is a distasteful task, but one which every football manager has to face up to at one time or another.

Every successful team is underpinned by a strong backroom staff made up of tried and trusted individuals who can be relied upon to provide support, advice, encouragement and, occasionally, comfort and reassurance. When I took over at Everton, Geoff Nulty was the club's assistant manager and Eric Harrison the first-team coach. Unfortunately, neither was part of my future plans.

The man I wanted at my side as I attempted to transform Everton into a major footballing power once again was Mick Heaton whom I had promoted from reserve-team trainer to first-team coach during my time at Blackburn. He knew the way my mind worked and we had developed a very close working relationship over a couple of years at Ewood Park.

Like so many managers, I felt that it was important I had my own man at my elbow. Although Mick and I are both tremendous enthusiasts, we are different characters in many respects and, as often happens, it was a case of chalk and cheese complementing each other. Mick and I have always worked well together which is why I had no hesitation in offering him a job at Manchester City shortly after I returned home from Spain.

Colin Harvey was another man on the coaching staff when I arrived and I was delighted when he agreed to stay on to work with the reserve team. I didn't want to lose him because I knew that his vast experience would prove to be invaluable.

Despite a number of untimely injury problems, I felt the club to be reasonably stable as we approached the 1981–82 season. After our opening seven League games, we were lying in seventh position but problems were already beginning to materialise on the horizon. We weren't scoring enough goals, there was a general lack of confidence and our away form was very disappointing. Attendances at Goodison Park began to drop and there was an underlying feeling of disquiet, both out on the pitch and on the terraces.

The team was performing well out on the training pitch but failing to deliver the goods when it really mattered—on a Saturday afternoon. Strangely, although we weren't picking up many points on our travels, we tended to play a lot better away from Goodison Park. Some players seemed far more relaxed on other grounds where the pressure was not quite so intense.

One of the major problems was that we were being over-run in midfield and it was this which prompted me to return as a player. To be honest, Mick Heaton had wanted me in the team against Birmingham City on the opening day of the season. I had only missed half a dozen games in two long and demanding seasons at Blackburn and I was still fully fit.

When I took over as manager, I retained my player's registration. In fact, Everton had paid a small fee for me because Blackburn had quite rightly pointed out that they were losing not only a manager, but a regular member of their first team. I had told Everton that I wished to retain my registration so that I could play in the reserves. The idea was that I would be able to closely monitor the progress of the club's youngsters.

The reason why I didn't start that season in the senior side was one of personal pride. I had left the club in 1974 as a more than useful player and I didn't want to tarnish my reputation. I didn't want to make a complete fool of myself in front of those supporters who had fond memories of the young Howard Kendall. However, Mick was insistent and it eventually got to the point where I had to concede that perhaps he was right and that I could provide the leadership which was lacking.

Another man who had urged me to extend my first-hand involvement with my players for as long as was possible was the late Bill Shankly. Bill would often come marching into our Bellefield training ground in his familiar bright red sweater, looking for a cup of tea and a chat.

He appeared one day, shortly after I had taken over as manager, and delivered a piece of sound advice. "Howard," he said, "the first thing to do when you arrive in the morning is to put on your tracksuit so that you are ready to go out training with the players at 10 a.m. If you don't do that, you will find yourself stuck behind a desk all day."

So it was that on 24 November 1981, I pulled on an Everton shirt for the first time in seven years. We drew 2-2 against Notts County at Meadow Lane and although I played my part, I left myself out for the next game, against Arsenal. After a dismal performance at Highbury (we lost 1-0) the players urged me to return for the home game against Swansea City on the following Saturday.

I talked the matter over with Mick and Colin and both agreed that I should play. It was a nostalgic occasion to walk out on to the Goodison pitch after so many years away. I finished the game with eight stitches in a badly cut lip but we played with a good deal more poise and ran out comfortable winners.

I played in four more games that season, my last ever senior appearance being in an FA Cup third-round tie against West Ham United at Upton Park on 2 January 1982. Trevor Ross missed a penalty late on in a 2-1 defeat. It was not quite the stirring finale which I would have hoped for.

Some people say that the job of player-manager is perhaps the hardest in modern football but I have to say that I relished the dual responsibility. The only problem with undertaking two quite different roles is that you become even more incensed when things go against you. During the course of my career, I think I only picked up seven or eight bookings but most of them came during the time I was player-coach at Stoke City and player-manager at Blackburn Rovers.

Five days after I had hung up my boots for the final time, I withdrew £700,000 from the Everton coffers—a club record at the time—to buy Adrian Heath from Stoke City. I had worked with Adrian at Stoke and although the fee was, perhaps, a little on the large size for a player who was still only 20 years old, I saw him as both a match-winner and a crowd-pleaser. The problems of living with such a large price tag weighed heavy around Adrian's shoulders for quite a while but once he had settled in, and won over the supporters, he became a vital member of the side. He will always be remembered for two goals, the equaliser against Oxford United in a Milk Cup tie in 1984 and the FA Cup semi-final winner against Southampton later that same season.

I was reasonably happy with the team I had assembled and although we never really threatened to return the League Championship to Goodison, there was progress made during the course of that season. Our final League placing of eighth was lower than I had been hoping for but it was certainly more attractive than the 15th position of the previous season.

Leading by example. One of my last ever games as Everton's player-manager in 1982

Ron Atkinson and Howard Kendall before the 1985/86 Charity Shield

That was the first season when three points was awarded for a League win. I worked it out that under the old two-point system we would have finished one place higher and qualified for Europe.

There had been an all-round improvement but I began to suspect that the team *WAS* playing to its full potential and that there was not a lot of room for improvement. I realised that we were never going to make the quantum leap forward from also-rans to genuine Championship contenders. I didn't think that we would win anything unless I again looked to make changes. We were doing nothing more than treading water, albeit at the shallow rather than the deep end, but I had not come back to Everton to run a team which was happy to regard mediocrity as some kind of achievement.

Looking back now at that first bunch of players I brought to the club, I wouldn't say that I regard the decisions I made as mistakes or errors of judgement, although I must admit that several of those I introduced did make largely disappointing contributions. I wanted to improve the position which Everton was in when I succeeded Gordon Lee and, to be honest, I couldn't see a viable alternative.

I could have spent all the money available to me on one player (as I tried to do with Bryan Robson) and then patiently waited for him to transform the team's fortunes, but I don't think that the Everton public wanted me to show patience. They wanted immediate action and I was happy to oblige.

All I can say is that had I joined Everton a little later, perhaps 12 or 18 months later, maybe I wouldn't have dived in and reorganised the playing staff quite so quickly. Perhaps I was wrong to sign players on the strength of their track record rather than because I really, really fancied them as individuals in their own right. You live and learn in football management and that first year in charge at Everton taught me a lot.

Although we had not made the rapid progress I would have liked, I did not feel under any significant pressure because my board was fully aware that it does take time to restructure a team. Shortly after taking charge, Sir John Moores, the club's majority shareholder, had said that he knew it would take me four or five years to get things right. Two things sprang to mind when he spoke those words to me. Firstly, I wondered if things really were that bad, and secondly, I thought I would settle for that length of time in the job.

That one comment, offhand though it may have been, showed that the directors were appreciative of the many problems I faced as the new manager of Everton. However, I realised that Sir John's comment could not, in any way, be construed as the promise of a job for life. It didn't even necessarily mean that I would be allowed to fulfil the four-year contract which I had signed.

The summer of 1982 was one of the most hectic I can ever recall as I approached positively the task of once again changing the make-up of the club's first-team squad. Although we had achieved a League position of some respectability and come a long way in a relatively short space of time, I was far from satisfied and began to scour the country for fresh talent.

I was anxious to clear the way for the arrival of new players so I decided to undertake a mini-clearout. Several experienced seniors were made available for transfer and when we did not receive any firm offers, they were told that they would be allowed to leave for nothing. Players can look at free transfers in two quite different lights. They can either see it as a golden opportunity to make a bit of money, a killing if you like, or they can panic and assume that because their present club no longer wants them, then no-one else will either. I think my decision came as a bit of a shock to certain individuals but all those players who were released did manage to find new clubs.

Alan Biley, who felt, wrongly in my opinion, that there was no security for him at Everton, joined Stoke City on loan before moving to Brighton.

In June, an unwritten agreement stretching back more than two decades was broken when Kevin Sheedy made the short journey across Stanley Park from Liverpool to Everton. For some reason it simply wasn't the done thing for the two Merseyside clubs to buy each other's players. It had already struck me as being rather stupid. Quaint, but stupid.

In the event, Liverpool were absolutely powerless to prevent Kevin leaving Anfield because his contract had expired and under the rules which governed the freedom of contract, he could join any club he wished.

Kevin had made only a handful of senior appearances for Liverpool and was anxious for regular, first-team football. Obviously, I couldn't promise him that—I couldn't promise any player that—but I think he realised that he would have a better chance of establishing himself at Everton. I know that Liverpool were loathe to see him go because although he had played only three first-team games, he had done exceptionally well. They had him earmarked as one for the future but like all promising footballers, he was impatient.

I was so keen to sign Kevin that I had missed our final League game of the previous season against Aston Villa at Villa Park to go watch him play in a Central League fixture at Preston. I was impressed by what I saw on that day and I will surprise no-one when I say that it was his ability to deliver sweeping, accurate passes with that famous left foot which really excited me.

Few people realise that the deal very nearly fell through at the last minute. I met Kevin to discuss terms but his demands were too great. As I left him I said: "I'm sorry. I hope you get fixed up somewhere else. Good luck." I left for the club's end-of-season tour to Israel convinced that I had missed out on a player I really wanted at Everton. We were halfway through that tour when I got a phone call from Goodison saying that Kevin had changed his mind and that he was willing to accept the terms I had offered.

After what had gone on, I was no longer sure that I wanted to sign him. I have always believed that players, if asked, should jump at the chance of joining Everton. Kevin hadn't done that; he had shown some reluctance to commit himself and his uncertainty had disturbed me slightly. I gave myself two hours to think things over before deciding that if the deal was right before I had left England, then it was still right. I paid £100,000 for Kevin and looking back now, it would have been a very big mistake to have scuppered the transfer.

Money was still very tight at this point but I desperately needed a forward with a proven goal-scoring record so I invested £100,000 in David Johnson, who had lost his place in the Liverpool side as a result of the emergence of Ian Rush.

Like Biley and Ferguson before him, David could boast an outstanding record and while he was not exactly in the first flush of youth, he was still fit and mobile. Unfortunately, it didn't work out. He just couldn't reproduce the sort of form which had won him international honours and it wasn't long before he was on his way to Manchester City after spending some time on loan at Barnsley.

David Johnson is one of a select band of players who have had the good fortune to enjoy two spells at Everton. Another is Andy King who played for the club between 1976 and 1980 and who returned to Goodison in July of 1982 in a player-exchange deal which saw Peter Eastoe join West Bromwich Albion. Andy is a man who loves Everton almost as much as I do and even after he had left to join Queen's Park Rangers, he kept in touch and was a regular visitor to the club.

He had spent some time training with us during the summer of 1982 and I was very impressed with what I saw. The skill was still there but more importantly, so was the burning desire to play for Everton. I don't know if he was actually lobbying for a return to the club during those informal kick-abouts at Bellefield but if he was, it worked.

He was a regular member of my side that season until he picked up an injury during a game against Sunderland at Roker Park in early March. It was a bad injury, a very bad injury, and although he did return to the side the following season before he left to join a club in Holland, I don't think he ever really recovered. He was certainly never the same flamboyant player again.

Andy was never a truly great player but he was a very good player and a very talented player. People on Merseyside tend to remember him only for his knack of scoring in derby games against Liverpool but he had much more to offer than the occasional brilliant finish.

The other player who joined the club around this time was Derek Mountfield who was signed from our near-neighbours, Tranmere

Rovers, for £30,000. I had been monitoring his progress for some time and had been impressed by his strength and his positional sense.

Having recruited four players for a sum total of just £230,000, I felt quite pleased with myself. I couldn't wait for the new season to begin but at about 4.45 p.m. on the first Saturday, I began to wonder whether or not I had wisely invested the money which my board had made available to me.

Our first game was against Watford at Vicarage Road, a fixture which did not appear to be particularly over-taxing on paper but which was made so very difficult simply because it was their first-ever appearance in Division One. The ground was packed, there was a carnival atmosphere and Watford were determined to mark the landmark in their history with a victory. They won 2-0 and I don't think Neville Southall will ever forget that day because he was controversially credited with an own goal after carrying the ball across his line.

Back in 1982, Neville was still something of a novice and after selecting him for our opening 15 games, I decided to drop him and recall Jim Arnold. Nev was lacking in experience and the one aspect of his game which was faulty was decision-making. After sitting back and counting up the goals which were down to his mistakes, I decided that he needed a rest. He joined Port Vale on loan but there was never any chance at all of him leaving the club. He was simply in the middle of a bad spell and it is sometimes difficult for a goalkeeper to play himself back into form.

My centre-backs at the start of that season were Billy Wright and Mark Higgins but that partnership was ended in curious circumstances in early December. Billy was an England Under-23 international and a very fine player but unfortunately his weight went up and down like a yo-yo. I was aware of the situation, or problem, and that was one of the reasons why I had made him club captain. I thought that the extra responsibility would help him to sort himself out. Some players can eat anything—chocolate, junk-food, chips—and not put on an ounce in weight, but Billy wasn't one of them.

During my days as a player with Everton, Harry Catterick used to weigh his senior players every Friday during the course of a season and every day during the pre-season build-up. I have never imposed such a strict regime but I do keep a check on the weight of my players. Early on in the season we held a "weigh-in" and I found that Billy was about eight pounds above what we had down as his playing weight. One or two pounds is acceptable but not more than half a stone.

I told him that he had to try and lose the surplus weight without resorting to a starvation diet. We put him on the scales a couple of weeks later and he hadn't lost weight, he had gained another three pounds. His excuse was that he had recently eaten a large meal. I was unconvinced.

I remember taking part in a sports forum a few days later where I was joined on the panel by Tommy Docherty. I told him about my problems with Billy and about the excuse he had proferred. The Doc turned to me and said, "What was he eating? Lead?"

I had no option but to pull Billy into my office and explain to him that he could not be considered for the first team until he had shed a few pounds. I told the media about my decision, never thinking for one moment that he would be ridiculed in print—but he was. The next morning virtually every newspaper carried the story with the same headline—"Billy Bunter".

We were playing against Ipswich at Portman Road the next day and I awoke in my hotel to hear the local radio station's sports headlines. In a dead-pan voice, the announcer said, "Ipswich will be unchanged but Everton have been forced to rearrange their defence because Billy Wright has failed a late *FATNESS* test."

You could say that the lad brought it upon himself in some respects but that didn't stop me really feeling for him. He must have been distraught with the coverage. Perhaps it was my fault for telling the papers in the first place.

The adverse publicity had a devastating effect on Billy and he never played for the first-team again. Six months later he was transferred to Birmingham City which was a tragedy in many respects because, at the time, he was the club's longest-serving professional and a popular figure within the dressing-room.

His absence from the senior side presented me with a problem because his natural replacement, Kevin Ratcliffe, like Higgins, was a left-sided player. I just couldn't see it working out with both players having such a positional bias in their play. For once I was happy to be proved wrong and the two of them forged an impressive partnership at the heart of our defence.

I had always admired Kevin and had actually tried to sign him while I was at Blackburn during a period in his career when he was playing left-back for Everton's reserves. I was later to discover that

I wasn't the only manager who coveted his obvious strengths, for Bobby Robson also tried to prise him away from Goodison while he was in charge at Ipswich Town.

Kevin, or "Rats" as he is known within the game, will, I am sure, hold up his hands and admit that he is not the most technically gifted of footballers, which is possibly why he kept telling anybody who would listen that his best position was centre-back. He was right too, because his natural aggression and speed of thought made him the perfect focal point for our defence.

After being left out of the team in December 1982, Kevin demanded a transfer and I circulated his name to all Football League clubs. He doesn't know it, but it was only a gesture to pacify him because I had no intention of letting him leave. Had any club actually come in for him, I would have quoted a totally ridiculous fee to end their interest. You don't sell your best, or your most promising, players unless you really have to. I knew that Kevin would make the grade and that he would serve Everton well for many years. As it is, he is now the most successful captain in the club's history.

With Kevin and Mark working well together at the back and the midfield compensating for a lack of goals from our forwards, we made solid progress and after two months of the season we were up into seventh position.

All was going well, the signs were generally encouraging, but then, on 6 November, we played Liverpool at Goodison. I wish that I could erase that afternoon from my memory, but I never will. In front of 52,741 people, on the day which mattered most to all Everton supporters, we lost 5–0. No, I shall never forget it.

The previous weekend we had lost 3–2 against Southampton at The Dell and our centre-backs, Higgins and Wright, were absolutely awful; they didn't put a foot right all afternoon. I decided that I just couldn't run the risk of a repeat performance against the team which boasted the most lethal strike-force in English football; I had to find an alternative.

I had taken Glenn Keeley on one month's loan from Blackburn and I thought he was worth putting straight into the side despite the importance of the fixture both in terms of local pride and points.

It wasn't as if he was a young, inexperienced player making his League debut because Glenn was a good defender who had been around for quite a long time. Of course, he had never played a game in the special, rarified atmosphere which is created when Everton face Liverpool, but I was confident that he would not let me down.

As the history books will tell anyone who cares to look under the category headed "Debacles", Glenn's Everton debut—in fact his entire career as an Everton player—lasted just 37 minutes before he was sent off.

Now, as the person who carried the can for including him in the first place, I might be slightly biased, but I still feel that he was a little unlucky to be dismissed. The game took place under the shadow of the first purge by referees aimed at cleaning up football. The idea was to outlaw the use of the professional foul—a well-meaning, if controversial, policy which seems to emerge every four or five years. Glenn's crime was to pull down Kenny Dalglish as he threatened to break clear into our penalty area. We were down to ten men and, not too surprisingly, Liverpool took full advantage of their numerical superiority and absolutely slaughtered us. The man who profited the most was Ian Rush. He played magnificently and scored four goals.

Without doubt, it was the most humiliating 90 minutes of my footballing career.

I felt very low for a few days afterwards but when I sat down to analyse exactly what had happened to my team, I drew some comfort from the fact that I could find mitigating circumstances. One of my players had fallen foul of a new ruling, we had played for 53 minutes with only ten men and one of the greatest strikers in world football had played at the very peak of his form. The defeat still hurt a great deal but I knew that I couldn't be seen to be down-hearted or despondent because players quickly pick up on things like that.

Even in defeat you must always try to be positive and while it is essential that you isolate the mistakes made by individuals, you have to accentuate the plus points. People might find it rather difficult to believe, but every performance yields something which can eventually be turned to good advantage—even five-goal drubbings by the old enemy.

In some respects, the dismissal of Keeley took the pressure off the team as a unit because the papers savaged him for his actions and me for selecting him.

Managers always like to believe that they do things for the right reasons. I believed it was the right decision before the kick-off and, who knows, had he not been so severely dealt with by the referee, he might have gone on and had a magnificent game. We certainly wouldn't have lost by five goals had we enjoyed a full complement of players for the entire 90 minutes.

Although Glenn still had three weeks of his loan spell left to run, he went straight back to Blackburn following the derby game; it would have been too much to ask him to turn out for us again because the pressure would have been unbearable.

I don't believe that our supporters were in a particularly rebellious mood after that game because I think that they accepted it for what it was, a one-off. Obviously, they were deeply upset, possibly slightly embarrassed, but defeats in derby games cause distress irrespective of whether you lose 5–0 or 1–0.

The major problem with any heavy defeat is that it can have a knock-on effect and disrupt the rhythm of a team for several weeks. I was expecting an adverse reaction and I got one. We didn't win any of our next six games, slipped down to 15th place in the table and went out of the League Cup in a third-round replay against Arsenal at Highbury.

We were trapped in a downwards spiral and I just felt that we needed someone with enough self-confidence to take games by the scruff of the neck. I needed someone who would not only shake up the players around him but who would also breathe fresh enthusiasm into the Goodison public. I had players in my team who were hiding during matches. A football pitch is a large area but it is very easy to make yourself anonymous, to go missing.

The man I chose for what was admittedly a difficult task was Terry Curran. He had tremendous talent, but more importantly, he was a genuine personality who had a reputation for entertaining the crowd. I took him on a month's loan from Sheffield United and his impact was such that I then attempted to make the deal permanent.

What should have been a simple, run-of-the-mill deal to complete was to become something of a saga and it was not until the start of the following season that Terry became a fully-fledged Everton player. After Terry's loan spell had expired, I agreed to meet United's asking price which was either £150,000 cash or £100,000 plus Trevor Ross, our midfield player who had spent the previous four weeks at Bramall Lane. I assumed that everything would be rubber-stamped but was then informed that United had increased their price.

It is not uncommon for clubs dealing with the so-called "Big Five" to suddenly demand extra cash at the eleventh hour. Everyone seems to assume that because they are involved in a transfer with Everton or Liverpool or Arsenal they can ask for, and get, more money. It just doesn't work that way because, like the smaller clubs, the larger ones also have to watch the pennies.

The deal was resurrected shortly before the March transfer dead-line but after meeting Terry and his agent at the Football League's headquarters in Lytham St Annes, it again fell through. This time it was my decision to call a halt because I felt that Terry's personal demands were far too excessive. I wanted him but I was not prepared to redefine the club's wage structure to satisfy his terms.

I was bitterly disappointed with Terry's attitude at that time because for weeks he had been quoted in various national news-papers as saying that the only thing he really wanted was the opportunity to perform in the First Division. I had given him just such an opportunity and he had thrown it back in my face.

I was eventually to get my man in September 1983 and, ironically, I only had to pay £90,000. Many people thought it was strange that I should have rekindled my interest in a player who had initially rejected the chance to move to Goodison but, as Terry explained, the previous disagreement had been prompted not by greed, but by personal problems.

After all that messing about I wish that I could say the story had a happy ending—but it didn't. Terry was plagued by injuries after joining us and he made very few senior appearances during his time at the club. He played his part for a time but sadly not for very long.

The other deal which I completed around the time of Terry's arrival on loan did work out—the signing of Peter Reid, a player who deservedly figures prominently in Everton's Hall of Fame.

I find it quite amusing to look back on what Peter achieved at Everton because, three months after his arrival, I honestly thought that I had made a dreadful mistake in buying him and was convinced that the transfer would prove to be a complete and utter disaster.

I had played against Peter and had no doubts at all about his pedigree; he was a smashing player who epitomised everything I looked for in a footballer. The problem was that like every other manager who admired his skill and his tenacity, I was worried about his fitness because he had suffered so badly from serious injuries that it was something of a miracle that the man could walk, let alone contemplate playing in the First Division.

His medical record would have done justice to a hospital soap opera because in the space of three years, between 1978 and 1981, he had broken both his right and left legs, had torn his knee ligaments and had undergone surgery to repair a damaged cartilage. It is very rare that a sportsman recovers from such a catalogue of disasters. It takes a very dedicated man; a very special man.

After he had forced his way back in the Bolton Wanderers side, the word began to work its way along the football grapevine that he was reproducing his old form and that he looked as good as new. Colin Harvey went along to watch him a couple of times and reported back that Peter was once again performing steadily. I was such an admirer of his that there was no question of my not buying him—just so long as he was fit.

We were not the only club interested. In fact, Sheffield Wednesday, who were then managed by Jack Charlton, had gone so far as to meet Peter and agree not only personal terms, but also a fee. I knew that I had to act very quickly or risk losing him. I matched Wednesday's fee of £60,000 and was given permission to open formal negotiations with Peter.

When I met up with him, his first words to me were: "You took your time, didn't you? I was just about to join Wednesday." I just said: "Well, you're not going there now, you're joining Everton." You could say that he gave me the distinct impression that he wanted to join us which didn't really surprise me a great deal because he is a scouser and just two-and-a-half years earlier he had been poised to move to Goodison.

My predecessor, Gordon Lee, had been similarly impressed by Peter's natural instinct for leadership and had lodged an official bid of £600,000—ten times what I was to pay for him. That deal had fallen through because of doubts over Peter's fitness.

Money was so very tight at that point that I actually had trouble raising the cash to finance the transfer. I was trying hard to improve the quality of my senior squad but to do so, I was having to scour football's bargain basement. Having to operate in such a manner can be a thankless task but when you unearth a gem like Peter Reid, it all seems worthwhile.

Although Peter was passed fit by our medical specialist, I knew that buying him was a calculated gamble. Bearing in mind the problems he had had in the past, I knew, all too well, that it was a decision which could backfire on me.

To say that Peter had a difficult start after joining Everton would be a gross understatement. To use footballing terminology, he had a nightmare. I threw him straight into the first team but he managed only seven games before damaging his knee ligaments. I remember Colin turning to me shortly after Peter had arrived and apologising for his part in setting up the deal. He said he was sorry for giving me the wrong advice and added that he now realised it just wasn't going to work out, either for player or for club.

There was definitely a point in those early days when I thought Peter was not going to be able to cope and that he would eventually have to be allowed to leave. As his manager, that would have been embarrassing for me but sometimes you simply have to hold up your hands and admit a mistake.

I decided that I would give him every opportunity to get fully fit and then see what, if anything, he had to offer us. The problem was that in the back of my mind I kept running through all his past problems and wondering if he ever would be totally injury-free again. I really hoped that he would, but I just couldn't be sure.

Peter was missing from the second half of that season but we managed to achieve a decent level of consistency and lost only six of our final 21 League games. The team hadn't taken shape completely but, again, the signs were encouraging. Some of the youngsters I had draughted in were beginning to look the part—players like Ratcliffe and Stevens.

We enjoyed a good run in the FA Cup that season but only after being given a real scare in a third-round tie at Newport County. We just couldn't find the target that day and but for a late equaliser by Kevin Sheedy we would have fallen at the first hurdle. After something of a struggle, we defeated Newport in the replay and then booked our place in the last 16 by overcoming Shrewsbury Town at home.

We encountered surprisingly few problems in overturning Tottenham Hotspur in the fifth round at Goodison but our efforts were not rewarded in the manner which I would have liked for we were drawn away to Manchester United in the quarter-finals.

We won a lot of friends on that afternoon despite losing to a Frank Stapleton goal deep in injury-time. We played brightly and intelligently at Old Trafford and were very unfortunate not to take them back to our place for a replay. We had certainly played well enough to deserve a second chance but that is cup football for you, totally unpredictable and prone to deliver immense disappointment at the very moment you are readying yourself for celebration.

I think that one performance against United, full of spirit and enterprise as it was, proved that I finally had the club on the right lines. We played Southampton at home three days later and a banner draped from the main stand bore the legend: "Everton—we are proud of you." It was encouraging to know that our supporters were more than willing to acknowledge publicly a highly commendable performance.

Our season finished with a welcome flourish, successive victories over Aston Villa, Queen's Park Rangers and West Ham United giving us a final League position of seventh. I was reasonably content but aware that managers are only rarely given more than three or four years to make their mark at the bigger clubs. I had spent two seasons building, dismantling and then rebuilding my side and I suspected that I had perhaps another 18 months available to me to turn the tide and to start disrupting the dust which had been slowly gathering in the Everton trophy room.

I honestly don't think that anyone connected with the club had expected me to walk in and transform things overnight by winning either the League Championship or the FA Cup in my first two years at the helm. Having said that, I knew that they wanted to see progress, substantial progress, during that time.

Football supporters are generally the same the world over, that is impatient for success. I can fully understand that because, to many, many people, their club is the focal point of their life; they live and die for match days. I think that the Everton public was more patient with me than they would have been with someone who could have been considered to have been an "outsider". I think that they were willing to give me the benefit of the doubt simply because many of them recognised me as someone with a deep-rooted affection for the club. Even so, I knew that my third season was going to be of crucial importance.

In the summer of 1983 we parted company with Steve McMahon. He had come to the end of his contract and he (and his agent) were looking for a deal which was bigger and better than the one which we were prepared to offer. I was disappointed to see him leave for Aston Villa but my sense of loss was tempered slightly because I was already working towards buying Trevor Steven from Burnley. Ideally, I would have liked to have signed Trevor *AND* kept Steve, but circumstances decreed that it was to be one or the other.

I was faced by a straight choice. I could either accede to Steve's demands or let him go and then use the money generated by his sale to finance a move for Trevor. I chose the latter option simply because of my desire to strengthen our right flank. Steve was an out-and-out central midfield player while Trevor had a great deal more width to his game. I felt that we badly needed a quality player down the right-hand side so, in the end it was no contest.

If I am totally honest, I would have to say that I am a little surprised that Steve has turned out to be the fine player he is today. I don't think that I saw the best of him because I suspect his mind was already on a move away from Everton when I joined the club. Steve is a competitive, aggressive player in the Peter Reid mould but above all he is now a winner. The move from Villa to Liverpool in 1985 was absolutely crucial to his development, for once surrounded by a team of quality players he began to prosper.

I had been linked with Trevor for several months before I actually signed him simply because I would go and watch Burnley play each and every time I found myself with a free night.

Burnley had quite a useful side around that time and Trevor wasn't the only player whose progress I was carefully monitoring. Michael Phelan, now of Manchester United, was there and although I was impressed by him, I just had slight doubts about his ability in the air.

Brian Laws, the Nottingham Forest full-back, was another one who caught my eye but I had set my heart on Trevor because he was exciting to watch and I thought that if he entertained me, he could do the same for the Everton public.

A few years later, Bob Paisley told me that Liverpool had been very interested in signing Trevor but that on the three occasions he had travelled across to Turf Moor to watch him, he had failed to last the distance. It would seem that Liverpool rejected him on the grounds of lack of strength.

My only real rival in the days leading up to the transfer was Terry Venables at Queen's Park Rangers. He wanted Trevor but, by using the £300,000 I had collected from the sale of McMahon, I was able to meet Burnley's asking price in full.

Like Peter Reid, Trevor initially struggled to come to terms with football at a higher level. He was a quiet sort of a person—not the type to knock down the dressing-room and shout: "I have arrived." His form in the early part of the season was very disappointing and after about a dozen games I decided to drop him. It was for his own good because I could tell that the pressure of trying to justify a large price tag was taking its toll. I wasn't unduly concerned because I knew that his time would come. He had far too much quality to fail.

Being the incurable optimist that I am, I was really looking forward to the start of the 1983–84 season. I should have known better than to have tempted fate because my darkest hour was a little over four months away.

CHAPTER NINE

Under Pressure

I wouldn't necessarily say that my third season in charge was a case of make or break, but the supporters were expecting better things and so was I. Unfortunately, after a bright start when we defeated Stoke City at home with a Graeme Sharp goal, things started to go wrong and after five games we had amassed the paltry total of five points and were struggling in 18th position.

The first tangible sign of discontent came in the form of attendances for our fixtures at Goodison Park. They began to fall dramatically and on 22 October, when we played Watford, just 13,571 people passed through the turnstiles to take their place on the terraces. Goodison Park is a magnificent stadium but it can be one of the most desolate places on earth when shunned by the public.

Managers and players alike are fully aware of when criticism is being channelled in their direction but usually it is a general atmosphere peppered with the occasional raucous shout of derision. Things were getting so bad at this early point in the season that I could not only hear the criticism but I could easily identify the person responsible. There were so few people attending our games that I actually began to recognise individual supporters.

When supporters prefer to miss games altogether, rather than turn up and voice their opinions, there is most definitely something wrong. We were down to the hard-core—those fans who will turn out to watch their team irrespective of results and performance.

I found myself faced by a similar situation towards the end of the 1990–91 season when just 14,590 people assembled for a midweek game against Wimbledon but that fixture took place shortly after our defeat by Crystal Palace in the Zenith Data Systems Cup final and at a time when our League position could not be significantly improved.

Those people who voted with their feet in the autumn of 1983 had told me, in no uncertain terms, that the pressure was on.

Although I was conscious of the fact that even a club of Everton's size simply could not exist on such meagre attendances, I was not over-concerned about my position as manager because the season was still very much in its infancy. So many clubs panic if things do not go well in the first few weeks. They scramble around looking for a quick solution and usually attempt to pacify their supporters by finding a scapegoat. This sacrificial lamb which is to be slaughtered on the altar of public opinion is invariably the manager. Thankfully, Everton is a club prone to adopting a more thoughtful, more realistic, approach whenever a crisis begins to loom menacingly on the horizon.

Shortly after that Watford game, I received a vote of confidence from my Chairman, Philip Carter. Now, a public display of loyalty of that nature, when issued on behalf of a football manager, usually means that the sack is not too far away.

Actually, it wasn't a vote of confidence in the traditional sense because Mr Carter had simply been asked by a newspaper whether or not my job was safe. He did the interview in good faith, spoke his mind, but more importantly from a personal point of view, he told me exactly what he was going to say.

In his piece, Mr Carter stated: ''We are not complacent about our present problems—we are most concerned—but let us state unequivocally that our manager, Howard Kendall, has the absolute support of the board. He is little more than halfway through a four-year contract and the board has not been, and is not, exerting any

Under pressure, 26 November 1983. We lose 0–2 to Norwich City at Goodison

pressure on him. We are looking forward to seeing an upturn in attendances, coupled with improved results. We have every confidence that the team will achieve under him. That is not just a club chairman trotting out a hackneyed phrase; I am stating that categorically.''

Mr Carter, who only rarely agrees to do interviews, was rather annoyed when the article appeared because the paper's editor had added a sarcastic footnote which said: "Well, we all know what a vote of confidence means, don't we?''

Knowing that my board was still behind me was a boost but I knew that things couldn't go on as they were for very much longer. The team was not playing well, the fans were totally disenchanted and the attendances were showing no sign of improving. Something had to give and I began to realise that I was staring dismissal full in the face. I knew that time—if it hadn't already expired—was running out very quickly.

I was constantly being asked by the media about what they construed to be a growing crisis at Everton but my answer was always the same—it was far too premature to even discuss such a notion. However, I wasn't blind to the situation in which we found ourselves and told the journalists to ask me the same question in February. I knew full well that if the topic was raised 12 or 14 weeks later and we were out of the two major Cup competitions and still struggling in the League, I would have no option but to agree with them. The only problem with that particular scenario was that I couldn't be certain that I would still be in charge in February. I knew that my board could not afford to fly in the face of the supporters' wishes for too long and had they opted to take some form of drastic action I would have fully understood their decision.

Obviously I was worried about my future but my feeling of insecurity paled into insignificance when laid alongside the bitter disappointment I felt at being unable to provide the Everton public with what it was they wanted so badly, namely success and entertainment. I felt as though I was letting them down and that the team which I had built was letting them down.

I admit to being baffled as to why it was we were playing so badly in our League games because at Bellefield, during training sessions, the players were producing real quality. I am sure that I was not the first manager to discover that his team was a damn sight more effective behind closed doors—away from the pressure.

I knew that I had some very good players in my senior squad and

I also knew that very good players do not become bad players overnight. It was a question of getting certain individuals to express themselves fully on match days. I had to make them believe in themselves and replace self-doubt and inhibition with assurance, composure, confidence and consistency.

All problems in life reach a head, a climax, at some point and the unease which had been shrouding the club since the start of the season finally burst through to the surface on 26 October, after a Milk Cup second-round, second-leg tie against Chesterfield at Goodison.

Three weeks earlier we had won the first leg 1–0, but my how we struggled to impose our authority in that second game. It was precisely what I didn't need, coming as it did just four days after that dreadfully low turn-out against Watford.

The game seemed to be going quite well for us because goals by Heath and Steven had put us completely in command and, with a healthy, three-goal aggregate lead, I was already beginning to think about our game on the Saturday. But as was so often the case around that time, we mysteriously stopped playing and Chesterfield gleefully began to claw their way back into the tie. They scored twice, late on, to draw level on the night and although we rediscovered sufficient poise to ensure our safe passage through into the next round, all hell broke loose as the final whistle sounded.

People began booing and shouting as my players made their way down the tunnel and as the reporters began to file their copy someone rushed across to the press box and threw dozens of leaflets into the air. The photostat sheets read: "Kendall and Carter Out. Thirty thousand stay-at-home fans can't be wrong. Bring back attractive, winning football to Goodison Park."

It obviously wasn't a spontaneous gesture because a lot of thought had gone into the preparation of the leaflets. I later wondered if the supporter who distributed them to the media would have done so had Chesterfield not launched such an unlikely late rally. The conclusion I drew was that the people behind this protest had simply been waiting for the most opportune moment.

It really didn't interest me exactly who was behind this action but I must confess that my pride was hurt when I read that leaflet. To this day I don't have a clue whose idea it was but, as I have always said, supporters *DO* have every right to voice their opinions, even if it can prove to be a painful exercise for the focal point of their discontent.

KENDALL

30,000
STAY AT HOME
FANS CAN'T BE
WRONG!

and

BRING BACK
ATTRACTIVE, WINNING
FOOTBALL TO
GOODISON
PARK!

CARTER
OUT!

26 October 1983. The 'Kendall Out' campaign gathers momentum. (Distributed after the 2-2 draw against Chesterfield at Goodison, in the second leg of the first round tie of the Milk Cup)

What had initially been slight pressure was now intense pressure and the most worrying aspect about the whole affair was that it was starting to involve, and affect, my family. I arrived home from training one day to find that the words "Kendall Out" had been painted across my garage doors. The same slogan was sprayed on a wall further down my road.

I suspect that my children were having a rather rough time at school during this period although, like all kids, they bravely tried to hide things which they knew would have upset their parents. They must have gone through a very unpleasant ordeal when it was nothing at all to do with them. Their only "crime" was to have Howard Kendall, the struggling manager of Everton, as their father.

As I said before, my family will always come first and after thinking carefully about the enormous pressures which they were having to contend with, I began to seriously consider packing it in.

Football managers are only human and while they like to promote an image of great strength and conviction, they can only take so much. It was clear that a sizeable section of my club's supporters had come to the end of their collective tether and I began to wonder if I had not reached exactly the same point. You can bang your head against a brick wall for so long before the pain reaches an unbearable level.

Three days after the leafletting incident we played against Leicester City at Filbert Street and I knew that if we were beaten I should steel myself for a repeat performance. We lost 2–0 and those people who felt that I should be sacked did not disappoint. A section of our travelling support made clear their opinion during the course of the game and afterwards a group gathered outside the ground to make the point a little more forcibly.

It was difficult to imagine that things could get any worse but in the run-up to Christmas, our form deteriorated further. After drawing with Aston Villa and Sunderland at home and losing at Queen's Park Rangers, we were comprehensively beaten by Wolverhampton Wanderers at Molineux on 27 December.

That game was the turning point. I had taken enough and decided to offer my resignation.

I am not the sort of person to sit around and wait for things to happen; I like to think that I am in charge of situations. It was obvious to me that my position as manager must have been the subject of some discussion at boardroom level, even if only on an informal basis. It would have been easy for me to sit back and wait for my employers to make the first move but I thought that to be unfair. I was the man in charge of a team which was struggling so it was my responsibility. I decided to take the bull by the horns and went to see my Chairman.

What I needed to know from Mr Carter was whether or not he still had faith in my abilities. I decided that if he gave the impression of no longer having confidence in me, I would resign on the spot.

During the course of our meeting, I told him that I had had enough and that I didn't think the present situation was benefiting anyone. In the bluntest possible terms I said that if he didn't think that I was good enough, I would go. I had absolutely no idea at all what his response would be. Had he turned around and said that he was accepting my offer of resignation, I really wouldn't have blamed him at all because the club was in a totally unacceptable position.

If Howard Kendall and Everton Football Club had parted company on that day, I would have left Goodison Park with my dignity still intact because the decision would have been prompted by myself. That was very important to me.

I suppose that my whole career was hanging in the balance as I awaited Mr Carter's reply. You can imagine my sense of relief when he said: "No, I am not accepting that at all." He told me that he and his fellow directors had every confidence in me and that they believed the work I was doing would eventually be rewarded.

There are two quite contrasting reasons why I have never before made public the offer of my resignation. Firstly, it was a confidence between the Chairman and myself, and secondly, it is not really a subject I care to discuss.

If you resign, it is virtually an admission of failure and that is something I have always despised.

I left the meeting feeling reassured and happy to be still in the job I had always wanted. Even so, despite this latest vote of confidence, I knew that something very dramatic would have to happen out on the field of play if I was to survive for more than another two or three months.

When the going gets tough for a manager, the pressure comes from many quarters, especially from the media. At a time when I needed as much support as I could muster, I was disgusted to read several articles in which former players and managers openly commented on my predicament. These people were so-called experts who had not even tried management or so-called experts who had tried management and not even got their careers off the ground. I was reading pieces by these ill-informed people virtually every day. They weren't discussing *WHEN* I was going to be sacked, but *WHY* I was going to be sacked. In their minds at least, the whole issue was cut and dried.

97

You have to remember that members of my family were also reading these thinly-veiled character assassinations and some of the things which were written around this time turned my stomach.

I am fully aware that the media has a job to do and that job can often be very difficult. I have always prided myself on my ability to undertake the necessary role of public relations officer for a football club and I would like to think that I have the respect of a very high percentage of those journalists whom I deal with on a regular basis, whether they be from newspapers, radio or television.

My relationship with the written media had actually started to flounder much earlier on in the season because I had cancelled my normal Friday lunch-time press conference before the game against Tottenham Hotspur at White Hart Lane on 17 September. That was only our sixth game of the season but I had already had enough of the sniping and criticism. I don't know whether or not certain individuals were actively trying to get me out of the job but I began to suspect that they were not simply reflecting public opinion, but fuelling it. There is a subtle difference. I just did not feel, at such an early stage in the season, that the criticism which was being levelled at me was warranted.

We won that game at Tottenham but I declined to discuss our victory afterwards, pointing out that if I was not talking to the Merseyside national journalists, it would be unfair to talk to their London counterparts.

A few days after that game, I got together with the local press and told them that while I felt they were out of order, I was willing to wipe the slate clean and start afresh.

I was disappointed with the attitude of certain journalists I had known for many years but I was more upset with the actions of the ex-pros who seemed to derive enjoyment from publicly discussing my plight. Possibly I was being naïve and showing my relative inexperience of such matters but it seemed totally ridiculous to attack me when my team was still in both the FA Cup and the Milk Cup and had played only a handful of League games.

Although my Chairman had pledged his full support, I was still walking something of a tight-rope and I am sure that many people felt I had finally tumbled off and hit the dirt on 2 January when Stuart Hall announced on Radio Two that the appointment of Mike England as the next manager of Everton was imminent.

I knew nothing at all about this "exclusive" story. It wasn't until

I got home that I was told, my wife turning to me and saying, "It says on the radio that you're being replaced."

I was so confident that my board would not treat me with such disrespect that I didn't even bother to ring the club to clarify the situation. Mike rang me shortly afterwards to ask what the hell was going on. He was clearly embarrassed by what was nothing more than fourth-hand rumour and speculation.

Two years after this period, which some people like to refer to as the "dark days", Philip Carter received a lot of praise for sticking by me and placing his own credibility on the line. He deserved each and every plaudit which was pushed in his direction. The Everton board had proved that a vote of confidence need not always precipitate a dismissal.

CHAPTER TEN

From a Whisper to a Scream

Having emerged unscathed from what amounted to a major personal crisis, I knew that I had to work quickly to repay the faith which had been shown by my board of directors. I knew that if I was to see out the remainder of my contract not only would my team's League position have to improve dramatically but those players who had so far failed to realise their true potential would have to prove to their supporters and their manager that they were not only capable of living with the best that English football had to offer, but that they were capable of bettering the achievements of their rivals. It was a very tall order.

A few weeks before I had offered to resign, I had completed a transfer deal which was greeted with some surprise and much scepticism. My decision to pay Wolverhampton Wanderers £200,000 for Andy Gray was ridiculed in some quarters because, like Peter Reid, he was a player with a poor fitness record.

In the face of a goal famine which was threatening to undermine our First Division status, I had been actively seeking a striker with a proven goal-scoring record. My search had taken me down to White Hart Lane to run the rule over Steve Archibald who had been placed on Tottenham's transfer list. However, I then decided that the Spurs player who most suited my requirements was Alan Brazil. I had made known my interest in Alan midway through the previous season when he was at Ipswich Town, but at that point I was unable to raise sufficient capital to fund a bid. This time, my directors told me that cash would be found if a top-class forward was to become available so I made my move. Keith Burkinshaw, the Spurs manager, said that he was not prepared to release him which was a big disappointment because Alan was young, a Scottish international and a consistent goalscorer.

Even if I had been given the go-ahead to make an official approach it is highly probable that I wouldn't have been able to afford Alan because the money at my disposal in no way constituted a king's ransom.

I had drawn up a sort of hit-list of those strikers who were available and who fitted the bill. Paul Mariner, Ipswich's England international, was on it but he was valued at between £600,000 and £700,000 which was way, way beyond my reach. Further down the list was the name Andy Gray who was ready to move at a price which I could afford. He was a player I had admired for many years but, like every other manager in football, I was fully aware of the injury problems which had blighted an otherwise magnificent career.

I had been to watch him in a Cup match at Preston and, to be honest, he looked awful. He clearly wasn't fit on that day but after enquiring, I discovered that he had played in more than 30 games in each of the previous two seasons. That was an acceptable figure as far as I was concerned so I contacted Derek Dougan, who was Wolves' managing director, and agreed a fee.

Andy's main problem was damage to both of his knees—general wear and tear—but our specialist was happy to pass him fit. In order that he could make his debut against Nottingham Forest on the Saturday, we had to go through the bizarre procedure of signing him on loan for 24 hours to ensure that he was a registered Everton player.

Andy is now, quite rightly, regarded as the catalytic force behind the club's remarkable transformation, but his signing was a major gamble. I knew that all too well because a fully fit Andy Gray would most definitely not have been available at such a bargain price.

Six days before Andy officially joined us, I admit to making a quite dreadful managerial blunder by leaving Peter Reid out of the side which played against Liverpool at Anfield. Peter had missed a few games because of injury but he was fit and available for the first Mersey derby of the season. I just didn't think that we were good enough to go to Anfield and compete with them on equal terms; I knew that they were a far better footballing side than we were. Subconsciously, I possibly opted for an exercise in damage limitation because I overloaded my midfield in a bid to stifle their most creative players. A 3-0 defeat was made even worse because that game was one of the first-ever to be broadcast live on television. Looking back now, it really was an awful mistake to leave Peter out because he was a Liverpool supporter as a child and he always loved playing at Anfield. He must have felt as despondent as I had when

Willie Bell dropped me for the same fixture during my days at Birmingham City.

The arrival of Andy Gray was like a breath of fresh air blowing through a shuttered room crammed with anxious, nervous people. He was a quality footballer—a big name—and his impact was immediate. The morning after I had bought him, John Bailey walked past me at Bellefield and said: "Great signing, gaffer." That comment brought home to me just how pleased the players were at the news of the deal.

On the Friday morning before the Forest game, we went out on to the training pitch to do some work on free-kicks and corners. John floated over a succession of crosses which Andy met firmly with decisive headers. After the session, Andy, who doesn't know the meaning of the word shy, wandered across to John and said: "That is the best quality of cross I have had in more than five years." Bailey, full of pride, stuck out his chest and replied: "That is the first time anybody has ever managed to get on the end of one of my quality crosses for more than five years." There was a rapport between new boy and existing players from the word go.

Andy is possibly the bravest footballer I have ever seen. He never once gave any indication of caring about his own personal safety and would happily dive in to head a ball which had already landed on the boot of an opposing defender. His instinct was not for self-preservation but for goals. In that respect, he was totally unique.

I had bought him to make things happen inside the penalty area, a skill which is all too rare but one which he had honed to absolute perfection. When he was fit, and when he was provided with a reasonable service, he was the best around. I can pay him no bigger compliment.

He was also a great man to have around in the dressing-room with his booming voice and his self-deprecating sense of humour. He was blessed with the rare ability to lift and amuse his team-mates at the same time. When things weren't going well, I knew that I could rely on him to instil a sense of confidence into those around him. He was invaluable to me, and to Everton.

It was around this time that I promoted Colin Harvey from reserve-team coach to first-team coach to work alongside Mick Heaton. Colin had done a tremendous job with the reserves and the respect for him amongst the seniors was immense.

Another notable episode which I am sure all good Evertonians will remember revolved around a Brazilian international forward called Nunes. An agent had contacted the club and regaled certain people with wondrous tales of how this one individual would single-handedly transform Everton into the most successful club side in world football. The plan was to bring him over on a month's loan but I objected on the grounds that we would look pretty stupid if he was to come over to England and then make a complete fool of himself.

I didn't want anything to do with this deal but, by way of compromise, I agreed to study a video of the player in action. I couldn't believe my eyes when I sat down to watch the recording because on a beautiful South American afternoon, Nunes was wearing gloves. I thought, hang on a minute, if he joins us in the middle of an English winter, what the hell is he going to wear to protect himself from the cold? I contacted my board and said there was no way I was going to let him join us.

At a point when I was trying to build up my squad, we lost a player when Mark Higgins was forced to retire from the game because of a serious injury problem. Mark had been suffering from a pelvic disorder and I really felt for him because he was a genuinely nice lad and a very good footballer. It is painful enough having to quit football because of advancing years so it must be devastating to have to hang up your boots when you are still a relative youngster. Having known Mark since he was a 15-year-old, I was delighted when he made a come-back, firstly with Manchester United and then with Bury and Stoke City.

After all the disappointments of the season's early months, the tide finally began to turn for us in the new year. A team which had been faced by a real threat of relegation around Christmas not only reached two Cup finals before the end of the season but also climbed up from 16th position to seventh in the League.

Just six months after the "dark days", my Everton side was being hailed as one of the finest in Europe. It was a combination of things which brought about this astonishing reversal in fortune but the key ingredients were the arrival of Gray, the emergence of Reid and the promotion of Harvey. The fact that it took just three men to turn sporting logic on its head reinforced my belief that the club *HAD* been on the right lines for some length of time.

Of our remaining 21 League games, we lost only three and the stark contrast between the two halves of our season was not merely reflected in an improved League position but in our scoring record. Thirty-three of the 44 goals we scored in the First Division came in the new year.

After such a dismal start, it was clear that we had no chance of forcing our way into the pack which had designs on the Championship but once the spectre of relegation had been banished we were able to turn our attentions to cup football.

Our Milk Cup campaign may have ended in the glory of the first-ever Merseyside final, but en route to Wembley we encountered some very difficult moments. Having defeated Chesterfield, we were drawn at home to Coventry City in the third round. We were trailing with only a few minutes to go but a late goal by Heath and a very late goal by Sharp were enough to see us run out 2–1 winners. The man who turned that game for us was Reid who climbed off the substitute's bench to deliver his first truly inspirational performance in a blue shirt.

In the fourth round we were drawn away to West Ham United and although we turned in one of our best performances of the season, they secured a replay with a late equaliser. Goals by Andy King, one of his last ever for the club, and Sheedy saw us through to the quarter-finals and a very tough tie against Oxford United at the Manor Ground.

Everyone tells me that had we lost that tie, I would have been sacked but I still don't know whether that was the case or not. Certainly, to have gone out of the competition to a club from a lower division would have increased the odds on my being dismissed but whether it would have happened immediately, I do not know. Possibly it would because when we took to the field on that night, we stood in 18th place in the First Division and there were still sections of the Goodison crowd who felt that I should leave.

Oxford, a more than useful side, had enjoyed a tremendous run in the Milk Cup and it seemed destined to continue when they took the lead through Bobby McDonald. We fought desperately hard to get back on to level terms but as we entered the last ten minutes, I just couldn't see any way back for us. We looked as though we were going to go out. We didn't, of course, because Adrian Heath picked up a dreadful Kevin Brock back-pass and scored a simple goal. Well, that is how most people saw our 81st minute equaliser.

From my point of view, there was nothing lucky at all about a goal which quite possibly saved my job. I maintain to this day that it was the product of good team-work and I would urge everyone to study it very carefully the next time it is shown on television. Peter Reid made the goal happen because he intelligently put Brock under an enormous amount of pressure after he had picked up a

105

Adrian Heath readies himself to score the goal which many people believe saved my job. (18 January 1984, in the fifth round tie of the Milk Cup against Oxford United at the Manor Ground)

loose ball just outside his own penalty area. Heath has always had a smashing football brain and having seen that one of his colleagues was pushing Brock into a very tight corner, he drifted forward to stop him making a pass back to his goalkeeper. Thankfully, Brock did attempt to find his 'keeper and Heath was sufficiently alive to the situation to intercept. That was actually the easy part because the pitch was very icy and Adrian had to display brilliant control to take the ball around the last man blocking his route to goal. Even then, I wasn't certain that he would find the back of the net because he had left himself such a narrow angle. He did, though. There has been a lot of talk about that goal and its obvious significance but let's remember, it wasn't an own goal, it wasn't a fortunate penalty, it was a piece of good play.

Oxford did not get a second opportunity to undermine my career prospects because we played extremely well in the replay and deservedly won 4–1.

Our opponents in the semi-final were Aston Villa. I was pleased with the draw because it kept ourselves and Liverpool apart and

106

prompted people to start talking about the possibility of blue meeting red beneath the twin towers.

Having been drawn at home in the first leg, I was anxious that we should build up some form of advantage to carry forward to Villa Park. After an eventful evening, we won 2-0 which I thought was just about enough. It was a memorable game for Kevin Richardson in particular because, early on, he badly damaged an arm after falling awkwardly. He was in considerable pain but was insistent that he wanted to carry on playing. It was fortunate for us that his bravery outweighed his common sense because he scored our second, crucial, goal with as sweet a shot as you could imagine. His other major contribution was to block a Villa shot on our goal-line with only a couple of minutes remaining. The Villa players were adamant that he had used his hand to stop a goal but the referee saw it differently and waved play on.

By the time we entered the second leg, Liverpool had already reached the final by defeating Walsall, 4-2 on aggregate. It made the prize on offer even bigger.

We started very, very well at Villa Park and had a Graeme Sharp effort gone in rather than striking the crossbar, our passage through would have been assured. Having dominated the game with a display of authoritative football, we foolishly allowed Villa to secure a lifeline when an Andy King back-pass fell well short of Neville Southall and Paul Rideout nipped in to score. After that it was just a case of backs against the wall. We defended exceptionally well and the final whistle was the signal for scenes of euphoric celebration, both on and off the pitch.

Just two months after I had offered my resignation, I was standing in front of several thousand delirious Everton supporters, raising my fists in triumph as we celebrated together the prospect of the club's first Wembley final in seven years. It was a very special moment for me because I knew that I had given our fans just what they wanted; I had finally delivered the goods.

Much had been made of the pressure I was under in the early part of that season, and of the crisis which seemed likely to cause my downfall, but that period in my life only really lasted for a couple of months. I must admit that it did seem longer at the time!

Believe it or not, we were actually delighted to be meeting Liverpool in the final. Obviously, it is hard to imagine more difficult opponents but we were just proud to be involved in what was an historic and, as it transpired, memorable event. Three weeks before

Relief. The final whistle blows and we have beaten Southampton 1-0 in the 1984 FA Cup semi-final at Highbury

The Everton team receiving a kiss-o-gram speech prior to leaving for the 1984 FA Cup final

the big day we had drawn with Liverpool in the season's second League derby at Goodison so we were full of confidence and raring to go. We were slowly beginning to climb up the table and there was a feeling of great optimism within the club. I could sense the amazing change of atmosphere.

The final took place on 25 March and it was a truly wonderful occasion; everything that I had hoped it would be. It became known as the "friendly final" and with good reason because the two sets of supporters travelled down together, stood together and sang together at the final whistle.

Even the game itself was played in a good spirit and, in some respects, the final score-line of 0–0 was perfect. It was a day when there were no losers because the fans of Everton and Liverpool had shown the whole of football just how to behave at a match.

I still feel that we were unlucky not to win. We certainly should have had a penalty in the sixth minute when Alan Hansen clearly handled Adrian Heath's goal-bound shot deep within his own penalty area. The referee, Alan Robinson, was perfectly positioned to see the offence and there was no excuse at all for not giving it. It was a fairly even game after that controversial incident with both sides creating, but squandering, several reasonable chances. Although we hadn't won, we had matched the best team in Britain in a major final and that was very important in terms of our maturing process.

The replay took place at Maine Road just three days later and it took a tremendous Graeme Souness strike to finally separate two evenly matched teams. We were disappointed but we knew that we were on the way if only because by that point we had already reached the semi-final of the FA Cup. In an ideal world that is how the script is supposed to read at the big clubs—as one door closes another swings open.

Our FA Cup campaign had opened at Stoke City in early January at a point when we were still struggling to find any rhythm or consistency. Bearing in mind that our home attendances had sunk so low, I just couldn't believe my eyes when we arrived at the Victoria Ground. Everywhere I looked there were thousands and thousands of supporters. I didn't have to do anything in terms of motivating the team. I simply opened the dressing-room window and said: "Listen to that." It worked a treat and we won 2–0 with goals by Gray and Irvine.

The fourth round was not quite so straightforward. We had drawn Gillingham at Goodison, but played like novices in a very unattractive goalless draw. The replay at the Priestfield Stadium again failed to produce a goal but we were very lucky to survive because, deep into extra-time, Tony Cascarino broke clear down the centre. I was absolutely certain that he was going to score but Neville Southall somehow managed to block his shot to keep us alive. Although we lost the toss for choice of venue, we played with a great deal more fluency in the second replay down there and won 3–0, thanks in the main part to Kevin Sheedy who played magnificently and scored twice.

We strolled through our fifth-round tie against Shrewsbury Town at home, 3–0, to set up a quarter-final against Notts County at Meadow Lane. Despite having to wear a light plaster-cast on the wrist he had damaged in the Milk Cup semi-final against Aston Villa, Richardson opened the scoring in the first few minutes. County, whom we had already beaten twice in the League, drew level, but we won the game with one of the most curious goals I have ever seen in my life. A cross was floated over from the left and, with not a defender in sight, it was obviously going to fall invitingly for Andy Gray. I naturally assumed that he would let the ball bounce before taking aim. He didn't. He dived full-length to head in a ball which could have been no more than six inches off the ground. It was a remarkable piece of improvisation.

Semi-finals are always great occasions—if you win, that is. The last four had a rather strange look that season because, with the greatest of respect to our rivals, we were the only really big club to have made it through. Watford were drawn against Plymouth Argyle, while we were paired with Southampton at Highbury.

Although I had left Graeme Sharp on the substitute's bench, I told my midfield players to deliver crosses into the Southampton penalty area at every opportunity and then ring the perimeter of the box in the hope that one of Peter Shilton's punched clearances would fall kindly for one of our supporting players. The ploy worked reasonably well but with Danny Wallace causing us all sorts of problems with his pace and trickery, the game was very, very tight.

We were still dominating as extra-time neared its end and I was still convinced that we would win without having to resort to a replay because it was clear that Southampton had shot their bolt and were on the verge of settling for a draw. The magical, priceless moment came with just a few minutes remaining when Derek Mountfield flicked on Peter Reid's cross from the right and Adrian Heath darted forward to head home.

Andy Gray heads in our second decisive goal in the 1984 FA Cup final victory over Watford. Some people said it was controversial . . . but it looked OK to me

The Milk Cup, League Cup, Rumbelow's Cup—call it what you will—is terrific, but the FA Cup is in a class of its own; it is *THE* knock-out competition.

The distance between London and Liverpool seems depressingly short when you have just won through to the Cup final. We wanted the journey home to last forever because the M1 was a sea of blue and white as our supporters blared car horns and hung out of windows waving scarves and flags.

111

Our coach driver was told to take it easy so that we could savour every last minute of that drive back to Merseyside. He could have driven at five miles per hour on the hard shoulder and nobody on board the team bus would have minded in the least, such was our sense of uncontained joy.

I felt that it was vital we win the FA Cup for three reasons. The first, and by far the most important, was that success would return one of the game's major trophies to Goodison Park for the first time in 14 long and often difficult years. Secondly, it would guarantee European football in the following season, and thirdly, it would pit us against Liverpool in the Charity Shield.

For us, the 103rd FA Cup final was our second game at Wembley in the space of three months. For Watford, who had risen from Division Four to become Championship runners-up in just six years, it was their first appearance at the famous stadium in the 62 years the final had been played there.

Listening to what Graham Taylor, the Watford manager, and his players said during the course of the build-up, it became clear that they were going out to enjoy the day. I am not suggesting that they did not have a burning desire to lift the trophy because I am sure that they did, it was just that I felt our appetite was that little bit more voracious. We were also going there to enjoy the day but our main priority, in fact our only priority, was to win. That meant everything. Second-best was not good enough; it was all or nothing. I sensed that, perhaps, Watford were just happy to have reached the final against all expectations. I also knew that I wouldn't be happy unless we headed back home with that cup nestling on the back seat of our coach.

We played some tremendous football in the weeks leading up to the final and I was so confident that we would defeat Watford that I had to keep pinching myself to regain a sense of perspective. There was a danger that my optimism would seep through to the players and that they wouldn't prepare themselves properly. I knew that if we performed as we could, as we had been doing, we would win. Strangely, after all the problems we had faced in the early part of the season, I also knew that we *WOULD* perform because confidence was starting to reach such a high level that my team was beginning to look upon themselves as the best.

In the early stages of the final, the feeling that it might not be our day began to surface. John Barnes and Les Taylor both missed presentable chances as we struggled to establish control in midfield.

112

Keeping it in the family . . . Cynthia and myself on our return home after the 1984 FA Cup final win over Watford

I guess that's why they call it the blues! Watford Chairman, Elton John, puts on a brave face after the 1984 FA Cup final

Adrian Heath (left) and Andy Gray with the FA Cup, 1984

Thanks, lads. Celebrations with Andy Gray and Graeme Sharp, who scored the goals which defeated Watford in the 1984 FA Cup final

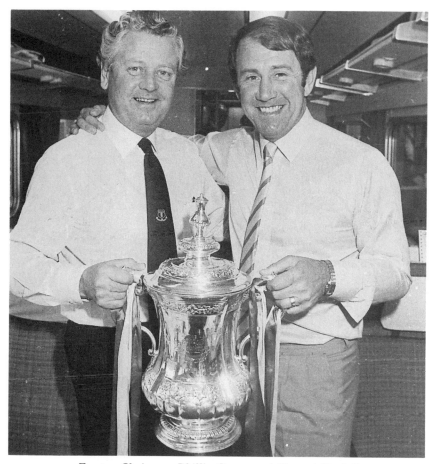

Everton Chairman, Phillip Carter, and Howard Kendall

Having settled down, we took the lead when Graeme Sharp showed lovely control before turning smartly to drive a shot into the bottom corner via a post. Several Watford defenders appealed for offside but Graeme was clearly in a legitimate position when he collected the ball.

Six minutes after the interval we scored again when Andy Gray rose superbly to head in a Trevor Steven cross. It is still regarded as something of a controversial goal because subsequent television replays showed that Andy had made slight contact with the Watford goalkeeper, quite possibly heading the back of his hands a split-second before making contact with the ball itself.

It doesn't matter how clear-cut a goal may seem, managers and coaches always do two things immediately the ball crosses the line.

115

Bob Paisley helps me celebrate the 1984 FA Cup final win over Watford

They look at the linesman and then the referee to make sure that there has not been an infringement. On this occasion, both officials were content with what they had seen, and so was I. Andy's goal destroyed Watford's spirit and effectively killed off the game. It was simply a case of waiting patiently for the final whistle.

The *Liverpool Daily Post* said that time appeared to stand still in the last few seconds of injury-time, the Everton supporters momentarily falling silent as the realisation of a dream approached. It was an unerringly accurate description.

I was in a very emotional state as Kevin Ratcliffe climbed the stairs to receive the Cup. I had twice been up those stairs as a player to collect a loser's medal and I was just so pleased that my lads were going up as winners.

From my point of view that success was not simply the end of a satisfactory season but the start of something much bigger; something much better. I said in my post-match press conference that the object was to become the best. To do that we would have to

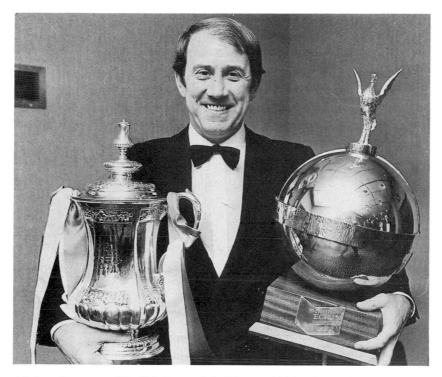

All that glitters . . . The FA Cup and the Liverpool Echo *Sports Personality of the Year award, 1985*

push Liverpool into the shadows which had been our home for so many years. I was at pains to point out that it is not necessarily the best team in the country which wins the FA Cup but it is the best team in the country which wins the Football League Championship. That was the next target.

At the end of a season which began in despair and ended in triumph, I won a Rothmans Football Award and I hope that I shall not be accused of boasting by reproducing the citation. I do this only because it succinctly condenses the contrasting emotions which I felt during the course of an unforgettable season.

It read: "In 1983–84, Everton came out from the Merseyside darkness which had shrouded Goodison Park since their last major honour in 1970 when they won the League Championship, a trophy which has since appeared to have become the property of their great rivals at Anfield.

"It was not an easy transition and often painful in the execution, but manager Howard Kendall kept faith with his ideals and persevered to a point where the second half of the season produced a respectable League position and a place in two major Cup finals. On top of this, the club's youngsters won the FA Youth Cup.

"In finishing as runners-up in the Milk Cup, Everton more than matched Liverpool over two absorbing games. In the FA Cup, they deservedly won the trophy for the first time in 18 years, marking a tribute to Kendall's honest and endearing approach to the rigours of management."

CHAPTER ELEVEN

Season In The Sun

The 1984–85 season may have been the most successful in Everton's distinguished history but it was too long—120 minutes too long to be precise.

Whenever I conjure up mental images to remind myself of that glorious campaign's many highlights, my sense of joy and pride is tinged with bitter regret for it ended on a depressingly low note. Even now, I can see Norman Whiteside cutting in from the right wing in the FA Cup final at Wembley to deliver the shot which robbed us of an historic treble. At the time it seemed a cruel and harsh footnote to add to a nine-month period of footballing excellence and my opinion has changed very little despite the passing of the years.

We wanted to win everything that season. We knew that we were good enough and it is somewhat ironic that our failure to rewrite the record books came about because we ultimately became the victims of our own enormous success. However, our defeat by Manchester United in what was our 62nd, and final, fixture of a gruelling marathon should not detract from an astonishing achievement.

Despite reaching two major finals in the previous season, I was still anxious to strengthen my senior squad because there is nothing quite like fierce competition to keep players on their toes. With this in mind, I paid Sunderland £250,000 for Paul Bracewell, a relatively small fee for a player who was to go on and achieve full England honours.

During my time at Stoke City, we had decided to start a youth policy by inviting 16 or 17 hopeful youngsters to work with the coaching staff for a fortnight during the summer. The idea was to assess their potential, select eight and discard the remainder. Paul was one of those kids but at the end of the course, we were not certain that he was suitable. We held an impromptu vote and, on a majority decision, he was told that he could join us. It was not a

119

unanimous verdict but we had been impressed by his enthusiasm and his work-rate. I followed his career very closely after he joined Sunderland from Stoke and when he became available, I had no hesitation in asking my board for the money to fund the deal.

Paul holds the rare distinction of having made his Everton debut at Wembley in the Charity Shield game against Liverpool. We won 1–0 to exact a measure of revenge for our Milk Cup final defeat.

The only other two major signings I completed that season involved players who were to enjoy hugely contrasting fortunes at the club. In September, I paid Birmingham City £90,000 for Pat van den Hauwe and in March, shortly before the transfer deadline, I bought Paul Wilkinson from Grimsby Town for £250,000. The former went on to win full international honours with Wales while the latter moved on to find success elsewhere after failing to fully establish himself on Merseyside.

Van den Hauwe, now there's a man with a colourful past, present and, I'm sure, future. Again, he was someone I had first encountered as a youngster because he joined Birmingham while I was there in the late Seventies. Mark Dennis, a player of the same ilk, I suppose you could say, was also at St Andrews at the same time.

I always thought that Pat had all the qualities to make a really outstanding defender because he was quick, aggressive and good in the air. Although he is a naturally right-footed player he was playing at left-back for Birmingham but that was actually in his favour as far as I was concerned because I have always believed that a right-footed left-back is much better than a left-footed left-back. Confusing though it may be, that is one of my firm beliefs.

I was aware of Pat's reputation when I bought him, insomuch as he had had his problems at St Andrews. I must stress that he wasn't alone in that. I just thought that if I could remove him from that particular environment and surround him with experienced, senior professionals at Everton, he would prosper. I was looking to the likes of Andy Gray and Kevin Ratcliffe to sort him out and put him back on the straight and narrow.

I sent Terry Darracott down to watch him and his report made very interesting reading. I asked if he felt he could step straight into our first-team and he said: "Yes." After I had completed the deal with Ron Saunders, the Birmingham manager, I asked Pat how much he thought I had paid for him. He stared at me for a few seconds before replying, "£30,000?" When I told him the real

Howard Kendall, manager of Everton FC, August 1984

figure, the colour drained away from his face. He was amazed at his value and obviously thought I had spent too much.

Pat quickly settled in with those around him because, by this point, the players were enforcing their own code of conduct, something which made my job a great deal easier. Our crowd took to him as soon as he was introduced into the first-team in October, which didn't surprise me at all. Pat is a very, very good footballer and despite all the stories which people may have heard about him, he is still playing in the First Division at the highest level. That speaks for itself.

The decision to replace John Bailey was a difficult one because he had been a tremendous servant. I knew that he would not be content with reserve-team football after two-and-a-half years in the senior side but I was reluctant to see him leave the club because he was such an inspirational character. His ability to illuminate a dressing-room with his infectious humour was valuable but not priceless, which is why I decided that I had to let him go when Newcastle United came in with an offer of £90,000 in October 1985.

Everyone at Everton has a favourite John Bailey story but I shall always remember him for his antics shortly before a derby game against Liverpool. He burst into our dressing-room with his number three shirt on the wrong way around and said: "God, they're in a right state; really nervous!" No-one could cheer up an apprehensive team quite like he could.

As is so often the case, our opening fixture of the season was very much a case of after the Lord Mayor's show, because we were beaten 4–1 by Tottenham Hotspur at Goodison despite taking a very early lead with a penalty. I don't know whether my players were still basking in the glory of their FA Cup win, but we were absolutely awful. Three days later we went to The Hawthorns and lost 2–1 to West Bromwich Albion.

After winning the Cup, I had set my sights on the Championship but just two games into the season people were already beginning to ask questions of us.

It was a case of trying to ignore those two results and starting afresh, something which we succeeded in doing in our third game when we won against Chelsea at Stamford Bridge. Of our next 16 League games, we won ten, drew five and lost only one, against Arsenal at Highbury. It was a tremendous run which was memorable for two things: moving to the top of the table after beating Leicester City at home and defeating Liverpool at Anfield courtesy of Graeme Sharp's spectacular volley from 25 yards.

Possibly our finest League performance of the season came seven days after that derby win when we took Manchester United to pieces at Goodison during the course of a 5-0 victory. It was a truly fantastic display.

During this period I kept repeating Bill Shankly's famous old saying that the Championship is not a sprint but a marathon. We were playing so well that I began to wish it was a 50-metre dash. We stayed ahead of the chasing pack until shortly after Christmas when a 4-3 defeat at Goodison by Chelsea saw us slip back into second place. It was disappointing but it sparked an even better run of 18 games which yielded 16 wins and two draws.

The performance which stands out from that particular spell of highly consistent football was the one against Sunderland at Goodison. We won 4-1 and the quality of the goals was quite unbelievable. Our football was flowing and the supporters were loving every minute of it. Whatever department of my team I looked at, I could see quality players performing at the very peak of their form. We were playing with style and flair in much the same way as had the Everton side of 1968-70.

I had played in a great side and I wanted to manage a great side. I knew that I was on the verge of achieving what was a very ambitious target. I was never once tempted to publicly draw a comparison between those two teams because, bearing in mind the transient nature of football, it would have been palpably unfair. Having said that, the level of entertainment which was being provided was so high that, had I not been in any way connected with the club, I would willingly have paid to watch Everton play during this golden period.

I knew that if we could maintain our form, the Championship would be ours. Things went so well that with eight games remaining, we only needed ten points to be assured of returning the title to Goodison for the first time in 15 years. With six games to go the target had dropped to just one solitary point. Our goal difference was so massively superior to that of our nearest rivals, Liverpool (who else?) that a draw against Queen's Park Rangers at Goodison on 6 May was going to be enough as far as the mathematicians were concerned. It was not, however, good enough for me and I told my players that there would be no lap of honour, no celebrations, unless we actually beat Rangers. I wanted to do things in style.

More than 50,000 people crammed into our ground on that day to see us complete the formalities with a 2-0 win.

How did I feel when the final whistle sounded? It was a mixture of ecstasy, pride and, I suppose, relief. Although we lost three of our last four League games, we still managed to finish up 13 points ahead of Liverpool. The margin would have been bigger had we not been forced to field weakened sides against Coventry City and Luton Town.

Forty-eight hours after clinching the title, we were presented with the trophy after beating West Ham United at Goodison. I felt an even greater sense of satisfaction than I had done 12 months earlier when Kevin Ratcliffe had lifted the FA Cup at Wembley. There is enormous strength in depth in the First Division and to finish at the top is a tribute to a side's character, stamina and footballing ability.

Achieving victory in style was so important to me because it is not without good reason that Everton Football Club is universally known as the School of Science. The dramatic improvement in League performance was reflected in the fact that we had not only won the title but had exactly doubled the number of goals scored in the previous season. It was an encouraging sign for the future that those goals, 88 in total, had been shared among so many players. Five men—Sharp, Steven, Heath, Sheedy and Mountfield—had reached double figures while Andy Gray weighed in with nine.

Any side with designs on the Championship cannot afford to rely exclusively on their forwards for goals. It is vitally important that they come from all departments. At the start of a season, I always find myself mentally pencilling in the number of goals I can expect from each member of my side. With certain individuals that is very easy because someone like Kevin Ratcliffe will be delighted if he scores just once. Personally, I think he should be capable of scoring at least two. If players who you have ear-marked for six goals finish up with ten, then you know that you are on the right lines and that your team is flourishing.

Derek Mountfield is a prime example. At the end of the 1984–85 season, his goal tally had reached 14, which is a magnificent achievement for a central defender. He managed to reach such a lofty total because, as a key member of a side which was playing well, he began to believe that scoring was just as much a part of his job as was heading clear corners at the other end of the field. Confidence is a priceless and infectious commodity within football.

Our defence of the FA Cup had started at Elland Road against a young but competent Leeds United side. The game was broadcast live on television, presumably because the TV moguls were sensing a major upset. It was perfect for them—holders v minnows; David v Goliath. It was a far from comfortable evening for us but goals by Sharp and Sheedy put us through.

We defeated Doncaster Rovers at Goodison in the fourth round, a game which, if nothing else, brought Ian Snodin to my attention for the first time. Ian played as a sweeper for Rovers and he looked to be a class above the rest of his team-mates. Almost exactly two years later, I paid Leeds United £900,000 for his services.

The fifth round presented us with the tie which, I suppose, all the leading clubs still left in the competition had really been wishing for—Telford United at home. In knock-out competitions, you can ask for nothing more than to be playing in front of your own supporters so to be paired with non-League opposition is an added bonus.

I went on a scouting mission to watch them and discovered that far from being the soft-touch many people possibly envisaged, they were very well organised and a useful little team. In fact, they were one of the best non-League sides I had ever seen. We won the tie 3–0 but, in some respects, the scoreline was a little misleading because they pushed us all the way.

The days when non-League clubs regarded a visit to grounds like Goodison Park as nothing more than a memorable day out have long gone. The gap between those sides within the Football League and those sides outside of it has closed quite dramatically over the past few years. Any game against non-League opposition is difficult these days as we found out shortly after my return to Everton when Woking gave us a few frights in an FA Cup fourth-round tie. As a manager, I am always pleased to see the back of any would-be giant killers.

In the last eight we were handed our third consecutive home draw, this time against Ipswich Town. It was a game which we very nearly lost yet one which showed the real character of my side.

We had started the game by producing the most elegant and stylish football imaginable. Those who saw it will probably remember our opening goal when Kevin Sheedy twice hit the back of the net with the same free kick. His first kick flew over Ipswich's defensive wall and into the right-hand side of the goal. Unfortunately, it was ruled out because the referee was still taking up his position. Undeterred, Kevin simply belted the ball over the wall into the left-hand side of the goal.

We defended very sloppily after that wonderful piece of improvisation and, by half-time, Ipswich were 2–1 in front, a lead which they were to hold until the dying minutes. The manner of our late equaliser said much about our determination because it was scored by Mountfield who, of his own volition, had wandered up front to find himself on the end of a van den Hauwe cross, not from the left, but from the right. Two players who were totally out of position had saved the day.

We won the replay at Portman Road with a Graeme Sharp penalty—an award which the Ipswich players did not like one little bit. Russell Osman was the culprit, handling an awkwardly bouncing ball just inside the area.

By the time our semi-final against Luton Town at Villa Park came around our season was really on the boil. We were on top of the First Division and embroiled in a fascinating European Cup Winners' Cup semi-final with Bayern Munich. Inevitably, people began asking me whether the treble was a possibility. After initially refusing to discuss the subject (one game at a time etc . . .), I made a deliberate point of changing my stance and stating publicly that we had an excellent chance of creating history. I knew that my players would not regard this as over-confidence on my part because they were similarly convinced that the impossible dream could be made a reality.

I knew that the Luton game was going to prove a stiff test of our mental and physical resources because it came just three days after the excitement and drama of our game in Munich.

The fact that we were the clear favourites to reach a second, successive final didn't help a great deal because the feeling of expectancy amongst our many thousands of supporters only served to increase the pressure on players who had performed so well in West Germany but who were obviously a little tired.

I thought that if we adopted a patient approach in the first 30 minutes or so, we would be able to ease ourselves back into the familiar rhythm. Unfortunately, Luton went hell for leather from the very first whistle. They had done their homework; they knew we would be suffering from battle-fatigue and they were determined to press home their advantage in the early stages. Ricky Hill opened the scoring for Luton before half-time but I still believe that it should have been ruled out for a foul on Gary Stevens during the immediate build-up.

I still thought that we would find enough energy to win the game but as the final whistle began to edge ever nearer Luton held firm. With just a couple of minutes left, I thought our chance had gone and I was resigned to defeat.

127

I should have known better because when you have men like Kevin Sheedy in your side, where there is life, there is hope. I think that it is fair to say that Kevin shouldn't even have been playing that day because he was carrying an injury and I knew that I was really gambling by selecting him. He hadn't played particularly well during the game and Kevin Richardson, our substitute, obviously thought he should have been picked because every time Sheedy made a mistake he turned and stared at me as if to say: "I told you so."

With a little over two minutes left, Kevin swept a 20-yard free-kick into the Luton net via the inside of a post. It wasn't what you could describe as a Sheedy special because, while it was accurate, it lacked power and seemed to bobble in. He was so desperately tired that it was probably all he had left to give but it was enough.

The whole Everton bench leapt forward on to the pitch and, I must admit, I felt such an overwhelming sense of relief that I momentarily slipped into a state of complete confusion. I turned to Colin Harvey and said: "Great. That'll do me. A replay. When is it?"

He replied: "What are you talking about—there's extra time!" Even though we had been forced into an extra 30 minutes by Southampton just 12 months earlier in the same circumstances, I thought he was joking. After my giggling colleagues had convinced me that the game was far from over, I was utterly convinced that we would score again. The psychological advantage we had gained by scoring so late in a semi-final was massive and I knew that the composure of the Luton players would have been badly affected.

Although we had weathered the worst of the Luton storm, they kept coming at us but our self-belief had been restored by Sheedy's strike and it was his cross which provided Derek Mountfield with the opportunity to head in the decisive goal. A tidal wave of determination and effort had carried us back to Wembley.

It would be wrong to talk about the final against United without first running through our Cup Winners' Cup campaign because the two competitions were interwoven to such an extent that I believe victory in one precipitated defeat in the other.

Our foray into Europe had begun not so much with a bang as a whimper because in the first round we had been paired with University College, Dublin. In many respects what should have been our easiest tie of the tournament actually turned out to be the most difficult. The first leg was away and people expected us to travel to Dublin and run up a cricket score. We didn't because although UCD had ground advantage, they played as though they were away from home. If it was an exercise in damage limitation, it certainly worked because they defended exceptionally well and held out for a goalless draw.

It was the first time in my career I had ever seen a home side put up the shutters in an attempt to keep the score down. I suppose I should have been flattered that they held us in such high esteem but I felt only disappointment on the journey home.

If anything, the second leg at Goodison was an even more frustrating experience because we again played poorly. The tie was to be eventually decided by a Graeme Sharp goal but we had a couple of very anxious moments towards the end, for had UCD scored we would have fallen at the first hurdle on the away-goals rule.

Still, we had achieved our objective of reaching the next round where we were drawn against Inter Bratislava of Czechoslovakia. This was to be the first real test because we were going into the unknown against a side I knew nothing at all about. I was naturally assuming that they would provide us with problems but you sometimes find that European teams do not have the fancy footwork to match their fancy names. This was just such a case because, over the course of the two legs, Bratislava really disappointed me from a footballing point of view.

We won the first leg in Czechoslovakia, 1-0, thanks to a rare goal from Paul Bracewell. The respect afforded to us by our hosts was such that we could, and possibly should, have had more goals. With the cushion of a crucial away goal, we romped to a comfortable 3-0 victory a fortnight later at Goodison to move forward into the quarter-finals.

Our opponents were the Dutch side, Fortuna Sittard, but this time the circumstances were slightly different because we were at home in the first leg, which was a distinct disadvantage. I needn't have worried too much because Andy Gray turned the game into a one-man show with a brilliant hat-trick. One of his goals was a typical diving header which left the Sittard defence dumbfounded at the man's lack of fear. We would have had to have delivered an absolute nightmare of a display to have lost the tie after Andy's heroics but, if anything, the return leg went even better for us with goals by Sharp and Peter Reid sealing an emphatic victory.

The other teams through to the last four were Bayern Munich, Rapid Vienna and Dynamo Moscow. People asked me which of the three I would rather be drawn against and my response was always the same—I didn't care as long as it wasn't Bayern!

When the news came through that we had indeed drawn the West Germans, I was disappointed because they were arguably the best team left in the competition and were the clear favourites to win it. The only consolation was that we would be playing in Munich's magnificent Olympic Stadium in the first leg. I knew that if we could produce a solid performance and keep the tie alive Bayern would not relish the prospect of playing in front of a packed Goodison Park.

Just three days before our FA Cup semi-final against Luton, we went out there and did a truly professional job in the most intimidating circumstances. I decided to use Alan Harper and Kevin Richardson wide in midfield with Trevor Steven floating up front to support Sharp. We played so well that Bayern were reduced to long-range shots long before the interval. We closed them down, denied them space in which to build and suffocated their talented midfield section. It was a brilliant performance; different class, as we say within the game.

1985 European Cup Winners' Cup semi-final. The first leg against Bayern Munich in the Olympic Stadium

Graeme Sharp scores our first goal against Bayern Munich on a quite unforgettable night. (Cup Winners' Cup semi-final, second leg at Goodison Park, 1985)

Andy Gray hits the second against Bayern Munich. (Cup Winners' Cup semi-final, second leg, at Goodison Park, 1985)

Trevor Steven scores our third goal against Bayern Munich. (Cup Winners' Cup semi-final, second leg, at Goodison Park, 1985)

We had successfully negotiated what amounted to one of the most daunting tasks in world football; we had been into the lion's den, and while we hadn't actually put the beast to the sword, we had emerged unscathed. Udo Lattek, the Bayern manager, said afterwards that the most important thing was that his side had not conceded an away goal. I would have tried to hide my bitter disappointment in exactly the same way had I been in his position.

That one result seemed to prove, beyond a shadow of a doubt, that the transformation of Everton was almost complete. I was not surprised at all that the media sought out my Chairman to establish his personal views on the great metamorphosis. Mr Carter was asked to reflect on the "dark days" and, for once, I really didn't mind this gloomy, and not too distant, past being discussed.

Mr Carter said: "If things had continued to go from bad to worse, we should have had to have admitted that we made a mistake, but it never came that close. It was not a question of sticking with Howard, but of giving continued support to the man I had selected in the first place.

"When we appointed him, we knew he had limited experience but a lot of potential. We realised that we were going to have a period of rebuilding and consolidation. What we said in effect was: 'We believe in you and your judgement, now go out and get it right.' We knew what Howard was trying to do and I think that he would be the first to admit that he has learned a lot in the last four years."

If I was allowed to carry just one footballing memory with me for the remainder of my life, it would probably be the second-leg tie

Andy Gray and Graeme Sharp celebrate the magnificent win over Bayern Munich at Goodison. (Cup Winners' Cup semi-final, second leg, 3–1, April 1985)

against Bayern at Goodison on 24 April 1985. What a night; what an unforgettable night.

There were just under 50,000 people in the ground as we emerged from the tunnel shortly before kick-off. The noise was deafening, the atmosphere electric.

When you are playing at home in the second leg of any competition there is always the danger that you will let your natural enthusiasm run away with you, and that your discipline will desert you. We played well in the first-half but one moment of slackness at the back cost us dearly because Hoeness climaxed a rare German breakaway by scrambling home a crucial goal for Bayern just before the interval. I have never known a ground fall so silent. It meant that if we didn't score twice, we would be eliminated on the away-goals rule.

The tension in our dressing-room at half-time was so palpable that you felt you could reach out and grasp it. I told my players not to worry but to carry on playing as they had been. One of the important things was that we would be attacking the Gwladys Street terracing in the second half, a section which is made up of supporters so fanatical that, at times, they seem to be almost capable of sucking the ball into the net. I tried to impress on a group of disappointed players that the game wasn't over simply because Bayern's one, solitary attack had yielded a goal. I was confident that if we could display patience and show character the Germans would eventually crack.

After exerting tremendous pressure, we were finally rewarded when Graeme Sharp headed in at the near post after the Bayern defence had failed to clear Gary Stevens' long throw. Our second goal was almost a repeat performance with Stevens again unhinging our opponents' defence with a huge throw-in. This time it was Andy Gray who profited. Bayern just could not cope with an unfamiliar tactic and seemed to be on the verge of capitulation.

Although we were playing hard but fair, Mr Lattek was not impressed. Shortly after one of his players had been forced to leave the field for treatment on a bloody nose, he leaned out of his dug-out and shouted: "Kendall, this is not football." Everyone sitting on our bench stood up and, to a man, told him where to go. There was no real malice involved—we were just so wound up. The Germans were well and truly rattled and we made sure of victory towards the end with a quite wonderful Trevor Steven goal.

The scenes at the final whistle were unbelievable as thousands and thousands of our fans roared their approval. I was on such a high that I knew it would take me hours to "come down". I rang home and told Cynthia that she would see me when she saw me. I was going to celebrate in style.

I went down to a restaurant in Liverpool's Chinatown with a few friends and just sat there, reliving a very special moment in my life. Even when I got home in the very small hours I couldn't relax. I'll always remember my kids coming down in the morning to get ready for school—I was still sitting in front of the television watching a video recording of the game.

It's funny looking back now because we hadn't won the Cup, just the semi-final, but I suspected that my joy was not unduly premature because, like virtually everyone else, I knew that we had cleared the biggest obstacle. That tie against Bayern, a team which was leading the West German Bundesliga at the time, *WAS* the final in my eyes. It didn't really matter who we faced in the final itself because it couldn't be any more difficult.

Rapid Vienna had beaten Dynamo Moscow, 4–2 on aggregate, so I went out to run the rule over them at the earliest opportunity. What I saw that night absolutely delighted me. They were nowhere

1987. We've made it. League champions for the second time in three seasons

Andy Gray celebrates his goal in the 1985 European Cup Winners' Cup win over Rapid Vienna in Rotterdam. (Also Graeme Sharp and Paul Bracewell, right)

Graeme Sharp holds aloft the Cup Winners' Cup—Everton's first European success

1985. The flight home after the Cup Winners' Cup win over Rapid Vienna in Rotterdam. Mick Heaton, Howard Kendall and John Clinkard (former physio)

near as good as Bayern and I knew that we could beat them quite handsomely.

I had to be very careful when I faced my players for the first time after seeing Rapid in action because they naturally wanted to gauge my reaction. Deep down inside, I knew that we would win the final—but I couldn't tell my players as much. Don't get me wrong, Rapid weren't a bunch of no-hopers but we were better; a lot better.

By the time we departed for Rotterdam, the League title was ours. It was good to know that my players would not have to lift themselves for the final three League fixtures if things were to go against us in Holland and, three days later, at Wembley in the FA Cup final.

The build-up to the Cup Winners' Cup final was wonderful as our supporters took over central Rotterdam and transformed it into a home from home. They played impromptu football games with the local police, charmed the hoteliers and inn-keepers with their wit and made friends wherever they went. In short, they were a credit to Merseyside.

The game itself went exactly according to plan even if I was a little surprised at our failure to underline our obvious superiority in the first half. We did not take the lead until the 57th minute when Graeme Sharp intercepted an under-hit back-pass and crossed for

Andy Gray to coolly convert from about eight yards. We were on our way.

One goal would probably have been enough to guarantee victory but my players were so determined to show a massive world-wide television audience that they were a vastly superior side, they just kept pushing forward. We doubled our advantage in the 72nd minute when Trevor Steven, lurking at the far post, drove in a Kevin Sheedy corner which had eluded the lunging boots of at least three defenders.

Our one moment of anxiety came shortly afterwards when Hans Krankl raced through to score a goal which Rapid really didn't deserve. He took his chance well but I have no doubts that he was in an offside position when he collected the ball.

About 30 seconds before Krankl placed the ball in the rear of our net, the man who was responsible for media liaison had approached me on the bench to ask if I would attend a press conference immediately after we had been presented with the Cup. At the precise moment he finished his question, Rapid scored. He was obviously a bad omen so I told him to clear off and leave me alone. He was sheepishly walking away when Kevin Sheedy raced up to the other end to fire in the third goal which clinched our win. I turned around and shouted: "OK. You can talk to me now."

Everton had won a European trophy for the first time but we couldn't relax because we had to go straight back home and prepare for the little matter of a Wembley date with Manchester United. It was astonishing to think that although we had achieved so much, our season was still far from over.

It was rather like being on a treadmill but I wouldn't have changed places with anyone, not for all the tea in China.

On our flight home, one of the sports writers told me of his post-match interview with Hans Krankl and how he had described us as possibly the best team in Europe. I revelled in those comments all the way to Liverpool airport. I don't know whether or not Krankl was correct in what he said because I was fully aware that the true test would come in the following season when we would be pitted against the very best—in the European Cup. Sadly, it was not to be.

Our preparations for the FA Cup final went very well, until, that was, I woke up on the Saturday morning and drew back the curtains in my hotel room. I had been silently praying for a cool, overcast day but the sun was beating down. It wasn't cracking the flag-stones, but it was very, very hot.

It had been a long season and after all the excitement of Rotterdam, I knew that my players would be shattered. It is never difficult to lift yourself for an FA Cup final but sometimes the body is not quite as willing as is the mind. It seemed almost cruel that a team which had performed with such distinction just three days earlier would be forced to chase a place in history in such unsympathetic conditions. What I wouldn't have given for a few clouds and a sprinkling of refreshing rain.

We desperately needed to get off to a flier and I still believe that had we managed to take an early lead, we would have gone on to win the game and claim that historic treble. We very nearly did score early on when Peter Reid had a shot kicked off the line by John Gidman, of all people.

To be honest, it wasn't a very good game at all because even though my players were showing distinct signs of tiredness, they did enough to hold United at bay. I suppose that the game is best remembered for the sending-off of Kevin Moran for his tackle on Reid—the first-ever dismissal in an FA Cup final at Wembley. Moran did commit a foul, there is no doubt about that, but he is a big, honest lad and I don't think there was any malicious intent. He shouldn't have been sent off—a booking would have been sufficient punishment.

Unfortunately, a warning wasn't enough for the referee, Peter Willis, a policeman who seemingly had his uniform on that afternoon. The foul looked far worse than it actually was because Moran caught Reid as he was off balance and sent him flying through the air like a top. Peter is the sort of professional who only rarely complains about fouls and he tried very hard to make Mr Willis change his mind.

That decision swung the game in United's favour. It is quite amazing how many times a team which has been reduced to ten men fights back to win matches. United became even more determined to win the Cup, probably for their disgraced team-mate, and we just had no more left to give. With seven minutes of extra-time left to play, Whiteside unleashed a long-range shot which flew past Neville Southall and into the bottom corner of our goal.

The decision not to allow Moran to go up and collect his winners' medal was absolutely ridiculous. Yes, he'd been sent off, but he had played his part in United's victory. In fact, he was more instrumental in that victory than possibly he will ever realise.

It was disappointing to lose but it wasn't a shattering blow because the season had been simply fantastic. My players were

Chairman Philip Carter joins me in celebrating our Championship success in 1987

Kevin Ratcliffe becomes the first Everton captain in 15 years to lift a Championship trophy, 1985

The marathon is over. My team celebrate the 1985 League Championship success

The true sign of success . . . an open-topped bus tour of the city, 1985. (Championship Trophy and Cup Winners' Cup)

1985. Tour of the city

Simply the best. Neville Southall and his FWA Player of the Year award, 1985

1985. Ron Atkinson and myself with English football's biggest prizes

obviously upset but I think they knew that they couldn't have given any more. It was just one game too many.

Don't get me wrong, this is not a case of sour grapes because United were the better side on the day and deserved to win.

For the players themselves the season also brought personal kudos. Peter Reid was chosen by the Professional Footballers' Association as their Player of the Year, Neville Southall was the choice of the Football Writers' Association. My season was made complete when I was named as the Bell's Manager of the Year.

We had emerged from the shadow of Anfield for a buoyant season in the sun and, with a young team, it was reasonable to assume that the sun would continue to shine over Goodison Park for the foreseeable future. It was a satisfying way in which to celebrate my 21st "birthday" as a professional footballer and manager.

1985 and we are the European Team of the Year

Personal success in the shape of the 1987 Bells' Manager of the month award

CHAPTER TWELVE

Heysel

Just three weeks after we had been crowned Football League champions, it became clear that we would not be allowed to have a crack at the European Cup in the following season.

On 29 May 1985, like millions of other football-lovers around the world, I sat in my living-room and watched incredulously as the horror of the Heysel Stadium disaster unfolded. It became clear early on in the television coverage that something was dreadfully wrong. They kept alternating between the studio in London and the live broadcast from Brussels as the assembled panel of experts attempted to place into something like perspective exactly what was happening.

After our success in the Cup Winners' Cup two weeks earlier, I was really hoping that Liverpool would defeat Juventus to lift the Champions' Cup. It would have been a memorable double for the city of Liverpool and no-one would have been able to dispute that Merseyside was, indeed, the capital of European football.

Watching it on television, I felt somehow detached from the whole wretched business because unless you are actually at an event it is difficult to fully grasp the implications. When it became clear that people were dying, I just found it totally unbelievable. It was a football match, for God's sake; a major sporting event; a day out for fathers and sons, mothers and daughters.

I was to experience the same feeling of revulsion after the Hillsborough disaster. I was working in Bilbao on that day, listening to the World Service on the radio to follow the progress of Everton in their semi-final against Norwich City. I remember the newsreader describing the scenes at Hillsborough as similar to those of Heysel and thinking that he was either ill-informed or over-exaggerating things. Sadly, he wasn't.

My own personal opinion is that the Heysel Stadium should never have been chosen as the venue for such a big, and important,

Old friend, old rival. Myself and former Liverpool manager, Joe Fagan

game in the first place. It became clear in the immediate aftermath of the tragedy that the ground was not suitable and that the organisation left a great deal to be desired. There was no real segregation of the opposing supporters, tickets were apparently on sale on the day of the match, the ground was in a state of disrepair—the list goes on and on.

At the time, I never gave a thought to the possibility of English clubs being banned from Europe; all my thoughts were with those poor people trapped on the terraces. There is a tremendous rivalry between Liverpool and Everton but I really, really felt for everyone at Anfield, especially for Joe Fagan.

Joe is a lovely man and after two years in charge, he had decided to relinquish the managerial reins. Heysel was supposed to be his glorious swansong—a fitting end to a brief, but hugely successful, spell in charge. He had announced his decision to step down shortly before the game and I cannot begin to imagine how he must have felt during and after that tragedy. My heart went out to him.

In the weeks after Heysel, I was asked many, many times for my views on UEFA's decision to impose a blanket ban on the participation of English clubs in the major European competitions.

150

I said that I found it an impossible subject to discuss because there were deaths involved. People had lost their lives as they followed a sport which they loved and, for once, football was a complete and utter irrelevance.

Six years later, it is still a very difficult subject to discuss but, in purely professional terms, the ban came as a massive body-blow to Everton Football Club. We had won the League and with it the right to contest what is arguably the most sought-after piece of silverware in world football. I had been so looking forward to seeing the cream of Europe playing at Goodison Park in front of one of British football's most knowledgeable crowds.

The first thing that came to mind was the Cup Winners' Cup semi-final against Bayern Munich and the fact that we were to be denied any more nights like that one. Although I understood why the decision had been taken, and my players understood why the decision had been taken, it was still a very bitter pill to swallow.

So, was it right to ban all the English clubs from Europe? Looking back on it, I would say yes, which will possibly surprise a few people.

At the time, English football had a bad reputation in the eyes of the game's administrators. We have always been fortunate at Everton to have a decent set of supporters who generally behave themselves and do the club proud. Many other English clubs could make the same boast with some justification but when UEFA met to discuss what had occurred in Brussels, they couldn't possibly have made judgements on individual cases and clubs—they could not take Heysel in isolation but merely as part of a much more expansive problem.

The footballing authorities in England had tried to do their bit towards rehabilitating our national game but it just hadn't worked. It seemed that the more measures they took, the more inventive the lunatic fringe became.

The ban hurt a great deal but I thought that if this swingeing action was going to sort out this dreadful problem once and for all, then I was totally behind it. All managers were aware that something had to be done; something revolutionary and drastic. It was vitally important that there were no more Heysels.

In professional terms, we were all stunned by the exile from Europe but it was just a case of sitting back and accepting the punishment in the belief that it would ultimately benefit English football. Several clubs were affected by the UEFA decision but

Everton suffered more than anyone because we were twice denied the opportunity to enter the European Cup. I know that many of our supporters still feel bitter about us being punished for something we had nothing to do with and I can understand that.

Obviously, it is difficult, if not impossible, to say how well we would have done in the Champions' Cup. Europe is full of great teams but I would like to feel that the Everton team of 1984–87 could be included in that bracket. I think that we could have had a right good go against the very best of them, I really do.

We had proved ourselves to be the best in England and we badly wanted to prove ourselves the best in Europe. It would be arrogant of me to say that we would have won the European Cup because I just don't know how far we would have progressed. What I do know is that there wasn't another English team better equipped than ourselves to tackle that most difficult of jobs.

I don't think that there was a real winner of the European Cup in 1985 because neither Liverpool nor Juventus were mentally prepared to play football after what had happened. People have suggested that the players involved did not fully appreciate what had gone on out on the terraces, that they had been somehow shielded from the reality of the situation, but I just can't believe that for one minute. They must have known and they must have been deeply affected.

The decision to actually go ahead with the game at a time when they were still treating the injured and ferrying away the dead must have been a very difficult one but I do believe it was the right move. If the game had been abandoned, who knows what might have happened outside the stadium and in the streets of Brussels later that night?

Possibly it would have been better had the two clubs been allowed to share the trophy for six months each, either that or make no award at all and leave a blank space in the sporting records as a permanent tribute to those who perished. As it was, the game went ahead under the darkest cloud imaginable. The most meaningless fixture in the history of football was eventually decided by a penalty, awarded for a foul which was committed some distance outside of the area. The Liverpool players did not even contest the award which says it all really. It meant nothing.

I am sure that the players, management and supporters of Liverpool could think of nothing else but getting back home to their families. When you have a tragedy like Heysel or Hillsborough, it puts sport into perspective. What does it matter who wins a football match when someone has lost their life?

It saddens me that it has taken two major tragedies to force football to start putting its house in order. I'm afraid that it is a classic case of bolting the stable door long after the horse has bolted. It is dreadful that supporters have to start dying before people decide to start taking measures which they probably should have taken in the first place. I sometimes worry about the lack of foresight within football, not just in this country, but around the world.

I believe the situation in Great Britain to be relatively healthy in terms of safety because we do have proper segregation of rival supporters, good policing and a sound policy as regards ticket sales. Whether or not we have done enough, I don't know. It really shouldn't take a tragedy to solve a problem. If an aircraft is sabotaged, security is tightened up immediately; football should adopt the same policy to help protect those who wish to attend matches. Surely we cannot tolerate a situation where people are going to a football match fearing for their safety?

Although I am not a native of Merseyside, the region is now very much my home and I shared the feeling of shock and sadness after Heysel and Hillsborough.

It is ironic that it should have been Liverpool Football Club which was involved in those two terrible events because they have some of the best-behaved and most loyal supporters in the game.

CHAPTER THIRTEEN

Double Disappointment

Unable to go back into Europe, I had no option but to train my sights exclusively on the domestic front and my long-held dream of a League and Cup double.

After two highly successful seasons, we had money in the bank and my board told me that they would back me up if I decided to move into the transfer market in a bid to strengthen my senior squad in readiness for the new campaign. The player I wanted—and the player I got—was Leicester City's Gary Lineker, who had finished as the First Division's joint leading scorer in the previous season with 24 goals.

Having won the Championship it would have been the easiest thing in the world for me to have sat back and placed my trust in the team I already had. While I am sure that nobody would have accused me of complacency had I done just that, I felt duty-bound to try and improve further the quality within the club. I didn't want Everton to become a one-season-wonder. That wasn't good enough; I wanted us to continue to make progress and dominate English football in the way Liverpool had done for so long. People always say that Liverpool have a settled and established side but they also buy and sell players at regular intervals to help maintain their enormously high standards.

Gary Lineker's most obvious asset is his astonishing pace. At the time, I don't think there was a defender in English football who could have lived with him over 30 or 40 yards. Although Graeme Sharp, Andy Gray and Adrian Heath were highly competent forwards with proven goal-scoring records they were not what you could call quick players. All three relied on their guile and bravery to help transform a little into a lot. I had absolutely no complaints at all about their contribution to the team as a whole but I just felt we needed a really pacey striker, particularly away from home where the visiting team so often has to rely on breakaways for their goals.

After I had completed the deal, Gordon Milne, the Leicester manager, told me that I had succeeded in buying a very special player indeed. That was the way I was looking at it too.

Gary was a tremendous success after joining Everton—it was actually getting his name on a contract which proved to be the problem. In many respects the negotiations between the two clubs constituted something of a grand farce as we haggled over the size of the transfer fee. When it became apparent that we were not going to reach a satisfactory agreement, it was decided to set the case before a tribunal.

The thing with tribunals in those days was that they seemed to sit down, look at the valuation of the selling club, look at the valuation of the buying club and then pick a figure somewhere in the middle. It was a complete nonsense really. Bearing that in mind, we offered £400,000 for Gary, even though we knew he was worth a great deal more. Leicester valued him at £1.25 million, even though they knew they would be forced to accept far less. It's a crazy system. The buyer deliberately lodges an artificially low bid because he knows that the seller is going to demand a ridiculous price.

In the end, the tribunal valued Gary at £800,000 while instructing us to pay Leicester a percentage of any fee received on a resale. It was a new club record but I was happy to pay that figure; it seemed just about right.

Although Adrian Heath was still recovering from a serious injury, Gary's arrival presented me with a major problem. I had one too many forwards and somebody had to go. I could see the potential of a Lineker-Heath partnership and a Lineker-Sharp partnership but I had my doubts as to whether a Lineker-Gray partnership would work out. With this in mind, I took the painful decision to allow Andy, the hero of Goodison Park, to leave the club.

In all fairness, after what the man had done for me and for Everton, I could not ask him to play reserve-team football. If I had done that it would have destroyed him. He was a big-name player who needed a big stage and if I couldn't offer him that stage then I wanted him to move on and find it somewhere else. I wasn't going to push him out of the door if he didn't want to go but I knew Andy well enough to realise that he would look at the situation logically and then take what action he felt to be appropriate.

Having reached one of the most agonising decisions of my managerial career, I knew that I would have to break the news to Andy as soon as was possible. I couldn't risk him learning that his

156

career at Everton was possibly over through the columns of a national newspaper.

Andy was in the process of moving house so I drove up to Formby to tell him that I had accepted a bid from Aston Villa. I arrived at his new home to find that he had still to have carpets fitted. There was a chap in the kitchen fitting a cooker. I looked at Andy and said: "Can you ask him to stop working for a minute?" He obviously realised why I had called on him and just said: "Oh, no."

We sat down and talked things over for a while but he was clearly distraught and very upset. He was such a good club man that I didn't expect any other reaction.

I think the fact that it was Villa who wanted him did help to soften the blow a little because he had enjoyed four very good years there in the late Seventies. I was also glad that it was Villa because I didn't want a player of his stature joining a lesser club where his natural enthusiasm for the game would have been submerged beneath feelings of regret and bitterness.

After talking to Villa, Andy joined them for £150,000, so ending a fairytale spell on Merseyside. I know for a fact that he looks back with great fondness on his days as an Everton player because he had such a tremendous rapport with our supporters. At a time when so many people had written him off, he had climbed back to the very top of his profession and won an FA Cup winners' medal, a League Championship winners' medal and a European Cup Winners' Cup medal. It is the stuff of which schoolboy dreams are made.

Many, many players have made significant contributions to the Everton cause over the years but none more so than Andy Gray. He deserves to be listed among the club's all-time greats even though he spent less than two years at Goodison Park. I will never forget the part he played in Everton's revival, both on and off the field of play.

Exactly what Andy means to the Everton public was emphasised during the 1990–91 season when Graeme Sharp was holding a series of testimonial functions. The organisers decided that it would be nice to hold an Andy Gray tribute dinner with the man himself as the guest of honour. So many people wanted to attend that they had to hold three in the end to meet the enormous demand for tickets.

I knew that many of our supporters would be mystified by my decision to sell the player whom they regarded as their club's saviour. Believe me, that decision was not taken lightly and was taken with Everton's best interests at heart.

Gary was fully aware that he was replacing a local hero and that he could not expect to be elevated to the level of idol overnight. He knew that it would take time to win over the doubters and the Gray fans. In fact, I don't think that he was fully accepted until Christmas of 1985, some six months after he had completed his transfer from Filbert Street.

I would say that Gary was the perfect man to replace Andy in more ways than one. Not only was he a quality footballer who could thrill a crowd with his skill and his goals, he was an intelligent and thoughtful person who appreciated the situation he found himself in. By utilising common sense, patience, good manners and humour, he succeeded in winning the affection of those supporters who had initially resented the manner of his arrival. By the time the 1985–86 season began to near its climax, Gary Lineker was arguably the most popular player on Everton's books and that in itself is a tribute to the way in which he approached an unenviable task.

Buying Gary was not, in any way, shape or form, a gamble, because every manager in the First Division admired his unique skills. Along with Ian Rush, he was the best at what he did.

The new season started very brightly for us with a 2–0 win over Manchester United in the Charity Shield. It was a particularly pleasing afternoon because Adrian Heath scored one of our goals in what was his first senior appearance for ten months. Adrian had been injured in December of the previous year during a League game against Sheffield Wednesday at Goodison. What was initially thought to be a simple knee ligament problem turned out to be far, far worse. The specialist who examined him in hospital told us that he had never seen such a serious ligament injury sustained during the course of a sporting event. He said that the damage which had been caused to Adrian's knee was consistent with someone having been run down by a bus. That is how bad it was.

There is never a good time to sustain a serious injury but in Adrian's case, it was doubly disappointing because it came at a point when he was probably playing the best football of his career. His form was so good that he was even being talked about as a contender for the full England international squad. Whether or not he would have eventually graduated to that level, I just don't know. He was, and still is, a very fine footballer, even if his goal-scoring record was not quite as good as perhaps it should have been.

It was good to have Adrian back in the frame because he had worked tirelessly to regain his fitness during the course of the summer months. Some players seem almost reluctant to fight their

Success on a plate . . . Bell's Manager of the Month during the 1985–86 season

way back into shape but there was no stopping Adrian. He spent hour after hour working with our physio, John Clinkard, to restore his health.

We started the League campaign as the bookmakers' favourites to retain the title which we had won in such style just a few months earlier. Although our early form was decidedly patchy, we recorded two excellent away wins, defeating Tottenham Hotspur 1–0 at White Hart Lane, and Sheffield Wednesday 5–1 at Hillsborough.

The First Division programme is long and demanding which made it all the more surprising to read in the *Daily Mirror* in early October that Manchester United had already won the title! This totally ridiculous piece of news was announced after United had won their tenth consecutive League game. True, they were 11 points in front of us but to suggest that the rest of English football's élite had already been reduced to fighting over the runners-up spot was plain crazy.

Although we hadn't faced United in the League, we had already played, and beaten, them in the Screen Sport Super Cup. Remember that marvellous little competition? The Super Cup was organised (with almost indecent haste) as some form of compensation for those clubs who had been denied a place in Europe because of the ban imposed in the wake of the Heysel tragedy. It was run on a home and away, round-robin basis with United and Norwich City making up our group. Having beaten United 4–2 at Old Trafford, and Norwich 1–0 at Goodison, we then had to go all the way down to East Anglia. It was a largely meaningless fixture because we had already guaranteed ourselves a place in the semi-finals.

A few days before the game at Carrow Road, one of the ground's stands had been destroyed in a fire which resulted in us having to get changed in a mobile cabin. As I launched into my pre-match speech about how important this game was to the club, I could see the disbelief written across the faces of my players. I couldn't pretend any longer and said: "What a waste of time this is—out you go."

Despite our total lack of interest, we somehow managed to finish up in the final where we played Liverpool over two legs. We lost 7–2 on aggregate but there weren't too many tears shed behind the closed doors of the dressing-room.

As our dogged pursuit of the "champions" Manchester United continued, I was forced to make another foray into the transfer market because of an injury to Derek Mountfield which, with the benefit of hindsight, marked the beginning of the end of his career with Everton.

The player I brought in was Scunthorpe United's left-back, Neil Pointon. He wasn't what you could call a household name and I could see some of our supporters mouthing the words: "Neil who?" when he made his debut against Arsenal a few days after completing his £50,000 transfer.

Neil may have been a relative youngster but he was certainly no novice, having already amassed a total of almost 200 senior games. Frank Barlow, an old friend of Mick Heaton from his playing days, was Scunthorpe's manager at the time and he was glowing in his praise of Neil whom, he said, was a model professional with a very good attitude. The thing which impressed me the most was that Frank said that Neil loved training, that he was always the last off the pitch and that he was often so reluctant to call it a day that he would willingly walk around picking up discarded bibs.

Attitude is everything to me because there are so many players who regard training as nothing more than a tedious chore which has to be endured on weekdays. Those sort of people turn up, get changed, train, have a shower, get dressed and go home without offering anything else to their club. Others can't do enough. They'll visit sick children in hospital, make presentations and generally get involved with the community within which they are living and working.

I travelled up to Preston to watch Neil in action and I was so impressed with what I saw that I actually rang my Chairman from the ground to ask for permission to open formal negotiations. I had seen enough in the space of 90 minutes and I wanted him at Everton.

The only thing which concerned me was his heading ability. It wasn't that he couldn't head a ball clear, it was just that during the game I had attended he hadn't been called upon to head a ball. Circumstances dictated that Neil was to make his debut in the week of his arrival and he swiftly allayed whatever fears I may have had because within a matter of a few minutes he had risen superbly to head away three dangerous crosses.

Neil isn't the most composed of footballers but he has so many different facets to his game that he must go down as one of my best-ever bargain buys. I am a great fan of his which explains why he was to join me at Maine Road during my spell in charge at Manchester City.

On 9 November Manchester United finally lost a League match, their 16th. They still held a seven-point advantage over second-placed Liverpool, and despite our emphatic 6–1 victory over Arsenal we were 14 points adrift in seventh place. I was not entirely despondent but I knew that we would have to put together a very impressive, unbeaten sequence if we were to force ourselves back into contention. I wasn't too concerned about United because they often fade after a bright start. It was Liverpool who worried me because you simply cannot allow them to open up a wide points gap.

Our form improved appreciably as the festive period began to draw nearer and by New Year's Day we were up into third place, ahead of Liverpool on goal difference, one point behind Chelsea and only three behind Manchester United, the rapidly faltering leaders.

I have always been a great advocate of the squad system and it was around this time, when our resources were being stretched by injuries to key players, that my unsung heroes began to emerge from the shadows and take their place, centre stage. The two men who best fit into this category are Alan Harper and Kevin Richardson who were to make solid contributions in both the 1985–86 and 1986–87 seasons. Both men could be relied upon to perform ably in virtually any position, with Alan in particular proving his versatility by playing full-back, central defender, midfield and even makeshift striker. They were invaluable to me because whenever I had a problem, irrespective of where it was, I could call upon one of them and have no worries at all.

Alan and Kevin were worth their weight in gold to the club but the only problem I had was keeping them happy because they were forever pointing out that they could not regard themselves as first-team regulars. I could fully understand their disenchantment but I couldn't do much about it as my team was established and almost picked itself when everybody was fit and available.

I had learned during my time at Blackburn the true value of what people tend to describe as utility players and I think that it is essential that every club has at least one man who could be said to be a Jack-of-all-trades.

We won six League games in a row early on in the new year and by mid-February were sitting proudly on top of the table. The Championship was already being hailed as the most exciting for several years as ourselves, Liverpool, Chelsea and West Ham United began to lock horns in earnest.

On 22 March we lost a League game for the first time in three months when we stumbled to a 2–1 defeat at Luton Town. It was a result which I firmly believe cost us the Championship. It is often difficult to pinpoint exactly where and when things went wrong but I have no hesitation in saying that we surrendered our title at Kenilworth Road.

Four days after that reversal, I received a phone call at home to tell me that Neville Southall had been badly injured while playing for Wales against the Republic of Ireland in Dublin. At first I was told that Neville had sustained a broken leg but after a specialist's examination, severe ankle ligament damage was diagnosed—a problem which can, on occasions, be even more difficult to treat than a straight fracture.

Thankfully, during the summer, I had paid Rotherham United £150,000 for Bobby Mimms who was an England Under-21 international with a great deal of natural talent. I had lost the man I believed to be the best goalkeeper in the world but I had every confidence in his understudy, despite his relative inexperience.

By this point, we had progressed through into the semi-finals of the FA Cup so I called Mike Stowell, our third-choice goalkeeper, into my office to tell him that he would be included in the travelling squad for the game against Sheffield Wednesday at Villa Park.

His response absolutely staggered me. He told me that he was cup-tied, having played in one of the preliminary rounds for Leyland Motors shortly before he joined us.

The situation was made even more desperate because Fred Barber, whom I had signed from Darlington a few weeks earlier, was also cup-tied. So there I was with three fit goalkeepers and only one eligible to play in the FA Cup.

I couldn't risk going into a major semi-final with just one goalkeeper so I spent an hour or so considering all my options. The solution I came up with forms the basis of the often-used quiz question—which Everton player won the most international caps? The answer to that question is Pat Jennings with 112.

Even now I come across Everton supporters who refuse to believe that Jennings was officially an Everton player, but he was. Although Pat had refused several tempting offers to come out of retirement, I was determined to get my man because he was the perfect, if not the only, choice. I made a few discreet enquiries and discovered that he was due to arrive back in England the following day after playing against Denmark in Belfast. Pat had finished with club football but was still turning out for Northern Ireland. I hurried down to Heathrow Airport not really knowing what his reaction would be when I put my proposition to him.

It was a peculiar scenario when I approached him, rather like an out-take from *This Is Your Life*. I pulled him to one side and explained my predicament and he agreed to join us on the understanding that he would only be called upon on a genuine emergency. Although Pat didn't train with us he did come up to Bellefield once or twice to have a few words with his new "team-mates". I think that he felt a little awkward actually, like an outsider looking in on something which he was not really supposed to be a part of.

Having been unexpectedly thrown into the defence of our League title, Mimms did ever so well. The fact that he knew he was to have an extended run in the first team obviously helped because he was aware that even if he was to make a mistake, he would still be between the posts in our next fixture.

With one month of the League season left to run, we found ourselves in second place, behind Liverpool on goal difference but with a crucial game in hand. A week in which Chelsea finally destroyed Manchester United's hopes by winning 2–1 at Old Trafford saw us faced with the daunting prospect of a trip to Arsenal while Liverpool seemed to have a far more straightforward task in the form of Coventry City at Anfield.

We had not won at Highbury for 11 years but Adrian Heath climbed off the substitute's bench to score the only goal of the game with just ten minutes remaining. However, it wasn't enough to take us back to the top because, at the same time, Liverpool were putting five past Coventry.

We did overtake Liverpool four days later by beating Watford 2–0 at Vicarage Road but just 24 hours later, Liverpool moved back into pole position by winning at Luton. It was very tight.

The penultimate Saturday of the season, 26 April, brought a double set-back for us. We were held to a goalless draw by Nottingham Forest and Peter Reid left the City Ground on crutches after damaging ankle ligaments.

As the great race entered the home straight, Liverpool were on top with 82 points from 40 games, we were second with 80 points from 39 games and West Ham were third with 78 points from 39 games.

The issue was to be decided on a Wednesday night when we lost against Oxford United at the Manor Ground while Liverpool were defeating Leicester City at Filbert Street. That was a game we really should have won because Gary Lineker had three or four excellent scoring opportunities. Normally he would have taken the lot but, for once, his killer instinct was missing. Because we suspected that a draw would be of no use to us, it was a case of throwing caution to the wind in the second half. The plan didn't work. Oxford caught us with a counter-attack and scored the only goal of a thoroughly depressing evening.

Liverpool's destiny was finally in their own hands and although we still had two home games left, against Southampton and West Ham, it meant that if our neighbours could beat Chelsea at Stamford Bridge, it was all over. We battered Southampton, 6–1, but it wasn't enough. A Kenny Dalglish goal in London gave Liverpool victory and the title.

I was pleased for Kenny, the first player-manager to win the Championship, because despite the rivalry between our respective clubs, I believe we shared a mutual respect for each other's abilities. Exactly one week after losing out on the Championship, our only other avenue of possible success was closed down when we were beaten in the FA Cup final by Liverpool. As we drove away from

Wembley the happiness of my mate, Mr Dalglish, was the very last thing on my mind.

After reaching the final in the previous two seasons, people almost took it for granted that we would enjoy another extended run in the competition. This belief was lent a measure of credence in the early rounds because we progressed through to the last 16 without too many problems, defeating Exeter City and Blackburn Rovers at Goodison.

Our fifth-round tie was a far more difficult proposition in the shape of Tottenham Hotspur at White Hart Lane. We lost Kevin Ratcliffe with an injury early on, but successfully papered over the cracks created by his absence and won 2–1.

Our quarter-final was against Luton Town at Kenilworth Road on the omni-turf I so despised. Despite my reservations about the much-vaunted "surface of the future", it was, I have to admit, a marvellous match. After falling two goals behind, I thought that we were dead and buried. With time running out, I decided to gamble by taking off a defender, Pointon, and throwing on a forward, Heath. Adrian had only been out on the pitch for a matter of seconds when Graeme Sharp rose well to head in a free kick to reduce the arrears. A few minutes later Adrian himself displayed great control within the penalty area to snatch an equaliser. Four days later, a fine solo goal by Gary Lineker was sufficient to carry us through into the semi-finals for a third consecutive season, this time against Sheffield Wednesday.

Our preparations for the game against Wednesday were disrupted by untimely injuries and although Heath and Reid were passed fit at the eleventh hour, we were without Lineker and Sheedy, both of whom had picked up knocks in a League game against Manchester United at Old Trafford.

Wednesday are a very difficult side to play against regardless of who is charged with responsibility for defining their tactics. Their team always seems to be crammed with giants, capable of combining a robust, physical approach with moments of subtle skill.

The first half was as uncompromising as I had expected, with Wednesday definitely creating the better of the chances as they chased a place in a major final for the first time since 1966. Our rhythm was disrupted during this period by the loss of Trevor Steven who was forced to limp away to the dressing-room after damaging a groin muscle. His replacement, Alan Harper, did not take too long to make a lasting impression. After 49 minutes he cleverly flighted the ball over the advancing Martin Hodge to give us the lead. However, our celebrations had barely subsided when Carl Shutt made the most of some defensive hesitancy to restore the status quo.

Once again we found ourselves forced into a period of extra-time, but I was not unduly concerned because, in the past, it had proved to our liking. So it was again, for Graeme Sharp scored with a glorious half-volley to take us back to Wembley—or Goodison Park South, as our fans were beginning to call the famous old stadium.

Upon entering our dressing-room, we learned that Liverpool had defeated Southampton, also in extra-time, to set up another all-Mersey final. Familiarity (or consistency) in football most certainly does not breed contempt for we were every bit as delighted to have overcome Wednesday as we had been to beat Southampton, two years earlier. It fell to us to try and stop our neighbours becoming only the third side this century to lay claim to the elusive League and Cup double. It is now a matter of history that we failed—but we gave it our best shot.

Our better moments came early on and had we been awarded a penalty in the 18th minute when Steve Nicol clearly held back Graeme Sharp as he attempted to reach a Gary Stevens' cross, the final result may have been totally different. Ironically, the referee that afternoon was none other than Alan Robinson, the man who had rejected our appeals for a penalty in the 1984 Milk Cup final against the same opposition.

My disappointment at seeing what I construed to be a clear foul go unpunished disappeared just ten minutes later when Lineker raced on to a Reid pass to knock the ball beyond Bruce Grobbelaar at the second attempt. At that stage I could envisage only one team winning, and they were wearing blue shirts.

We were still well on top when Liverpool equalised in the 57th minute. Gary Stevens is still blamed for that goal but while he was responsible for surrendering possession with a sloppy, cross-field pass, Liverpool still had much work to do before Ian Rush stole in to beat Bobby Mimms. The fact that I took Gary off shortly afterwards and replaced him with Heath suggested that I was annoyed by his basic error of judgement but it wasn't that, I was simply shuffling things around in a bid to liven up my side. Managers are always wary of substituting a player who has made a mistake because it usually serves to compound his misery. The withdrawal of Gary was a tactical move and most definitely not an act of public admonishment.

Having drawn level, Liverpool began to prosper. Craig Johnston put them in front five minutes later when he climaxed an excellent, sweeping move and with six minutes remaining, Rush plundered a third when he swept home a Ronnie Whelan cross.

The next day the papers described our season as disappointing simply because we had failed to win a trophy but I could not subscribe to that viewpoint at all. We had lost the title by two points and had been beaten in the FA Cup final after leading with 33 minutes left on the clock. A bad season? It was a very good season because we had got within just two games of winning the double ourselves.

The worst aspect of our Cup final defeat was not having to walk off at Wembley as losers, but having to travel home on the same plane as our conquerors the next morning. On top of that, we had agreed to tour the city with them as part of a dual home-coming celebration. Believe me, having to crawl around the streets of Merseyside on an open-topped bus, watching your greatest rivals wave in the air English football's two greatest prizes is no fun at all. It was cruel; very, very cruel. Even though it must have been hard for our supporters to stomach, they turned out in their thousands. It was a display of loyalty which we all appreciated.

We were actually a man short on that journey of "celebration" for Peter Reid had not travelled home with us from London. The story was that he was negotiating a move to a Swiss club but I still have my doubts about that. I know how upset he was after the final and I believe that he just couldn't face the prospect of being forced to sit through a day of uncontained joy for the red half of the city.

CHAPTER FOURTEEN

Severing the Links

For the second successive summer, I found myself faced with the unpalatable task of having to explain to my club's supporters why it was I had decided to sell one of their favourite players. Having risked upsetting the Everton public 12 months earlier by off-loading Andy Gray to Aston Villa, I found myself treading the same precarious path by sanctioning the sale of Gary Lineker to Barcelona.

The reasons behind what is still widely regarded as a controversial decision were numerous and diverse but the simple fact of the matter is that Gary himself wanted to move to Spain and while I regarded him as one of the best two strikers in British football at the time, I felt it would be totally unfair to stand in his way.

Many people still believe that it was Gary's goal-scoring exploits during the course of the Mexico World Cup finals which prompted Barcelona to move in with such a massive offer. Nothing could be further from the truth. Indeed, had Gary not finished as the tournament's leading scorer with six goals, it is conceivable that he could still be an Everton player.

Barcelona, who were then managed by Terry Venables, had made contact with me several months before England departed for South America, to express an interest in Gary and to enquire about his availability.

There was nothing underhand about the dealings I had with them for while they circumvented the more traditional system of discussing would-be transfers on a Chairman to Chairman level by coming directly to me, I did keep my board fully informed about each and every development.

It is difficult, if not impossible, to keep such things secret in football and, inevitably, Gary found out about the enquiry. He quickly let it be known that if the offer was genuine, and not just speculation, he wanted the opportunity to at least meet up with Barcelona's representatives. Understandably, he saw it as an opportunity he dare not miss. We informed Barcelona of our asking price during the course of what were nothing more than provisional negotiations and they agreed to meet that price in full.

Knowing the way in which the big continental clubs operate, I think that it is highly likely that the deal would have been abandoned had Gary endured a miserable World Cup. However, once Gary had returned to England as something of a national hero, there was no doubt in my mind that he would complete his transfer.

As Gary still had three years of his contract left to run at Everton, we could, of course, have blocked the move and made him stay but there would have been no point in that at all because he had his heart set on a move abroad. It wasn't as if we were selling him to some obscure, little club which no-one had ever heard of; it was Barcelona, one of the most famous names in world football. I felt that I could not deny him the opportunity to further his career— and earn the sort of money which would put him on a sound financial footing for the rest of his life.

Naturally, my main concern was the future of Everton but I was convinced that Gary's departure would not cause irreparable damage to the team which had so narrowly missed out on the double in the previous season. Now, that may seem to be a very strange thing to say, bearing in mind that Gary had finished that season as the First Division's leading scorer with the remarkable total of 40 goals.

Obviously, we were going to miss him but we had won the Championship without him in 1985 and I was convinced that we could do it again. I was certain that my team was strong enough and skilful enough to once again replace Liverpool as English football's premier side.

It is somewhat ironic that Gary should have scored so many goals during his one season at Goodison Park and yet left the club empty-handed in terms of winners' medals. His arrival had prompted a slight change in our play but it was nothing that was practised out on the training pitch. It is sometimes the case that individual players determine the way in which a team plays and Gary proved to be one of those players. His style was really suited to a method of playing which coaches refer to as "squeezing". That is to say, moving forward quickly, concentrating play in midfield and then springing your opponents' offside trap.

With Kevin Sheedy's marvellous passing ability and Gary's great pace, the system worked perfectly. To utilise to the full Gary's speed off the mark, we were knocking long balls down the centre and over the top rather than using our wide, midfield players to construct attacks as we had done in previous seasons.

Like Ian Rush, Gary was so adept at timing his runs forward that he was constantly finding himself in a one-to-one situation with the goalkeeper. The only problem was that while he was having no trouble in finding the target, those players who had been scoring regularly in our Championship-winning season saw their contribution, in terms of goals, drop quite appreciably. The season before, we had five players reach double figures but during the 1985–86 campaign only Lineker, Sharp and Heath managed to achieve that target. Having seen the way in which we had performed before Gary's arrival, and the way in which we had performed with him in the side, I felt that we could not only live without him, but make even more progress.

It would be totally wrong to suggest that I was not very disappointed to see Gary leave Everton because I think that he had proved he was at the peak, or nearing the peak, of his potential. Naturally, I took some flak, both from supporters and from the media in the weeks immediately after he had left for Spain but I believe the decision to have been right for I can see no point at all in retaining the services of a player who has made it clear he is unsettled.

Liverpool faced an almost identical situation when Juventus came in for Ian Rush. They were exceedingly loathe to see him leave but, again, it was a case of placing the interests of an individual before the interests of a club. The important thing to remember is that we managed to achieve success without Gary—and Liverpool did the same without Ian.

I was even accused of selling him simply because Barcelona had made such a handsome offer—a quite ridiculous notion. Although we netted in excess of £2 million from the deal we did not really need the money after three successful and financially rewarding seasons.

CHAPTER FIFTEEN

Do It Again

Our Championship success in the 1986–87 season, the first post-Lineker campaign, was a source of even greater personal satisfaction than had been the triumph of two years earlier simply because, as a manager, I was pushed to the very limit.

We used no fewer than 23 players in our League games that season, a quite staggering figure which proved once and for all that football is not just about a first team of 11 men but about a sizeable squad of fully committed professionals who are willing to undertake whatever task is asked of them.

It is amazing how swiftly a few minor injury problems can be transformed into a major crisis and as Kevin Ratcliffe was presented with the Championship trophy on 9 May, I reflected on the transfer deals I had completed ten months earlier and offered a silent prayer of thanks.

By their very nature, injuries are invariably ill-timed and totally unexpected. A manager has no idea at all when the curse of the groin strain or the saga of the hamstring pull is going to strike his team. All he can do is try to prepare for every eventuality by building up as powerful a senior squad as he can. This most necessary of tasks is obviously a great deal easier at the more affluent clubs than it is at those clubs where money is tight and a shoe-string budget is the order of the day. Sadly, a very high percentage of the Football League's members now fall into the latter category.

While I was convinced that we stood an excellent chance of reclaiming the position of England's premier club side, I sought to strengthen my squad during the summer of 1986 just to be on the safe side. It is better to have too many players than too few. I wasn't anticipating making any major signings but with money available to me I was looking to provide cover in several key positions. Yes, some of the money collected from the sale of Lineker was spent during this period but to be honest, I could have completed my mini-refit without dipping into it.

The biggest of my signings was Dave Watson who joined us from Norwich City for £900,000 in August. Although I had long been an admirer of his, the transfer was arranged in some haste, midway through a pre-season tour of Holland, when it became clear that Derek Mountfield was not going to be fit enough to play in our first League game against Nottingham Forest at Goodison Park. Derek had been suffering from a knee injury for some considerable length of time and, with a new season only a matter of a few weeks away, we just couldn't see any signs of improvement. He was working hard to rectify the problem of muscle wastage but his progress was rather slow.

I knew that if we were to have a real crack at winning back the title from Liverpool, we would have to get off to a good start—something we could not expect to do with only one fit centre-back. Ian Marshall had played in the Charity Shield game against Liverpool, but I felt him to be too inexperienced to cope with an extended run in the first team.

My only alternative was to find a defender of proven ability. I rang Ken Brown, the manager of Norwich, and said that I wanted to buy Dave. Initially, he said that there was no way he would sanction the deal because, to use his words, losing Dave would be like losing an arm. Having worked with Dave, I understand exactly what he meant.

Although I backed up my initial interest with a firm bid, Ken's determination to keep Dave at Carrow Road was such that it was not until I made him the proverbial offer he simply could not refuse that he relented and gave the deal the green light. I think it is fair to say that every player has his price.

Like Lineker, Dave found it hard to gain acceptance in the months which followed his transfer because he too was faced by the daunting prospect of having to win over supporters who were understandably loyal to another player. The pressure of trying to make our number five shirt his own property took its toll on Dave in the early days and after two months of the season I left him out of the first team and recalled Derek whose fight for fitness had been accelerated by the introduction of a rival. I never once feared that Dave would give up the battle—he's not that sort of person—and after forcing his way back into my plans in early December, he not only became a permanent fixture but a firm favourite with the crowd.

I am a little surprised that Dave has not won more England caps than he has and that his career at international level petered out mysteriously back in 1988 at a time when he was performing so capably at club level. With the current trend for two markers and a sweeper, I still believe that he has every chance of resurrecting his career with England because he is so well suited to that particular system. Very few players in English football can match Dave Watson for determination, courage and concentration.

Other players to arrive in the build-up to the new season included Wayne Clarke, Neil Adams and Kevin Langley.

Langley is an interesting example of a lad who had virtually everything that is required to make a top-class footballer—virtually everything. I had paid Wigan Athletic £120,000 for him with the expressed intent of nurturing his talent in the reserve team, but with Peter Reid sidelined through serious injury his learning process was suspended and he was thrown in at the deep end from the very first day. He played in our opening 16 League games and did exceptionally well until he suffered a loss of form. After spending some time at Manchester City and Birmingham City, Kevin eventually returned to Wigan. His Everton career may have been short but he does have a Championship winners' medal to remind him of his time on Merseyside.

Adams, whom I bought from Stoke City, was another player with potential but another youngster who was possibly a little out of his depth in the higher echelons of the First Division.

Possibly the most interesting transfer I was involved in that summer was the one which brought Paul Power to Goodison from Manchester City. Many, many people were really surprised by that deal but for an outlay of just £65,000, I picked up a model professional.

Having been told that Pat van den Hauwe would be absent for several months because of a serious ankle injury, I desperately needed a versatile player who could fill the left-back berth. Paul may have been 32 years old and entering the twilight of his career but when I asked City if he was for sale, they told me that not a close season had gone by without someone asking about his availability. He was reliable, dedicated and very much in demand. He was very keen to join us but the stumbling block was a testimonial game he had provisionally arranged against Manchester United. We surmounted that problem by promising to take United's place and play City at Maine Road later in the season.

Paul had a truly magnificent season playing not only at left-back but also on the left-side of midfield. I am certain that he never once regretted his move to Everton because at the end of a season when he figured in all but two of our League games, he was a winner for the first time in his long and distinguished career.

The only time I ever had to take Paul aside and point out exactly what playing for Everton represented was after our League game against his former club at Maine Road on 29 November. We won 3–1 and Paul was one of our scorers. Having turned the ball into the net, Paul displayed not one ounce of elation or emotion and simply headed back towards his own half of the field to await the restart. Clearly, he did not know what to do. He obviously felt that he couldn't leap up in the air and was embarrassed about the whole episode, which was perhaps understandable after having spent so many years with City.

The only other time I can recall a player almost regretting a goal was when Denis Law scored for Manchester City and condemned his former club, Manchester United, to relegation. It is a difficult situation but it is important that players remember exactly where it is their priority lies.

During the course of that season, Paul proved that those players who look after themselves in a physical sense need not be unduly worried about the passing of the years.

Despite having to select inexperienced players and having to chop and change my line-up at regular intervals, we started the season with something of a flourish, steadily accumulating points even though we lost three consecutive League games in late September and early October.

I have always regarded the Christmas and New Year programme as arguably the most important period of a League campaign and it was our inspired form between 20 December and 17 January—when we won six games in a row—which was ultimately to prove decisive. By winning at places like Newcastle United and Aston Villa we had sounded a chilling warning to our closest rivals.

If a team can enter January in good form, the psychological effect can be immense. It is almost as if players, having passed the half-way stage, can see the finishing post in the distance. They can see where they are going and if they are still in with a shout, they collectively gird their loins and redouble their effort.

It was a similar run in March and April, when we won seven games on the trot, which was to virtually guarantee us a second

Championship in the space of three seasons. The crucial afternoon during that spell came on 28 March when a Wayne Clarke goal gave us victory over Arsenal at Highbury while Liverpool were unexpectedly being beaten at Anfield by Wimbledon. That was the turning point.

It was a near-perfect day, actually, because that evening I managed to get my hands on some tickets to see *Phantom of the Opera* in London. I was sitting way back, up in the 'gods' as they say, but I felt so happy that it really didn't matter.

The title was clinched at Carrow Road when a rare goal by van den Hauwe after just 45 seconds gave us victory over Norwich City. I'll never forget that goal for more reasons than one.

As the ball hit the rear of the net, I jumped up from my place in the directors' box to show my delight. After applauding my players, I moved backwards to sit down only to discover that my seat had disappeared. To the amusement of everyone within 30 yards, I crashed to the ground.

Ridiculous though it may seem, exactly the same thing happened midway through the second half after I had moved down to the substitute's bench. Whoever decided to put tip-up seats in a dug-out and a directors' box wants his head examining! The second incident was captured for posterity by the television cameras and I am certain that the clip will eventually find its way on to *Question of Sport* under the ''What happened next?'' category.

We had won the biggest prize of all again and it gave me great pleasure to ask the Football League to supply us with a number of extra winners' medals. We may have won the title but that season actually brought disappointment as well insomuch as we lost an FA Cup tie outside of Wembley stadium for the first time since March 1983. Our aim had been to reach the final for a fourth consecutive season. I suppose that was a crazy notion bearing in mind the unpredictable nature of knock-out football but we honestly thought it was a distinct possibility.

Having beaten Southampton and Bradford City in the third and fourth rounds respectively, we seemed to be in with a fair chance of accomplishing this mission-impossible. Our winning goal against Bradford had been scored by Ian Snodin who, a fortnight earlier, had joined us from Leeds United in a £900,000 deal. That transfer was only completed after Ian had taken the bold step of rejecting the chance to join Liverpool, who had matched our fee and also negotiated personal terms.

I think that Ian possibly felt that Livepool already had so many central midfield players that he would end up playing wide on the right. I told him that he would definitely play in the centre if he joined Everton and I think that influenced his decision.

Shortly after he had joined us, Liverpool knocked us off the top of the First Division and the papers were full of articles calling into question the wisdom of that decision. He had the last laugh when he picked up his Championship medal and I was genuinely pleased for him because there are very few players brave enough to turn down an opportunity to move to Anfield.

During the time I was attending Leeds matches at Elland Road to run the rule over Ian, many people thought that my target was John Sheridan, another fine player who is now blossoming at Sheffield Wednesday after a difficult and unproductive spell at Nottingham Forest.

There were two main reasons why I wanted Ian at Everton—his tremendous pace and his powers of leadership. Ian has now undertaken the role of full-back and I am sure that had he not suffered so badly with injury problems over the past two seasons, he would now be a regular member of the full England side. He's had a lot of bad luck but if anyone has the will to force his way back to the very top, then it's Ian.

Anyway, our FA Cup run was to end in the fifth round against Wimbledon at Plough Lane despite the fact that Paul Wilkinson turned home an Adrian Heath cross to give us an early lead.

Sadly, we were overpowered in the second half and Wimbledon scored three times to run out emphatic winners.

The most distressing aspect of a thoroughly miserable afternoon was the reaction of the Everton supporters who had travelled south. As we left the ground, a small section of our fans who had gathered outside the main entrance began to jeer and hurl abuse at myself and the players. It was only a minority but they were really out of order. They seemed to think that because we had reached three consecutive FA Cup finals, we had some sort of divine right to play at Wembley each and every May.

Our performance at Plough Lane had been so disappointing that I took my entire senior squad out for a meal the following day to try and give them a bit of a lift. It was an informal sort of affair where problems and ideas were discussed in an open and frank manner. It was a useful exercise.

Cup football wasn't particularly kind to us that season because we went out of the League Cup to Liverpool and were dumped out of the Full Members' Cup by Charlton Athletic. The latter was not what you could call one of our major priorities but it did yield an amusing story because, following our exit, I was accused of having conceded defeat before the final kick of the game.

Charlton beat us 6–4 on penalties after our second-round match at Goodison had ended all square after extra-time. A few days after the game, I received a letter saying that the paying public had been conned, the suggestion being that because I had shaken hands with Lennie Lawrence, Charlton's manager, immediately before the last penalty kick had been taken, I was prematurely congratulating him on his side's victory.

So, just to set the record straight once and for all, it wasn't a fix or a con!

CHAPTER SIXTEEN

Memorabilia (Shadows and Reflections)

The old adage which suggests that managers are nothing more than supporters in tracksuits is far more than an endearing cliché, for every individual who has graced the professional game has his own, very personal, list of favourite teams and players. I am no different and after more than 30 years involvement with football I have a treasure trove of fond—and not so fond—memories to remind me of the many differing phases of my career.

During my time as a player the team which stood out as arguably the best of the lot was the only one assembled at Leeds United by Don Revie in the late Sixties and early Seventies. It is often said that Revie's famous side was cynical, sly and ruthlessly uncompromising and while it is true that they gave a whole new meaning to the term professional, nothing should be allowed to detract from the quality of their football.

From back to front, from number one to number 11, that team was crammed with footballers of the very highest calibre and, like everybody else, I am still at something of a loss to explain why it was they so often had to settle for second-best when it came to the big honours. With players like Norman Hunter and Jack Charlton at the back, the likes of Billy Bremner and Johnny Giles in midfield and men like Allan Clarke, Peter Lorimer and Mick Jones up front, they were always formidable opponents.

The Leeds team of that era was perhaps the first to fully acknowledge the importance of camaraderie both on and off the field of play. They worked, lived and breathed together, their sole aim being the pursuit of excellence. At a time when many clubs placed the quality of performance above a burning desire for success on their priority list, Leeds wanted to win; they simply had to win at all costs. This attitude was derided, berated and criticised on a grand scale but I quite admired a defiant stance, which almost seemed to be designed to infuriate those contemporaries who sought parity in terms of tangible achievement.

Leeds were good but, my word, they were a hard bunch. I remember once going into a tackle with Giles and bundling him on to the dirt track which used to surround the pitch at Elland Road. I didn't go over the top or anything like that; it was a good, solid challenge. After Giles had picked himself up and dusted himself down he walked back on to the pitch and just glanced at Charlton, Hunter and Bremner while nodding in my general direction. It was like having a contract put out on you.

You had to have eyes in the back of your head when you played against Leeds in those days. People talk about one-touch football but believe me, when you played them it was down to half a touch. It was a case of getting the ball and then releasing it as quickly as was possible. It was just the way Revie's players had been brought up but, to be fair to them, they were so good that they didn't really have to resort to intimidation.

Leeds had many so-called "hard" players in their line-up, the most celebrated of which was Hunter. You couldn't wish to meet a more polite and friendly man off the pitch but once the whistle went he was a totally different person.

During one game at Elland Road, I sent a pass fully 30 yards to Johnny Morrissey and the ball had actually arrived at his feet before Norman clattered into me.

If you were scheduled to meet Leeds, you had to make sure that your girlfriend of the time was a very understanding woman because it was inevitable that you would turn up for your date on Saturday night covered in plasters and bruises.

Like most of the Leeds players, Norman was hard—very hard— but usually fair. The thing is that no matter how tough you are, you simply cannot survive in the First Division unless you also have a great deal of talent. It is a pity that Leeds' reputation for occasionally accentuating the physical side of the game overshadowed their great qualities for they had some really marvellous players. Eddie Gray is a perfect example because I am convinced that had he not been so unfortunate with injuries, he would have established himself as a major world star.

The other two outstanding teams of the time were Liverpool and Arsenal, which possibly goes to show that very little has changed in English football despite the passing of two decades. Biased though I may be, I must include the Everton side of 1968–70 in my list because some of the football we produced during that period was delightful.

In terms of individuals I would turn to the famous Manchester United side which contained people like George Best, Bobby Charlton and Denis Law. Best was the greatest player I ever came up against. The man was quite remarkable and, it must be said, unique. George had everything—close control, great pace, bravery, wonderful heading ability, stamina, tremendous balance and vision; what a player. The almost unanimous choice as the greatest player of all time is Pele but I would have George Best right up there alongside him. George was unfortunate inasmuch as he was never really given the world stage upon which to perform because Northern Ireland never managed to qualify for the finals of a major tournament when he was at the very peak of his powers. That was something which Pele never had to worry about.

The other players who would make up my all-time top five individuals are Maradona, Franz Beckenbauer and Johann Cruyff. That might sound a little predictable but the best judges of footballers are the fans themselves and those names would figure prominently on anyone's list.

It is not too difficult to isolate the outstanding teams of the last decade because since I first moved to Goodison Park in May 1981, only three teams have managed to win the League Championship—Everton, Liverpool and Arsenal.

It almost goes without saying that Liverpool have had a succession of outstanding teams but if I had to select the one player who I believe underpinned their continued success it would be Alan Hansen. Alan was a wonderful footballer and I honestly do believe that he was, in many respects, Liverpool's best attacker. Whenever Everton played against Liverpool I would always tell my two forwards to move into the centre and mark Hansen and his partner if the opposition full-backs were in possession.

If you didn't do that, and if Hansen was allowed to amble forward, he would feed Dalglish who would feed Ian Rush who would probably score. The message I tried to drill home, time and time again, was: "Stop Hansen."

I think that the loss of Hansen is potentially more damaging to Liverpool than was the loss of either Kevin Keegan or Kenny Dalglish. When Keegan left, Dalglish stepped in; when Dalglish finished playing there was ample cover in the shape of Peter Beardsley, John Barnes and Rush. The partnership which Hansen forged at the heart of the Liverpool defence with Mark Lawrenson, who was another brilliant player, was the envy of every other club in the Football League. It was a marvellous pairing.

The other two truly great players to have graced Anfield over the past ten years or so are Dalglish and Rush. Along with Gary Lineker, Rush has proved conclusively that the offside trap need not be feared by strikers who are intelligent enough to combine timing and pace. So often it is not a case of a defence racing out and leaving a forward stranded in an offside position, it is more a case of a forward racing ahead into illegal positions. I would urge every young player to watch Ian and Gary very carefully and learn from what they see. There are many players in English football who are exceptionally quick off the mark but in the end it comes down to timing and Rush in particular is a past master at leaving defenders for dead with his speed of thought.

Although Rush is one of the greatest strikers I have ever seen, he was fortunate to have a man like Dalglish in midfield delivering the ammunition. Similarly, Lineker had much to thank Kevin Sheedy for during his one, glorious season at Everton. If you have a quality striker and a quality midfield player working on the same wavelength, you are halfway to a very successful team.

Rush is actually a far better all-round footballer than many people give him credit for. He never stops working and the number of times he forces defenders to surrender possession is remarkable. I wasn't too surprised when I heard that Ian was to cut short his career in Italy with Juventus because it is far more difficult for forwards to make their mark in that country than it is for defenders or midfield players. He is not the first quality striker to make a swift return from Italy because Denis Law and Jimmy Greaves before him also discovered to their cost that trying to survive on a starvation diet of half-chances was not to their liking. Players like Ray Wilkins, Graeme Souness and Liam Brady found life a good deal easier and duly prospered.

In June 1990, Paul Gascoigne was an enormously gifted player who didn't seem to have a care in the world. At the time of writing this book in June 1991, Paul Gascoigne is still an enormously gifted player but one who is burdened with a multitude of problems. Ever since George Best departed from a game which he illuminated with his unique brilliance, the media have been desperately searching for someone who could play out the role of football's *enfant terrible*. Unfortunately, they seem to have found their man.

Let's get one thing straight—yes, the lad can play. He is very talented but because he has only been around at the top level for a relatively short period of time he cannot be said to be in the same class as men like Best, Dalglish, Charlton and Rush.

To be classed as a legend you have to sustain your brilliance over many, many years. Whatever Paul Gascoigne does in the future he will be long remembered, but we shall have to wait and see if he becomes a legend for the right reasons or not.

I feel desperately sorry for Paul because I think there is a very good chance that he will be lost even before he has really started. I am not only talking about his desire to move abroad. I just think it will be impossible for him to carry on as he has been doing. He is like a good club comedian who finally gets to appear on television and then realises that he must constantly change his script because everyone has heard his jokes. He is going to find himself looking for new ways in which to surprise people, searching for something different to eclipse what has gone before. That won't be easy.

Paul returned home from the World Cup finals in Italy not just a sporting hero but a 22-carat national celebrity. His image was inflated by the media and I just get the impression that he himself feels as though he has to do something different, something quirky, each and every time he is in the public eye.

I just wish that he would buckle down and concentrate on his football because, in the final count, if you take that away from him, he will be left with next to nothing. An impish sense of humour and a cheeky smile is all well and good but he should remember that it is his skill out on a football pitch which has endeared him to so many people.

There is no doubt that Paul has contributed to his own problems because, by delving into the world of pop music for example, he has helped to create a larger than life image which is difficult to live up to and difficult to sustain. In a very short space of time, Paul has managed to live out the fantasy of millions of young lads up and down the country inasmuch as he has risen from a working-class background to become one of the most famous faces in Britain. If we are not very careful we will end up seeing less of him than we did of George Best and that would not only be a terrible shame but a terrible waste.

I don't think there is any doubt that Paul is now running the risk of burning himself out—long before he realises his full potential as a footballer. To be fair to Terry Venables, I think he has done a tremendous job in trying to concentrate Paul's thoughts and efforts solely on football.

It would be wrong to suggest that I know Paul Gascoigne well because I have only met him on a couple of occasions. He has always struck me as a really smashing lad. But if Paul were to carry on in Italy as he has occasionally carried on over here, I think he will swiftly find himself at odds with his new club. He is always looking to do something different . . . well . . . he'll have to do that over there . . . he'll have to start behaving himself!

There is a completely different attitude to player discipline on the continent and if he was to step out of line, they wouldn't think twice about fining him a week's wages. The big foreign clubs pay their players fortunes but they take fortunes off you if you don't fall into line.

If he does go over there, does well and then returns home in two or three years as a truly great player then I shall be the first in the queue to offer my congratulations.

I know that Paul can be his own worst enemy at times but even so I really do doubt that even half of the stories we read about him are true. They can't be—no-one could possibly get up to so much and still perform well in the First Division and on the international stage.

Would I like him in my team? It is difficult to say because he is the sort of player who almost demands that everything revolves around him. You would have to place his name on the team-sheet first and then construct a side around him.

To say that Paul was hyped up for the 1991 FA Cup final against Nottingham Forest would be to go nowhere near the full truth. Once again, I think the problem was that he was attempting to top his previous appearance at Wembley when he had played so magnificently in the semi-final win over Arsenal. Having scored such a memorable goal in that game, he was desperate to go one better. The two other key factors were that it was possibly going to be his last game for Spurs and he was carrying an injury which he probably realised was going to restrict him to 30 or 45 minutes.

He was so wound up that possibly even he couldn't account for his actions during his brief spell out on the pitch. Rather ironically, I think the fact that Paul was on such a high before, and during, the Cup final may have actually helped Spurs to defeat Forest. It may well have been that the rest of the Spurs side had no time at all to be nervous in the minutes before they left the dressing-room because they were either laughing at Paul's antics or trying to calm him down.

I know that many people now rate Paul as a genuine, world-class, all-time great player but, in all honesty, I couldn't put him in that bracket just yet. In my opinion, he is still some way from surpassing the achievements of men like Alan Ball and Trevor Francis.

The time to pass judgement on Paul Gascoigne will be in about five years' time. Let's just hope he is still around.

As a manager I have great respect for his natural ability. He can go past players, he can run a game, he has great change of pace, tremendous physical strength and terrific passing and shooting ability. When Paul left Newcastle for Spurs in 1988, both Liverpool and Manchester United expressed more than a passing interest in buying him, which says everything really.

However, the first time I ever came across Mr Gascoigne he did not leave me with a very favourable impression because he spent most of the game shouting and swearing at the Everton dug-out. He was only a kid at the time but, even so, his attitude left a lot to be desired.

I was full of admiration for his performances in the World Cup but the one thing which did annoy me was his tearful performance before the penalty shoot-out against West Germany in the semi-final. There is nothing wrong with public displays of emotion—that is only natural—but the tears he shed were for himself; he was upset because he knew that the second booking which he had picked up would rule him out of the final if his team-mates had succeeded in making it through.

His attitude should have been: "Come on, lads—I can't play in the final, but you can. I'm right behind you."

I just felt that his priorities should have been with his colleagues as they began to prepare themselves mentally for the difficult task of taking penalties. If I had been the manager of England I would have felt bitterly disappointed because Paul was thinking about himself and not his team.

The other great outfield player currently plying his trade within the Football League is John Barnes—one of the most dangerous forwards in the country without a shadow of a doubt.

It is true that John has never really managed to reproduce his club form at international level but with so much expected of him all the time, that possibly isn't too surprising. I always feel like grabbing hold of John shortly before he runs out for games and telling him not to worry about turning on the magic every time he collects the ball. He seems to feel as though he has a duty to go past two or three defenders every time he is in possession.

I had to laugh after John had been praised for his performance in a more central position during the England v Argentina friendly at Wembley in the summer of 1991. After goodness knows how many international appearances, people were saying that perhaps he had finally found his true role. I wish I'd been given 60-odd chances to find my best position for my country! I would have settled for one chance, however brief.

I am still a big fan of Bryan Robson because he has performed with great style at the very highest level for such a long time. His career may have been blighted by injury but he has still managed to serve both club and country with great distinction.

In the last few years, English football has seen the introduction of what coaches and managers tend to refer to as "floaters", that is to say, a player who performs just behind a team's two strikers. United have never needed one of these specialists because, throughout his entire career, Bryan has always combined the roles of midfielder and supporting striker.

As far as goalkeepers are concerned, I believe that Neville Southall has been the best around for many years now. The biggest compliment that I can pay him is to say that he deserves to be compared with the all-time greats like Gordon Banks and Lev Yashin.

The problem is that goalkeepers who play in good teams don't

Neville Southall . . . one of the most dedicated professionals I have ever encountered

188

always get the credit they deserve because they are often well-protected by their defence. I have seen Neville turn in a faultless display yet only be awarded six points out of ten in the Sunday papers simply because he had so little to do.

If Neville had been English, and not Welsh, he would be a household name the world over by now. The lack of opportunity afforded to him at international level means that he is one of British football's best-kept secrets.

I might be biased but two other players who more than deserve a mention are Trevor Steven and Kevin Sheedy, both of whom are quite outstanding talents. I am amazed that Trevor has not been a permanent fixture in the England side over the past five or six years. I have always regarded him as the natural replacement for Steve Coppell.

My choice as the 1990-91 Player of the Year would not have been Mark Hughes or Gordon Strachan but Nottingham Forest's Stuart Pearce. Having scored countless crucial goals and having provided inspiration when his team most needed it, he was the obvious choice.

CHAPTER SEVENTEEN

Say Hello, Wave Goodbye

My decision to leave Everton during the summer of 1987 and accept the position of coach with one of Spain's leading clubs, Athletic Bilbao, was not one taken in haste or on the spur of the moment, for I had long desired the opportunity to try my luck abroad.

I must make it clear that I was in no way disenchanted with life at Everton. Why should I be? We had returned the League Championship to Goodison Park, the team I had assembled was winning widespread acclaim for its purity of football and the future was unquestionably bright. Life was good.

I just felt the need to move into the continental arena where the working environment was totally different and where the challenge was, if not more severe, then of a contrasting nature. It was a longing which burned deep inside of me and one which I knew that I had to get out of my system.

I know that many people were astounded when the news of my departure broke on 19 June but there was a small select band— comprising family, friends and close associates—who were not in the least bit surprised. They were the people who knew how close I had come to leaving England 12 months earlier, when I had been made an offer I simply could not refuse.

On that occasion the club which attempted to prise me away from Merseyside was not Athletic Bilbao but Barcelona.

As was the case when Barcelona came in to buy Gary Lineker, they didn't stand on formality in any way at all. English protocol demands that all negotiations, whether they be about a manager or a player, are conducted at the very highest level. Unfortunately, this is not the Spanish way of doing things. If a leading Spanish club wants someone, they go straight to the individual concerned; they don't mess about unravelling what they regard as red tape.

The contact was direct. Towards the end of the season, they simply rang me up and said that their manager, Terry Venables,

191

Farewell Everton—for the time being I leave after announcing my intention to join Athletic Bilbao. Also pictured is Jim Greenwood, Everton's Chief Executive

was likely to be leaving during the summer and that I was the man they wanted to succeed him. I was staggered. I couldn't believe that one of the five biggest, most famous clubs in the world had virtually offered me the job of manager.

Although I was very happy at Everton the idea really excited me. I don't believe that there is a manager within the Football League who would not have felt elated and flattered by an approach like that. I knew that if the offer was to be confirmed, I would have to think very carefully about the implications, both for myself and for my family—but I also knew that I would accept. It was a dream scenario, one lifted straight from the pages of a fantasy novel.

I announce that I am to leave Everton to take over at Athletic Bilbao. Also pictured is Philip Carter, Chairman, now Sir Philip

Off to Spain—but not before I explain the reasons behind my decision

I am not the sort of person to go behind the backs of my employers so I immediately informed my Chairman, Philip Carter, of Barcelona's interest. I promised to keep him fully informed of any developments and that is exactly what I did.

A meeting was arranged in London where I was introduced to members of the Barcelona hierarchy including Jose Luis Nunez, the President, Gaspart, the Chief Executive, and a couple of the club's influential directors. It was top-level stuff being conducted by the men who mattered so I knew that initial speculation was on the verge of being transformed into harsh reality.

Over breakfast, we verbally agreed that if, as was expected, Terry decided to leave, I would take over. I even went so far as to sign a provisional contract. I still have that document. I have kept it for old times' sake; to remind me of what might have been.

I returned to the task of steering Everton towards the League title with a feeling of great anticipation. I couldn't believe my good fortune. There I was managing the club I had loved for so many years and in my desk drawer was a piece of paper which said that I was to be the next manager of Barcelona.

It didn't work out, of course, because a few weeks later, Terry announced that he was to stay on in Spain. I was very disappointed because I would definitely have joined them. What few people realise is that my board, who were resigned to my departure, had already offered the job of Everton manager to Colin Harvey. I had told Colin that I was on the verge of going to Spain and I said that I wanted him to go with me as my assistant. He said that if he was not offered the chance to succeed me at Goodison Park, he would also leave and join Barcelona. It was only logical that Colin should be offered the Everton job if I were to leave and, to be perfectly honest, I never doubted for one moment that my board would take any other course of action.

Inevitably, one of the major reasons why I felt so drawn to the continent was the UEFA ban on the participation of English clubs in the European competitions, imposed in the wake of the Heysel Stadium tragedy. I missed those nights of European glory very much indeed.

I can't say whether I would have been successful at Barcelona because football is a game full of ifs and maybes. Terry had done exceptionally well out there, winning the Championship, and the club was very happy with the English style of play which he had introduced, hence their interest in me.

194

My chance to join Barcelona had gone but the seed had been planted; my appetite had been whetted and in the back of my mind I knew that one day I would leave England to become a manager abroad.

That day actually arrived a good deal sooner than I had been anticipating, thanks in the main part to a man called Fernando Ochoa who entered my life around April, at a point when we were on the verge of clinching the League Championship. Fernando, the General Secretary of Bilbao, rang me at home and said that he was in Liverpool and wanted to speak to me as a matter of some urgency.

We met up and it quickly became clear that Mr Ochoa was a most persuasive man. If he had been sent over to England to try and "sell" Athletic Bilbao to me, he did a very fine job indeed. He spent a couple of hours detailing the internal workings of his club, its strengths and weaknesses and his own hopes and aspirations for the immediate future.

The one thing which he kept stressing was that Athletic Bilbao was a Basque club, was proud to be a Basque club and was determined to continue its policy of using only Basque players in the same way which Yorkshire Cricket Club until recently restricted itself to those players actually born within the county.

He said that Bilbao was struggling near the foot of the Spanish First Division and that the club's board of directors had come to the conclusion that the best way to arrest a worrying slide in fortune was to appoint an English coach and that I was the one who had been chosen. Fernando said that he wanted someone who was capable of nurturing the young talent within the club; someone who could help to produce a whole new generation of first-team players.

The more I thought about his offer, the more it appealed to me. The thing which particularly excited me was the prospect of becoming a real trainer once again; getting out on the pitch and working closely with players. I was given the distinct impression that I wouldn't find myself hindered by the administration duties which are such an integral part of every English manager's job. I would be free to pull on my tracksuit and get down to the basics of technique and coaching.

I was so interested that I agreed to fly over to Spain to attend a secret meeting after I had returned from our post-season club tour of Australia, New Zealand and Hawaii. It was supposed to be a cloak-and-dagger style of operation but, as is so often the case, it turned into a real pantomime.

I had decided that I would need someone with me to offer advice so I contacted Jonathon Holmes, a well-respected agent-cum-personal manager who had helped Gary Lineker negotiate the terms of his contract with Barcelona. Upon my return from Hawaii, I met Jonathon in London and we made our way to the airport to catch a flight to Madrid, where the meeting was to take place. In an attempt to conceal my identity, Bilbao had left the tickets not in my name but in the name of a Mr Robinson. I realised that with a ticket saying Robinson and a passport saying Kendall, I probably wouldn't get very far so we spent ages messing around having the names altered.

When we eventually arrived at our hotel in Madrid, the problems started again. I approached the reception desk and said: "I believe that you have a room reserved for Mr Kendall." After much shuffling of papers, the answer was: "No."

Remembering my alter-ego, I said: "Room for Mr Robinson?" More shuffling of papers, "No."

The girl behind the desk was clearly suspicious of this foreigner who didn't seem to know who he was and asked to see my passport. She glanced at it, smiled and said: "Oh! Mr Howard. Nice to see you."

The meeting went a good deal more smoothly than had my check-in. I found the Bilbao officials to be warm, friendly and very efficient. They knew what they were doing and they knew what it was they wanted.

Although I didn't want to appear over-excited by their offer, I was hooked. My mind was made up. I wanted the job.

I returned home to discuss with my family the obvious logistical problems of my working in Spain, then Cynthia and myself flew out to Bilbao to look at some schools. It wasn't long before we both realised that to uproot our three children and place them in a totally alien environment would prove to be very traumatic.

It just didn't seem fair so I took the painful decision to leave my family behind and go to Bilbao by myself. Being separated from those people you love is always unpleasant but looking back now, many of my fears proved to be unfounded.

Obviously, it was difficult for a time but the ironic thing is that during my first 12 months in Spain, I actually saw more of my wife and kids than I had done during my final season in charge at Everton. I used to come back to England whenever possible and my family would come out to Bilbao during the school holidays. All in all, it worked out very well.

I think my leaving Everton when I did possibly helped my children because it meant that they could turn up at school on Monday morning not having to worry about how their dad's previous club had fared at the weekend. I am sure that they felt a great release of pressure when I left Goodison Park for the last time. Well, the last time for three years, anyway.

It was while I was in Spain with my wife that I actually took the plunge and committed myself to Bilbao by signing the contract which had been previously agreed.

It is perfectly understandable that people should think I left Everton to pursue a personal fortune (Spanish gold?) but that was not the case at all. In fact, Everton came up with a fantastic offer in an attempt to persuade me to remain at Goodison Park. I still had two years of my existing contract left to run but that did not stop my board drawing up a new, four-year deal. In terms of an increase in salary, it was a really tremendous offer.

If it was money I was after, I could have stayed where I was because the deals set before me by Everton and Bilbao were almost identical. Those people who know me well will confirm that I am not a money-motivated individual. I have always tended to accept what people are offering, happy in the knowledge that I am being paid the going rate for a particular job.

The other suggestion at the time was that I left Everton because I had taken them as far as was possible, that for the first time in so many years, the only way was down. Interesting though that idea may be, it is also totally false because I was convinced that the club had sufficient strength and depth to maintain both its standards and its success.

I left because it was the right thing for me—as a person and as a football manager.

My argument that I wished to revert to my more favoured role of tracksuit trainer was also greeted with some scepticism. Those who believed my decision to be based on monetary, rather than footballing, considerations asked why it was that I did not delegate responsibility to allow me more time with the players. Perhaps I could have done that but the simple fact is that the more successful a club becomes, the more desk work there is for the manager. However efficient your secretary is, the paperwork piles up, the phone never stops ringing, the queue of people outside your office door never seems to recede.

Perhaps the most important thing from my point of view was that

I did not feel, in any way, that I was leaving Everton in the lurch. I was not walking out, leaving them with the difficult job of having to scour the country for a new manager because my successor was not so much on the doorstep as in the front-room.

Colin Harvey is a modest and quiet man and although he said at his first press conference that he was somewhat shocked when asked to take over the reins, I know how delighted he was to be appointed manager of Everton. I was thrilled for him. I knew that I was leaving the club in the best possible hands. He was not only the perfect choice but the popular choice because I am certain that if the club's supporters had been asked to select the man they wanted in charge, 99 per cent would have raised their arms to vote for Colin.

I also thought that if I was ever to take a chance, a gamble, with my career, there would never be a more opportune moment. I had done well at Everton and, without being conceited, I thought that I would have a reasonable chance of finding another job in England if things did not work out for me in Spain.

It was very, very hard to leave Everton behind for many reasons. I knew that I was disappointing many people, particularly my directors who, I think, believed that they would succeed in keeping me at Goodison Park. When I signed my provisional contract with Barcelona, they made no real effort to talk me out of leaving because they were fully aware of the prestige which goes with managing a club of that stature and importance. I think they viewed Bilbao in a completely different light.

Very few people in this country appreciate just how big a club Athletic Bilbao is. It may not have the glamour of clubs like Juventus, Real Madrid—and Barcelona—but, believe me, it is a *VERY* big club.

Shortly after I had left Everton, Brian Clough aired his opinions on my move in his programme notes and said that he would have understood me joining Barcelona but that he was at a loss to explain why I had gone to Bilbao. People should not talk about things of which they have no understanding; things which they know little, or nothing, about. It is unfair and extremely naïve.

After I had completed the formalities of my contract, it was decided that the news of my departure should be announced at simultaneous press conferences in Bilbao and Liverpool. It was a nice, neat idea but I wasn't in the least bit surprised when the news leaked out 24 hours early. The speculation started in Spain and by the time I arrived back in England everyone seemed to know the full details of what was supposed to be a closely guarded secret.

Inevitably, I was besieged by journalists who wanted to know exactly what was happening. I was determined to keep my part of the bargain and said nothing at all even though television crews and photographers spent the best part of the night camped outside my house. It was not until the following day, at the official press conference, that I broke my silence.

I don't know whether the Everton supporters were disappointed at the news or not. I do know that they were delighted to hear that Colin had been named as my successor.

The fans I spoke to outside the ground as I left after the press conference were tremendous. They wished me the best and said that I would be welcome back at any time. It was lovely to part company on such amicable terms.

Although I was excited about what lay ahead, I did feel great sadness as I left Goodison Park for what I assumed would be the final time because the club had become such an integral part of my life. Although I felt it was time to move on, and although I was confident that I had made the right decision, I couldn't help but reflect on those many glorious moments of triumph and celebration as I drove home.

I only ever once regretted my decision to join Athletic Bilbao and that was a few weeks after I had finally severed my ties with Everton.

My new club rang me up and invited me over to Spain to watch their domestic Cup final between Atletico Madrid and Real Sociedad. My trip was to be a little more than the first instalment of what I feared was going to be a difficult familiarisation programme because there were a couple of Basque players involved whom Bilbao were interested in signing.

I flew over to Spain and drove down to Zaragoza, accompanied by my President and General Secretary. The two other people who joined us on the trip were Iribar, the famous Spanish goalkeeper whom I had succeeded as coach but who had been placed in control of Bilbao's second team, and Rojo, who was to be my assistant.

I just couldn't believe what I saw during the course of that game; it horrified me.

Because of the politics involved, the two sets of supporters were at each other's throats from the moment they arrived in the stadium. The Sociedad fans were obviously all Basques while the

Madrid fans were all pro the King. When the King and Queen took their places on a special balcony shortly before kick-off it sparked an astonishing, ugly war of words. Worse was to follow when the game actually got underway. Bottles and cans rained down on the pitch throughout the entire 90 minutes.

The atmosphere was absolutely awful and I remember sitting back in my chair, closing my eyes and wondering what I had let myself in for. Not wanting to upset my new employers, I kept my feelings to myself but I was deeply worried in case the scenes I was witnessing were commonplace. I just didn't know what I was going to do if each and every game in Spain was played out against such an intimidating backdrop.

I left that game honestly believing that I had made the biggest mistake of my entire life. There is nothing finer in football than a large, partisan crowd whipping up fervour but what I saw in Zaragoza on that day had nothing to do with sport at all. I wish those people who continue to insist that we have the worst hooligan, or crowd control problems in European football could have been sitting alongside me at that game because their brains would have had trouble believing what their eyes were seeing.

Although baton-wielding police dragged many supporters from their seats and threw them up against the security fences, things got so bad that a loudspeaker announcement made it clear that unless the trouble was halted, the game would be abandoned. There I was, watching the showpiece of the Spanish football season and someone was telling me the game was on the verge of being abandoned! We might have our problems here in England but at least our Cup final is a dignified and orderly occasion.

Under these circumstances, I did find it rather difficult to study the performances of those players I had been instructed to watch but I did my best. The men who were under close scrutiny that day were Bakero who is now with Barcelona, Lopez Ufarte and a lad called Uralde, who was the player I ended up signing.

The deal, which was negotiated while I was at home in England, resulted in Goicoechea, the legendary "Butcher of Bilbao", leaving to join Atletico Madrid. I wasn't overjoyed about this arrangement because Goicoechea was the club captain and something of a hero with the local crowd.

As I stressed earlier, I believe a new manager's first transfer deal to be of paramount importance. It has to be right and it has to be well-received among the rank and file of the supporters. In as subtle a way as was possible, I suggested to my President that perhaps selling Goicoechea was a little undiplomatic. It is true that new brooms do tend to sweep clean but I was mindful of upsetting the Bilbao public even before I had moved to the city. I made the point but to no avail. I was repeatedly told that the deal was a good one because Uralde was unquestionably the man to solve Bilbao's goal-scoring problems.

The determination of my board to complete the signing of Uralde brought home to me the problems I would face in attempting to transform my new club's fortunes while working within the rigid, inflexible framework of the highly restrictive, Basque-only policy.

In England, if money is available, the task of bolstering your senior squad is relatively straightforward inasmuch as you take in as many matches as is possible, isolate those individuals who show promise and then buy them. That is an option—or a luxury—which is not open to the manager of Athletic Bilbao. During my time in Spain, I saw many, many players I would have loved to have bought; players who would have made a big difference to the quality of my side. I couldn't sign them, however, because they were non-Basques.

In the early days, it was all a little frustrating but I quickly settled into the rhythm of things and began to flow with the tide. I realised just how proud everyone connected with Athletic was of being the national club of the Basque country. They accepted that their policy of refusing admittance to "outsiders" served to greatly reduce their chances of success but it didn't matter.

The decision of Real Sociedad, the other leading Basque club, to break with tradition and open its doors to foreign players (John Aldridge, Kevin Richardson, Dalian Atkinson etc) only strengthened Bilbao's determination to pursue its historical policy of splendid isolation.

With big-money transfers something of a rarity, Bilbao places a very heavy reliance on its youth and junior policies. The simple truth of the matter is that they just cannot afford to let anybody slip through the net. The club actively begins to nurture talent from the age of eight or nine. The youngsters are brought along to the training ground, kitted out in the official club colours and coached. It really is a joy to see the enthusiasm and excitement of kids who hope to form the next generation of Basque footballers. The system does work very well because the junior team quite often finishes as champions and the reserve team, Bilbao Athletic, who play in the Spanish Second Division, also has a very good record.

If I am honest, I must admit that the Basque-only ruling was something of an attraction in a peculiar sort of way because the fact that I was not expected to walk in and win the Spanish Championship in my first season helped to reduce the pressure a little.

Bilbao was a club in a very poor state of health when I arrived to take over. They had only narrowly managed to avoid relegation in the previous season and there was much work to be done. I discovered the main weakness of the club to be a reluctance to upset their own people; those who had been around for several years.

I think that the reasoning behind their decision to appoint me was a desire to clear away the dead wood which had accumulated. They wanted someone to come in from the outside and make the hard decisions which they could not make for themselves. They knew exactly what needed to be done but because of the club's family atmosphere they just couldn't do it. I wasn't exactly a hatchet-man but I was expected to sort out the problems I encountered and put the club back on the right lines. It was a lovely job really because I felt like the managing director of a big company who had been called in by a rival to offer assistance and advice. A trouble-shooter, if you like.

Having reluctantly left my family behind, I moved to Bilbao during the summer and took up residence at my new club's training ground. There is nothing quite like living close to the office!

Bilbao's training centre, which was used by England during the 1982 World Cup finals, is beautifully located up in the mountains and is simply enormous with seven pitches and numerous bedrooms. Those rooms were used by Bilbao during the course of pre-season training for what they call "concentration", that is, the senior players would retire to them in between sessions to get themselves mentally prepared for what lay ahead.

I took up the offer of a small apartment with a bedroom and a bathroom. It seemed the logical thing to do because the alternative was to closet myself in a city-centre hotel where, I'm sure, I would have felt totally isolated. Living at the centre, alongside one of the club's former players and his family, helped me a great deal, particularly with the problem of trying to learn a foreign language. The fact that my neighbours did not speak English made me determined to grasp the basics of Spanish as quickly as was possible. It was a case of either learn or stay silent.

Although I was provided with an interpreter to help me communicate during the course of my business duties, I was very much on my own at the end of the working day. I took lessons in Spanish several evenings a week but I did not find it easy. I was probably a little long in the tooth to start grappling with the complexities of a completely alien language. I never fully mastered Spanish but by the end of my time in Bilbao I knew enough to get by.

As a city, Bilbao is not dissimilar to Liverpool in that it is an industrial port. I grew to like the place a great deal. Bilbao's stadium is a magnificent place to play football despite the fact that it is relatively small by European standards, holding just 42,000 people.

It is known in Spain as "The Cathedral" and Sammy Lee, the former Liverpool star, said it was the best stadium he had ever played in, which is high praise indeed.

Although I had been bold enough to sanction the sale of their hero, Goicoechea, I was warmly received by the supporters who were aware that I had enjoyed quite a bit of success in England. They were probably a little wary, a little suspicious, but they gave me the impression that I would be given a fair crack of the whip.

During my first few weeks in Spain, I did a little research to help build up a basic knowledge of my new club's history and was astonished to discover that Bilbao has very strong links with my native North-east. The club was formed by the city's shipbuilders in the 1880s at a time when much of the trade between England and Spain was channelled between Newcastle and Bilbao. In fact, the bond between the two countries was so strong that Athletic Bilbao's first-ever trainer was a chap with a bowler hat and a large cigar called Mr Petland. To this day, he is the most revered of all the club's many coaches—and he was an Englishman.

The Basque people love the English style of football because, unlike most continentals, they like to see fast and furious action. Several people told me that when Liverpool played a European Cup tie in Bilbao in 1983, the home supporters stood and applauded at the final whistle even though a goal by Ian Rush had denied them victory and a place in the competition's quarter-finals.

The dictionary definition of the word "fanatic" is: "a person whose enthusiasm or zeal for something is extreme or beyond normal limits". That just about sums up your average Spanish football supporter. It was commonplace for several hundred people to turn up at the training centre and on one occasion, when our junior side was playing Real Madrid, more than 7,000 assembled. They were there to look at the kids because those frail-looking youngsters were the future of Athletic Bilbao.

The squad I inherited was a mixture of the good, the bad and the indifferent. Although I felt there to be the nucleus of a potentially useful side, too many of the younger, less experienced players were just not good enough.

It quickly became apparent that the mentality of the Spanish footballer was totally different to that of his English counterpart. Our first away game in the League was against Logrones who, after winning promotion the previous season, were playing in the top flight for the first time in their history. After conceding a goal in the opening few seconds, we fought back well to earn a draw. I had never seen a dressing-room so elated after a disappointing draw in my entire life. You would have thought my team had just won the European Cup such was their sense of joy.

I sat them down and, through my interpreter, I told them, in no uncertain terms, that they shouldn't be celebrating because their opponents were an awful side. I tried to impress on them that it was vitally important that we set our sights a good deal higher. I don't know whether or not the message got through because these were players who, from a very early age, had been told that a draw away from home was a major triumph. All they kept saying to me was: "One positivo." Now, a positivo is not a League point but a merit point. Confused? So was I in the beginning.

In real terms, the positivo system is totally worthless as anything other than a form guide. Teams are awarded two positivos for an away win, one for an away draw and none for an away defeat. For home games the scoring is: none for a win, -1 for a draw and -2 for a defeat. When I left Bilbao in 1989, the club's score was $+1$ and I was told that I was the first coach ever to leave with a higher than zero rating. A small achievement in itself.

Just as I had in England, I was determined to try and forge a good working relationship with the Spanish media but the fact that my club was insistent that I should tackle this job on my own—without an interpreter—did not help at all. Looking back now, I feel it was a mistake to leave me to fend for myself because I am sure that many of the journalists had me marked down as evasive and unco-operative when, in fact, the only problem was that I simply could not understand their questions or did not have a vocabulary suffi-ciently expansive to formulate a meaningful response.

Even after I had mastered the basics of Spanish, I struggled because the people in the south of the country seem to speak a completely different language. I am sure that if a Spaniard were to become the manager of, say, Sunderland, he would struggle to understand what was being said on Merseyside. Local dialects and strong accents are as prevalent in Spain as they are in England.

It was easier to communicate with my players because if they could not understand my instructions out on the training pitch, I would simply pick up a ball and show them. I was thankful that my level of fitness was still sufficiently high to enable me to take part as we practised new techniques and strategies. The players worked hard for me, but, more importantly, they were keen to learn.

It was quite amusing to lay the problems I faced at Bilbao alongside those I had faced at Blackburn Rovers and during my early days at Everton. In England it always seems to be the case that managers have a list as long as their arm of players they would dearly love to sign but are unable to sign because of a lack of money. In Spain, I had plenty of money available but a very short list of Basque-born players who were suitable. It was a sharp—and confusing—contrast.

The other major structural difference at Bilbao was the make-up of the squads—or panels—for the first and second teams. At the start of every season, the coach will select those players who will form the basis of his senior squad, usually 22 men. The remainder will fight for places in the second team, Bilbao Athletic. The problem is that because both first and second teams are playing within the League, once a player has made ten appearances for the former he is ineligible to play for the latter. This leads to some very tricky decisions because if a youngster starts off in the senior side, plays eight or nine matches and then loses his form, the coach must decide whether to keep him where he is or ask him to step down to the reserve team. Once he has made ten appearances there is no decision to be made.

After studying my first-team panel, I decided that two of the youngsters would be far better off dropping down to the second team to help further their footballing education. I just couldn't see the point in them sitting around for months awaiting a call-up which might never come. There was the distinct possibility that the two of them would have gone through the entire season without once being called upon to take to the field of play. I thought that was a ridiculous prospect so I decided to do something about it.

I pulled them to one side after training and explained that they needed to get as many games as was possible under their belts if they were to improve. It seemed quite logical to me but they were devastated. They were horrified at the prospect because, like all

Basque players, they had spent years working their way up through the ranks to reach the senior panel. They had finally made it to the top and there was I, telling them that they had to drop down to a lower level. I tried to console them by telling them that they could still train with the seniors and that they would be recalled if they proved themselves to be good enough.

Again it was down to the difference in mentality. I never once had a member of my first-team panel knocking on my door seeking an explanation as to why he wasn't being selected to play. They were simply happy to be a part of the club's élite. Training hard is all well and good but there is nothing quite like real matches to sharpen up a player, be he Spanish or English.

Although we went out of the Spanish Cup, the Cup of the King, to Castilla, the second team of Real Madrid, over two legs, I enjoyed a very successful first season in charge.

Because I knew that we stood little, or no, chance of winning the title, I was bitterly disappointed with our exit from Spain's only knock-out competition because I desperately wanted to win something if only so that I could savour the Basque equivalent of a victorious homecoming. In England, a team which has won a major trophy tours its home city on top of a double-decker bus—in Bilbao they board the club's own boat and sail up and down the river. I was shown a video of just such an occasion and it was unbelievable. I wanted some of that. I knew that I was not going to spend the rest of my working life in Spain and I wanted to leave them with at least one lasting memory.

We finished in fourth place that first season and everyone at the club—directors, players, supporters—was delighted. After the disasters of the previous season, winning a place in the UEFA Cup was success in itself. I wasn't exactly a hero at the end of that season but I did feel that I had been accepted. I think they appreciated the work I had put in.

It was around this time that I went close to making a long-term impression on Spanish football. At a meeting of all the country's leading coaches, I proposed that Spain should follow in the footsteps of England and consider awarding three points for a League win. I just thought it was the only way to rid the country's football of the negative, unattractive tactics which were being employed by so many of the leading teams. Surprisingly, a very high percentage of my colleagues were in full agreement and pledged their whole-hearted support.

The proposal was put to the Spanish Football Association but they turned it down. Their argument was that to increase the number of points awarded for a victory would only have served to underline the gap between the bigger clubs and the smaller clubs. They felt that if Barcelona or Real Madrid were ten points clear at the top of the First Division instead of only six or seven, people would quickly lose interest in the destiny of the Championship. It is a shame that the plan was not accepted because I am confident that Spanish football would have benefitted handsomely in the long run.

Our success, or our relative success, did not go unnoticed outside of the Bilbao area because, during the summer recess, it became clear to me that the more fashionable Spanish clubs were a little wary of what our change of fortune might ultimately lead to.

We had possibly made the fatal mistake of finishing above mighty Barcelona. They were not amused at all and were not slow to use their cheque-book in an attempt to rectify the situation. Their aim was simple: not only did they want to improve the quality of their own team but they wanted to make damn sure that I couldn't improve the quality of my team!

The only sure way of doing this was to descend on Real Sociedad, who had also finished above them in the final table, and sign all their best players—Basque players. Although it was a highly cynical operation, I couldn't help but have a sneaking admiration for their sheer professionalism. Our supporters were somewhat dismayed by this act of sporting piracy but I tried to take the heat out of the situation by telling the media that I had renamed Barcelona, Basque-elona.

CHAPTER EIGHTEEN

Spanish Sighs

With my options severely limited in terms of introducing new blood, I knew that my second season in Spain was going to be a good deal tougher—and so it proved. The honeymoon period was over.

Again, we did reasonably well in the League, finishing in sixth place and missing out on a UEFA Cup place only by a solitary point. Had I been able to bring in a couple of new, influential players, I think we would have emulated our feat of the previous season and again qualified for Europe.

The one transfer deal which I did complete that summer did not exactly endear me to the Bilbao supporters. Although the Basque policy was to place a heavy reliance on the enthusiasm and exuberance of youth, I decided that we desperately needed a touch of experience so I bought a mature full-back from Murcia called Nunez. Nunez, who was 31, had spent the early part of his career playing in the Bilbao area and he had done ever so well against us in the previous season. I put him straight into the first team but he proved to be an immense disappointment.

Our assault on the UEFA Cup began well with a 2-1 aggregate win over AEK Athens. Unfortunately, in the next round we were paired with Juventus. The first leg was in Turin and we lost 5-1. It was a strange sort of a game because our goalkeeper didn't make a save all night, everything they hit went straight in. We just weren't good enough and they ran riot.

Because most of our supporters were already resigned to the fact that we had lost the tie, our stadium was only half-full for the return leg a fortnight later. That special, big-time atmosphere was missing. Juventus scored before half-time to further extend an already commanding advantage which left us facing the distinct possibility of complete and utter embarrassment. I tried to lift my players during the interval by demanding a show of pride and commitment. My words probably had a hollow ring to them because, like everybody else, I was fearing the worst. However, football is a funny game the world over and, for no apparent reason, we were a team transformed in the second period. We absolutely bulldozed Juventus and scored three times in a ten-minute spell of wonderfully fluent and incisive play.

I knew that Juventus were well and truly rattled because several of their players kept looking across at their coach, Dino Zoff, as if to say: "What the hell is going on here?" If we could have scored one more goal to pull back to 6–5 on aggregate, I think we would have gone on to record one of the greatest fightbacks in the history of the competition. We pushed everybody forward but the final goal of an extraordinary night went to the Italians. We were out—but honour in defeat was ours.

My contract with Bilbao expired at the end of that season but they were obviously happy with the progress which had been achieved and I was offered—and was delighted to sign—a 12-month extension.

Under the terms of the deal which I had agreed when I left Everton in 1987, I had the option to return to England at the end of that second season as a totally free agent. If an English club wanted to employ me they could do so without having to worry about the question of compensation. That was not to be the case with clubs from any other country; they would face a hefty bill.

The prospect of having to pay substantial compensation obviously did not unduly bother Barcelona because, for the second time in three years, they sought to make me their manager.

I met with their representatives in Madrid and listened to what they had to offer. Although the idea of being in charge of one of the world's biggest clubs did still appeal to me, I found myself backing away from the proposed deal.

It would have been harder for me to have left Bilbao for Barcelona than to have left Everton for Barcelona. Everyone at Athletic had been so good to me—so friendly and helpful—that I just couldn't turn around and kick them in the teeth. To end speculation which was being fuelled by the Spanish media, I rang Barcelona and told them that I was not interested in the job. I was flattered by their continued interest but I think they fully understood my reasons for wanting to remain at Bilbao.

My third term at Bilbao coincided with the club's Presidential elections, an event which occurs every three years and one which leads to sweeping changes at boardroom level. In typical political style, the new members of the club's hierarchy were anxious to make an immediate impression so they sanctioned the purchase of a player called Loren from Real Sociedad. He cost £1.5 million but, in truth, he wasn't worth that sort of money. He had played in defence in the early part of his career so I used him as a centre-back for the last ten minutes of a pre-season game in Holland. It was only an experiment during the course of a meaningless friendly but the newspapers slaughtered me the next day, claiming that I had paid out big money for a player of highly dubious quality.

The 1989–90 season was still very much in its infancy when I began to suspect that the pressure was beginning to mount. I wouldn't say that I felt my job was on the line but one or two little things happened which led me to believe that not everyone was happy with the job I was doing. We were being heavily criticised in the newspapers for our poor and inconsistent League form and my discontent at this potentially damaging coverage finally reached a climax on the day I was approached by one of Spain's most distinguished sports journalists.

This particular writer was clearly neither an admirer of myself nor of the English tactics which had infiltrated Bilbao's football since my arrival at the club. We had a dreadful row, one which annoyed those members of my board who were mindful of the possible implications of alienating Spain's influential media.

A couple of weeks later, my side was faced by one of the most daunting, eight-day programmes imaginable. On successive Sundays we had crucial League fixtures against Seville at home and Real Madrid away. Sandwiched in between was the small matter of a Spanish Cup second-round, first-leg tie against Barcelona in Bilbao. We lost to Seville, lost to Barcelona and then got battered 4–0 in Madrid. It had not been a good week and I was expecting repercussions.

I wasn't in a particularly good mood as I entered the press conference after the defeat by Real. As is always the case after a big game in Spain, the whole thing was being broadcast live by television and radio.

Explaining away heavy defeats is never easy at the best of times but it is even more difficult when you have two dozen microphones and hundreds of cameras dangling a matter of only a few inches from the end your nose. It was like a three-ring circus in that room.

I tried really hard to keep my cool and answer the questions in a civil manner but I was being pushed to deliver an acceptable excuse for my side's dismal performance.

In the middle of this undignified free-for-all, a radio journalist from Bilbao asked me a question. The problem was that in an attempt to make himself heard above the growing pandemonium, he was shouting and he was speaking far too quickly. I answered what I thought was the question. I had obviously misheard him because he shouted the same thing again, only this time at an even greater pace.

Believing that I had already supplied him with the response he was looking for, I stood up, said, "Goodnight", and walked out. You just don't do that sort of thing in Spain.

That night, as I enjoyed a meal with my wife and a couple of friends who had flown out for the game, I decided that I'd had enough. I told Cynthia that I felt two-and-a-half years to be long enough and that I was ready to go back to England. I was really pleased that she was there with me because it was a big decision and I needed some moral support.

Shortly after we had finished our meal, a television crew turned up at the hotel and asked me, quite bluntly: "Do you think you will be in charge of Athletic for the next game?"

I told them to put the same question to my President. They did and he said: "I don't know." I knew then that my time was up.

First thing on Monday morning I went down to Bilbao's main office to see Fernando, the man who had enticed me to Spain in the first place. He told me that my position as manager was to be discussed at a board meeting later that same day. Just as I had done at Everton in late 1983, I decided to make things easy for my employers by offering my resignation. I told him that I wanted to go.

Fernando phoned the President and told him that I was quitting. My resignation was immediately accepted. It is rather difficult to say whether I resigned or whether I was sacked because I am 99 per cent certain that my contract would have been cancelled during the course of that board meeting. I don't suppose it makes a great deal of difference, really.

It was a very emotional few hours for me because I had really fallen for the club in a big way.

The most pleasing aspect of my departure was that I left on very good terms with everybody connected with Athletic Bilbao. I have the greatest respect for all those people who made me feel welcome in a foreign country. I have been back to Bilbao on several occasions since that day and I have always been made to feel welcome. Many of the people I worked with in Spain I now regard as not merely associates, but good friends.

Only time will tell if I made any sort of lasting impression on Athletic Bilbao. If nothing else I think I possibly helped to establish a stronger bond between the club's players and supporters. Because Spanish footballers are aware that their public is very much in awe of them, they are sometimes a little reluctant to mix freely with those admirers who, in the final count, pay their wages.

I remember one New Year's Day when hundreds and hundreds of Bilbao supporters turned up at the training ground to watch a training session. I was so impressed by this display of loyalty that I felt it should be rewarded. I gathered my players together and said that I wanted them to shout, in unison, "Happy New Year." They refused to do it until I pointed out that the alternative was a brisk, five-mile run up and down the nearest mountainside. My threat, light-hearted though it was, stirred them into action and they shouted out the greeting. I have never heard a response quite like it. The fans, young and old, roared their approval.

I have no regrets at all about my two-and-a-half years in Spain; in fact, I am certain that the experience has made me a far better manager. I never did get my boat-trip down the river but I would like to think I did a reasonably good job in difficult circumstances.

*　　*　　*　　*

When I left England at the end of the 1986–87 season I did so with a completely clear conscience because I was confident that my departure, surprising though it may have been to many people, would not unduly disrupt the progress of Everton. I left them as Football League champions and I could see no reason at all why the club should not move forward and consolidate its position at the very pinnacle of the English game.

It is now a matter of history that things did not run quite as smoothly as I had anticipated. Indeed, had the club's success story been extended to embrace the late Eighties, there is no doubting that I would be writing these words from a totally different viewpoint. If the flow of silverware to Goodison Park had not been stemmed, it is inconceivable that I would now be the manager of Everton Football Club.

In the days after I had returned home from Spain in November 1989, people were almost queueing up to ask me the same question: had I kept in touch with Everton's progress while working in Bilbao? The question was as obvious and predictable as it was ridiculous. Of course I had monitored Everton's progress. My departure from Everton had done nothing at all to lessen my affection for what I still believe to be the biggest and best club in the entire Football League.

The decision to appoint Colin Harvey as my successor was a logical one for, like myself, he is openly passionate about every facet of the club. After serving Everton in so many different capacities (player, youth-team coach, reserve-team coach, first-team coach) Colin had finally realised a long-held dream by landing the top job. I boarded that plane to Bilbao knowing full well that I had left the club in the best possible hands.

Over the past couple of years it has been suggested that had I rejected Athletic Bilbao's overtures and accepted Everton's offer of a new, extended contract, the club's decline as a major footballing power would have been averted. Personally, I think that is a quite ludicrous thing to say because in a mystifying, unpredictable game you can never tell what is going to happen from one minute to the next. What would have happened to Everton had I remained at Goodison Park is one of life's great imponderables because I just don't know. Who knows, the club might be in the Second Division now!

On the day Colin assumed control, he admitted that his job would be a difficult one and that only by keeping the Championship pennant flying over Goodison Park could he hope to satisfy the demands of supporters who had grown accustomed to success.

In many respects, I feel that Colin took over at the worst possible time because when you are on top of the pile, the only way is down. It is to his eternal credit that he accepted a job which had a distinct Catch 22 feel about it. It was the classic no-win situation. If Everton continued to sweep all before them, people would say they expected nothing less. If Everton didn't sweep all before them, people would want to know why.

The League positions achieved during his three full seasons in charge may not have been quite as good as in the previous few years but they weren't disastrous by anyone's standards. On top of that, in 1989 Everton reached the finals of both the FA and Simod Cups. At practically any other club in the country, that would have been regarded as success but Colin was eventually to pay a heavy price for his side's failure to emulate the feats of the team which he himself had helped to assemble and coach between 1984 and 1987. It was ironic that his past should so blight his future.

I was surprised that Everton failed to win a trophy of any description during my absence but I do feel there were mitigating
circumstances. It is true that my respect for Colin knows no bounds
and that he has been one of my closest friends for more years than
I care to remember, but if the ties which bind us are ignored—if I
analyse the problems he encountered from a position of complete
neutrality—I think I can begin to understand what happened, what
went wrong.

The team which Colin inherited was unquestionably one of the
best in Europe; that had been proved in 1985 when the Cup
Winners' Cup was won in such style. However, no team can afford
to lose several key members without suffering some form of adverse
reaction. While I was away in Spain, men like Peter Reid, Gary
Stevens, Trevor Steven and Paul Bracewell left Everton for a variety
of diverse reasons. These weren't your run-of-the-mill footballers
who come and go at regular intervals, these were proven, top-class,
international stars who had formed the back-bone of a highly
successful side. Take four players of that calibre out of any side in
the world and problems—major problems—are not so much a possibility as an inevitability. For example, how on earth do you replace
a man like Reid? He is the sort of player who only comes along
every five or six years if you are lucky.

Having seen some of his most influential players drift away, Colin
was faced by the same problem which befell Harry Catterick back
in the early Seventies; he had money in the bank but few logical or
comparable replacements readily available to step in.

I think that I am right in saying that Colin spent in excess of
£10 million on new talent in an attempt to keep Everton at the
forefront of the English game. Some of his transfer deals were criticised but the fact that he was always actively seeking to improve the
quality of his senior squad only goes to prove that he was determined to get things right. He was not content to sit back. He took
the action which he felt was required at the time.

As I am now working alongside many of those players who were
brought to Goodison Park by Colin it would be totally wrong, if not
unethical, for me to comment on whether or not I thought they
were good purchases. Colin and I spoke a great deal while I was in
Spain but he never once asked me for advice—and I never once
offered advice. We both knew how important it was that he ran
Everton his way. He simply had to be his own man. It was only
natural that we should discuss the progress which was being made

by our respective sides, Everton and Athletic, but that is as far as it went.

In a funny sort of way, I am a bit disappointed to be once again at the helm at Everton because if things had gone well at the club between 1987 and 1990, I would now visit Goodison Park only twice a year, as the manager of another team. Were it not for two decisions I took during the early part of the 1988–89 season, I think it is debatable whether I would ever have returned to Everton for a second spell in charge.

After a reasonably successful first season at Bilbao, I was beginning to settle into the Spanish way of life when I received two tempting offers to return to England in very quick succession.

The first came in October 1988 from the club which I had supported as a youngster, Newcastle United. Having sacked Willie McFaul, United had placed Colin Suggett in charge of first-team affairs on a temporary basis. I think they turned to me after Arthur Cox, the manager of Derby County, had declined an invitation to return to St James Park. Gordon McKeag, who was then the Newcastle Chairman, contacted me and said that he wished to fly over to Spain to discuss the vacant post. I said that I would meet up with him for an informal, no strings attached, chat. Unfortunately, the news of our meeting was leaked to the press back in England and within 24 hours the Spanish papers were running stories speculating that I was to resign.

I was very annoyed that a so-called private meeting had become public knowledge because my meeting with Mr McKeag took place just a few days before my side was to face Juventus in an important UEFA Cup tie. The very last thing I wanted was for my players to go into such a difficult game believing that their manager was on the verge of quitting. In an attempt to allay the fears of my directors, I immediately contacted them and said that I had turned down Newcastle's offer and would be remaining at Bilbao to honour my two-year contract.

When we arrived in Turin the day before the Juventus game, I confess to making a very bad error of judgement during a meeting with the Spanish press. Not too surprisingly, they wanted to know if I was going to return to England. Although I had already told my board that I was staying, I decided to maintain a diplomatic silence. I said that I was unwilling to discuss anything other than the forthcoming game.

I should have known better because my silence was construed as an admission that something was going to happen. That little saga with Newcastle haunted me until the day I finally left Athletic Bilbao because whenever things were going badly, I knew that one of the papers would resurrect the story about the day I nearly returned to my native North-east. Actually, that wasn't the case at all because I was never even close to taking the job. I was very, very flattered to be approached by one of the most famous clubs in British football but the offer came at totally the wrong time as I had been in Spain for less than 18 months.

The second club which tried to lure me back home was Leeds United but as their offer came shortly after Newcastle's, I found myself citing the same reasons when I turned them down.

Again it was a case of a club which had dispensed with the services of its manager approaching me with a view to taking over. I have always made it clear that I will not enter into negotiations with any English club which still has a man in control. If there is a vacancy, then that is a different matter altogether.

Leeds, who were then in the Second Division, were looking for a successor to Billy Bremner, one of my old sparring partners from my playing days, who had been fired after failing to return the Yorkshire club to the top flight.

I have never believed there is anything wrong with talking to anyone so I agreed to meet with Bill Fotherby, Leeds' managing director. Mr Fotherby is a most persuasive man. No-one could have sold Leeds United to me in the way he did during the course of that meeting. He did everything possible to try and persuade me to quit Bilbao and move to Elland Road.

Even though I knew that I would eventually announce that I was going to stay put, I went so far as to listen to the terms of the contract which Leeds were offering. It was intriguing to say the very least.

Now, unless I'm mistaken (I don't think I am) the main stipulation was that I had to guarantee that Leeds United would definitely win promotion from the Second Division at the end of my first, full season in charge. Managers can guarantee many things but they can never guarantee something like promotion. It wasn't made clear to me what would happen to my contract if I failed to end the club's lengthy exile from the First Division. You'll have to draw your own conclusions.

The second stipulation was that I should work closely with the media to maintain the club's good public relations record. Mr

Fotherby was well-prepared for his meeting with me but he obviously hadn't done his homework on that particular subject because, as I have said before, I have always prided myself on my ability to deal with the press.

Having turned Leeds down, I was absolutely delighted when they found the man they were looking for in the shape of Howard Wilkinson. Without any doubt, he is one of the best managers in the country and his record since moving from Hillsborough to Elland Road speaks for itself. Bill Fotherby told me that Leeds were going to go places in the next few years and I think he will be proved right.

CHAPTER NINETEEN

The Maine Chance

Because I knew that I would one day return home to England to take up a fresh challenge within the Football League, I consciously made an effort while in Spain to keep track of events back in England.

The problem with any job in football is that you have no idea at all exactly how long it is going to last. It doesn't really matter what length the contract you have put your name to is because the axe can fall at any time. Many a manager who has felt his immediate future to be secure has later rued his sense of complacency.

I didn't want to come back and find that I was totally out of touch with the English game. Two-and-a-half years may not constitute a lifetime but things can change very, very quickly in football. Consequently, I gathered and devoured every scrap of information I could, whether it be about transfers, tactics, the international arena or the politics of the game. I had all the major football magazines sent over to me on a regular basis and I would enquire about what was happening whenever anybody rang me from England. One of my greatest joys was receiving the *Liverpool Echo* Saturday sports paper. Ken Rogers, one of the *Echo*'s senior sports writers, was kind enough to send the "Pink" to me every week and although I didn't receive it until several days after publication, I used to love catching up on all the Merseyside gossip.

When I came home, the plan was to sit back, relax, take stock of the situation and then decide on my next career move. I was in no great hurry to get involved with another club. I was really looking forward to turning up at matches as nothing more than an interested onlooker but I quickly realised that even this harmless pastime was going to cause problems.

From the minute I stepped off the plane from Bilbao, the papers were linking me with various managerial jobs, up and down the country. It was ridiculous really. All I wanted to do was watch some football yet I found myself studying the fixture list to try and find a game which involved two clubs who were doing well and whose managers were not under any pressure. Every time I attended a match, my presence was reported the following day. Every time I attended a match, I was linked with one of the two clubs I had been innocently watching. I began to feel like some sort of pariah.

The very last thing I wanted was for people to start thinking that I had returned with the expressed intent of immediately searching out a new job. It began to read like the script for a low-budget horror movie—"The Scalp-hunter . . . starring Howard Kendall."

The first game I went to see was Blackburn Rovers against West Ham United at Ewood Park. It was fast, furious, full of excitement and goals and it made me realise what I had been missing during my time in Spain. I said afterwards that I had seen a £1 million footballer that day, without naming the player in question. Initially the papers thought that I was referring to Scott Sellars but after I brought Mark Ward to Maine Road from Upton Park during my time at Manchester City, they decided it was him.

It wasn't. The player who had so impressed me was West Ham's Stuart Slater, the man who was instrumental in ending Everton's FA Cup run in March of 1991.

I would have been naïve in the extreme had I not expected my name to be linked with at least some First Division clubs, particularly those in the North-west. I knew that it would never be suggested I was readying myself to take over from Kenny Dalglish at Liverpool. That was unthinkable for the obvious reasons. The prospect of a return to Everton never once crossed my mind so that left the two Manchester clubs, City and United.

Although City were struggling at the wrong end of the table, their manager, Mel Machin, had taken them back into Division One the previous season so most people seemed to assume that his position was relatively safe. Those journalists who were looking for a story, or a "line" as they call it, simply removed three clubs from a provisional list of four and homed in on the name which was left—Manchester United.

Several stories were printed saying that as Alex Ferguson had failed in his bid to return the League Championship to Old Trafford, his board was ready to dismiss him. The inference was that I would be approached to succeed him. I felt so awkward about this situation because it was totally unfair on Alex, a man whom I respect greatly. I even received phone calls from a couple of writers asking me to comment on Alex's situation at United. I just kept repeating that I would not talk about any job in English football unless it was vacant.

People who were reading these stories must have thought I was hawking myself about looking for one of the top jobs when, in fact, nothing could have been further from the truth.

I am sure that the more experienced managers ignore completely what appears in some newspapers. If everything which was printed was underpinned by even a smattering of truth, clubs would be changing their managers almost every other week. One or two of this country's more popular papers should have a small sachet of salt stapled to their back pages.

The first inkling I had that my plan to take things easy for a while was likely to be abandoned came in late November. Twenty-four hours after Manchester City had sacked Mel Machin, I received a phone call from a third party asking me if I would be interested in taking over at Maine Road.

I had to admit that I was interested because City is a very big club. I knew that my holiday, or sabbatical, could not last forever but, to be honest, I did not think things would happen so quickly.

Much has been said and written about what happened in the days between the departure of Mel on 27 November and my appointment on 6 December, so I think now is the time to clear everything up and set the record straight once and for all.

I met the City Chairman, Peter Swales, at his home where we discussed exactly what was on offer. When we came to the question of the contract, he outlined his terms and I did the same. From my point of view, there was nothing unusual or outrageous about these terms—or demands as the papers called them—because they were the same ones which had been agreed by all three of my former clubs, Blackburn Rovers, Everton and Athletic Bilbao.

As I had done in the past, I simply wanted to protect myself by attempting to cover every eventuality. The clause which I wanted written in to any contract would guarantee my release if another club was to agree to meet a set figure of compensation and would guarantee me a pre-arranged sum in compensation if I was to be dismissed.

The other point which I was insistent about—and which led to a breakdown in our negotiations—revolved around the possibility of my being offered the job of England manager.

While I was in Spain, I had received a couple of calls asking me to outline my contractual situation with Bilbao. The man who made those calls was not a member of the Football Association but he made it clear that he was acting on their behalf. Although Bobby Robson was obviously going to lead England into the Italian World Cup Finals, the implication was that he was going to step down as manager once the tournament was over. The FA was doing no more than I was trying to do with City—they were trying to cover themselves in as professional a way as was possible.

I am not saying that the FA had decided that I was going to be the next manager of our national team because that wasn't the case at all; they were just making a few preliminary enquiries. I told this go-between that my contract with Bilbao was such that I would be free to leave and that there would be no bill for compensation.

During the course of my talks with Mr Swales, I said that I wanted a clause which would release me to become the England manager *IF* the FA was to offer me the job and *IF* I wanted it. I was worried in case he thought I was being arrogant or big-headed but I do believe that he understood my situation fully.

Obviously, he was concerned about the possibility of my taking the City job and then walking out, a few months later, to manage England. He said that he felt his club should be entitled to receive compensation if that was to happen. I disagreed and pointed out that my previous employers had been more than happy to insert the disputed clause in my contract.

At this point I honestly wasn't sure whether I would have accepted an invitation to manage England had one been forthcoming. I just knew that the possibility of my being asked to succeed Bobby Robson did exist and I wanted to keep all my options open. I don't think I was being deceptive or using underhand methods in any way at all. I certainly wasn't looking to use Manchester City as a stepping stone en route to an even more prestigious job. Wherever football may take me in the future, I shall always insist on the same contract.

It was clear to me when I left Mr Swales' home that we had reached an impasse. I headed for home believing that I would never manage Manchester City.

A couple of days after it had been announced that talks between myself and City had floundered, Joe Royle was installed as the clear favourite to pick up the reins at Maine Road. Joe had done such a wonderful job at Oldham Athletic that he was an obvious choice. From what I can gather, Joe was on the verge of accepting City's offer—until he discovered that he was not the first choice. After he

I leave Goodison Park for what I thought would be the last time as manager

had spoken to Mr Swales, Joe rang me at home to ask whether or not I had been officially approached.

I suppose that I could have paved the way for his appointment by being economical with the truth but I had known Joe for such a long time that I felt it only fair to level with him. Once I had confirmed that I had indeed held talks with City, Joe said that he was pulling out. He is a very proud man and the idea of only being second-choice did not appeal to him one little bit.

I was at Manchester airport waiting for a flight to Spain where I was to tie up a few loose ends when City approached me for a second time. A club representative told me that Mr Swales had agreed to my contractual clauses. I shook hands with him and told him to tell his Chairman that he had found himself a manager. I was absolutely delighted. I couldn't believe my good fortune, for less than a month after returning home I had been placed in charge of one of the biggest and best-supported clubs in Britain.

After completing the formalities of my departure from Athletic,

I flew straight to Southampton where my new team was playing a League game. After being introduced to the City directors, I went into the dressing-room to meet the players. Tony Book was in charge of first-team affairs on that day so I simply wished them luck and said I would see them on the training pitch, first thing Monday morning.

When I took over at Maine Road, City were at the bottom of the First Division table; rock-bottom in more ways than one. It will surprise no-one to learn that my brief was to safeguard the club's Division One status. For City to have been relegated just 12 months after winning promotion would have been a complete and utter disaster—not just in purely financial terms.

The first thing I wanted was an assistant—a reliable, tried and trusted, right-hand man. The person who fitted that bill to perfection was Peter Reid. Peter was playing for Queen's Park Rangers at the time but it did not take me too long to negotiate his release on a free transfer. I still thought that he had the stamina to perform at the top level and I knew that he would be invaluable in terms of motivating and encouraging those players of lesser experience within the dressing-room.

After I had left Manchester City, Peter Swales went on record as saying that, in his opinion, the signing of Peter Reid was one of the best pieces of business his club had ever completed. I think most City supporters would readily agree with that sentiment—whatever they might think of me.

With Peter at my side, I sat down to assess what I had in terms of players at Maine Road. In all fairness, without picking out individuals for criticism, I quickly realised that my squad was just not good enough. After studying the players closely in training I quickly understood that our position at the bottom of the table was not a false one. I wasn't surprised at all that we were filling a relegation place. I had to ask myself a very simple question. Could I see the team I had inherited climbing to a position of safety without the introduction of new talent? The answer was an unequivocal no.

I firmly believe that had I not made immediate changes it is conceivable that Manchester City would have been relegated.

I was then faced by two choices; I could leave things as they were, let the club slide back into the Second Division and refuse to take the blame by saying it wasn't my team in the first place, or I could ask my board to make money available for transfer market activity. Because I was thinking long-term, because I was expecting to spend

a considerable length of time at the club, because I was determined
to transform Manchester City into a team which was capable of
winning the League Championship, I held out my hand and asked
for the cash.

I knew that Alan Harper was having a bad time at Sheffield
Wednesday so I contacted Ron Atkinson and agreed a £150,000
deal. During his time at Everton, Alan had proved himself to be a
manager's dream. Although he was forever complaining that he was
one of Goodison Park's "nearly men" inasmuch as he spent a great
deal of time sitting on the substitute's bench, he was versatile,
composed and very professional. I couldn't believe that no-one had
been in to snap him up during the time he was in and out of
Wednesday's senior side.

I remember telling my coaching staff at City that if the club was
to develop along the same lines as had Everton, I wouldn't be
happy until Alan was unable to guarantee himself a regular, first-
team place. I wanted to build a side which was so good that Alan
would once again have to resort to knocking on my office door to
complain about lack of opportunity. I was using Everton as a bench
mark but I could see nothing wrong with that because the record
books showed that between 1984 and 1987 they were the best that
English football had to offer. All I was doing was setting a target for
everyone at the club to aim for in the years ahead.

The fact that my first two signings had both enjoyed highly successful spells at Everton under my managership did not seem to
cause any bitterness or resentment. I think the supporters were just
pleased that someone was doing something in an attempt to arrest
a fall from grace which appeared to be accelerating.

It was my next deal, my next big decision, which was to create
such an enormous gulf between myself and the man on the
terrace—one which I was never to bridge.

On 28 December I signed Mark Ward from West Ham United in
a package deal which saw Ian Bishop and Trevor Morley move to
Upton Park. Because of the complex nature of transfers which
involve more than one player, it is rather difficult to say precisely
what the valuation of each individual was but I was more than
satisfied with the terms.

What happened in the days and weeks after that deal was completed continues to baffle me. I wish that I could say baffle *AND*
amuse me, but there was nothing humorous about a situation which
began life as a mole-hill but which very quickly became a mountain—

a mountain which appeared, overnight, in the space between myself and my club's supporters and which severed all lines of meaningful communication.

When the news of the transfer was made public there was absolute uproar. It wasn't so much that I had bought a third player with Everton connections, nor was it the fact that I had sold Morley; it was my decision to let Bishop leave which so angered the general public.

I could use the excuse that, having been at the club for only a short space of time, I had no idea how popular Bishop was with the fans but I won't do that because I was fully aware that he was a firm favourite. However, the backlash was so strong that you would have thought the lad was a living legend who had been a key figure in the City side for many years. I couldn't believe that anybody could be that popular in a team which was not performing well and which was struggling at the foot of the table.

With all due respect, I had been brought to Maine Road to try and sort things out. I was trying to build a better future for a club which had moved up and down between the First and Second Divisions like a yo-yo. I hadn't taken the job for a laugh. The way some people were talking in the immediate aftermath of Bishop's departure, you would have thought I had taken over at City with the expressed intent of ruining the club.

I was looking for a quick solution to a serious problem and if that meant that I had to sell players who were popular with the supporters then so be it. If you are not single-minded in my line of work then you don't get anywhere. You stand and fall by your decisions in football management and my decision to let Bishop leave was made with the best interests of Manchester City at heart. I thought it was the right decision at the time and I still think it was the right decision now.

The supporters, or a very high percentage of them, may have been upset and mystified by the action I took, but I was working *FOR* them, not *AGAINST* them. I did not want them to be watching Second Division football in the following season and, believe me, that was a distinct possibility.

The Bishop situation developed into a saga, the like of which I have never experienced in football before. As I say, had he been the focal point of the Maine Road crowd's adulation for several years I could have understood the sense of outrage but he'd only made a handful of senior appearances since moving from Bournemouth. I think one of the problems was that he had played very well, and scored, during the 5-1 victory over Manchester United earlier in the season. I got the impression that many City fans were happy to hang on to the sweet memory of that one game and ignore everything else that was happening. The attitude in some quarters seemed to be, Oh well, if we go down, at least we beat United.

When I decided to sell Bishop, I was fully aware that the papers would point out that it was the second time I had shown him the door because in 1984, when he was at Everton, I had sold him to Carlisle United. He had nothing more than raw talent and potential in those days and I felt it was best that he moved on to gain valuable experience.

Let me make one thing perfectly clear—I have nothing against Ian Bishop either as a footballer or as a person. He has developed into a very fine player and I am sure that he will enjoy a long and successful career. He was sold because I felt that Mark Ward would be more valuable in our fight against relegation.

To be fair to both Bishop and Morley, I must say that neither wanted to leave the club. They would have been perfectly entitled to dig their heels in and refuse to move but I think they realised that their best interests would be served by a clean break.

The sad thing about the controversy which was stirred up by Bishop's sale is that it almost obscured the fact that I had brought a very fine footballer to Maine Road. What people possibly don't realise is that I was faced by the stiffest of competition in the days before I clinched the Ward deal.

When I rang Lou Macari, who was then the manager of West Ham, he said that he was only interested in a player exchange deal and that Bishop and Morley were the two players he would like. I said that we would need some money in addition (about £200,000) if the transfer was to go through.

Mark Ward was one of football's hottest properties at the time. Lou told me that Liverpool had tried to buy him but that they were unwilling to sell the two players he wanted, namely Jan Molby and Mike Hooper. Nottingham Forest had also been in, but their offer of Lee Chapman plus cash had been rejected. When a player is being pursued by the likes of Liverpool and Forest he is obviously no mug.

I was anticipating staying at City for as long as they wanted me and with that in mind, I was building for the future. I didn't just

Friendly rivals. I take my Manchester City team to Goodison Park for a League game. Also pictured is Colin Harvey

want to stave off the threat of relegation and then find ourselves faced with the same scenario in the following season, I wanted us to make giant strides forward. I have always been an ambitious man and I wanted City to start every season with a real chance of winning the game's major honours.

I am not saying that City didn't have some very good, young players, because they did. The problem was that these youngsters had been forced to live through the trauma of firstly fighting for promotion and then fighting to prevent relegation. They needed a period of stabilisation; a period when the pressure was lifted and they didn't have to keep looking over their shoulders.

The whole thing about the sale of Ian Bishop still puzzles me. I was astonished by the reaction his departure prompted but I was staggered by the length of time it went on. In fact, it is still going on because every time I meet a Manchester City supporter, that is the first topic which is raised.

I will never, ever forget my first game as the manager of Manchester City. Ironically, it was against Everton at Goodison Park. I suppose the writing was on the wall that day because I relegated Bishop to the substitute's bench. It was not a popular move. I walked out at 2.55 p.m. to hear my supporters chanting: "There's only one Ian Bishop." Nice welcome, that was.

Another one of my decisions which did not exactly endear me to the City faithful was the infrequent use of Clive Allen, a natural crowd-pleaser who often found himself confined to the substitute's bench during my time at Maine Road.

I have the greatest admiration for Clive. He is one of the most clinical goal-scorers I have ever seen and, despite his disappointment at being unable to hold down a regular first-team spot, he was an absolute joy to work with.

The realisation that I was not the most popular man working in the Moss Side district of Manchester did not deter me from bringing to the club another player with Everton connections. Because I felt that my squad needed a forward with a proven goal-scoring record, I arranged a deal which brought Wayne Clarke to Maine Road and which saw David Oldfield, plus a cash adjustment, go to Leicester City.

Wayne, who has played his entire career beneath the enormous shadow cast by his more famous brother, Allan, is a far better player than people give him credit for. His only problem is that he does need to be in a good team if he is to prosper. If he is surrounded by creative midfield players who are capable of delivering telling passes into the penalty area, there are few better finishers in the English game.

Those supporters who were still angry about the sale of Ian Bishop did not welcome the arrival of a fourth former Everton player. They seemed to think I was pursuing a policy of jobs-for-the-boys. The fans began to chant "Everton reserves" during our matches and the suggestion was that I was seeking permission to change the colour of City's strip from light blue to royal blue.

I must admit to being slightly annoyed at what was happening because from my point of view it really didn't matter which clubs my players had previously been at. You can't judge the quality of a footballer simply by looking at his curriculum vitae—you have to study his performance out on the field of play. All I wanted was for the supporters to give my new boys a chance; a fair crack of the whip. Sadly, that just wasn't happening.

Mick Heaton, my former number two at Everton, must have been pleased he was a coach and not a player when he joined City as my assistant in early January. I brought Mick in because he had, obviously, an expansive knowledge of the players I had brought to the club. The other members of the back-room staff, Tony Book, Glyn Pardoe, Jimmy Frizzell and Roy Bailey, were similarly adept at dealing with those players who had been at the club before my arrival. The balance was just right.

The relationship between myself and the supporters was subjected to even more strain in February, when I bought Adrian Heath from Aston Villa. If I am honest, I must admit that I was somewhat reluctant to buy yet another player who had made his name at Goodison Park because I knew exactly what the reaction would be on the terracing. Although I was convinced that Adrian would prove to be a valuable addition to my staff, I was wary of perpetrating the groundless myth that you had to have played for Everton at one time or another if you were to be allowed to join Manchester City.

In the end the decision as to whether to sign Adrian or not was taken by Mick. Obviously, as the manager, I had the final say but it was Mick who travelled down to Birmingham to watch several of Villa's reserve-team games and pass final judgement. He convinced me that Adrian was still full of enthusiasm and that the passing of the years had not in any way eroded his skill. That was good enough for me, so I bought him.

I must point out that during this period of reconstruction, not once did my Chairman question the wisdom of my transfer deals. He gave me his full support at all times and was always 100 per cent behind me. He deserves great credit for that.

Like Clarke before him, Adrian endured a baptism of fire. I named him as a substitute for the home game against Charlton Athletic on 24 February and when I sent him on he was jeered all the way from the bench to the pitch. The problem was that to make way for Adrian, I had pulled off Steve Redmond for the first time in his entire career. The whole ground erupted as the supporters chanted: ''What the **** hell is going on!''

The whole thing was getting out of hand. The supporters may not have realised it but those former Everton players I brought to the club were proud to pull on the shirt of Manchester City. It is supporters who live on past glories, not players. When a player leaves one club for another, his allegiance switches completely. Players like Reid, Heath, Harper and Clarke may have enjoyed great success during their time at Goodison Park but, believe me, nothing gave them greater pleasure than playing against—and beating—Everton. They looked upon it as a God-given opportunity to show that their old club was wrong to sell them in the first place.

I was absolutely thrilled when we defeated Everton at Maine Road towards the end of the season. Yes, I still had a great affection for Everton but they were no longer my concern. I was the manager of Manchester City and Manchester City was the only thing that mattered to me. Even now, at a time when City have re-established themselves as one of this country's leading clubs, I don't feel as though a section of the Manchester public honestly believes that I was committed to the cause during my time at Maine Road. Words rarely change opinions so all I can say is that my commitment to that club *WAS* total.

The fact that there was so much abuse and criticism being tossed in my general direction meant that the progress which we were making was almost forgotten. One month after I had taken over we had risen from the bottom of the table to 14th place; the spectre of relegation was slowly being banished. Had we managed to enjoy a long run in the FA Cup, perhaps people would have been slightly more tolerant but unfortunately we fell at the first hurdle, losing a third-round, second-replay tie against Millwall at The Den.

With the benefit of hindsight, that most precise of sciences, I can pinpoint several reasons for the cavernous gulf which separated me from the City supporters, not least my working relationship with the local paper, the *Manchester Evening News*.

When you accept a new job in management the very last thing you want to do is rub people up the wrong way—especially those people who have been connected with your new club for many, many years. To say that I got off on the wrong foot with Peter Gardner, the sports writer who had covered City for the *MEN* for more than 25 years, would be a gross understatement.

Shortly after I had arrived back from Spain to watch City play at Southampton, I was shown the edition of the *MEN* which covered the news of my appointment. Peter's article was made up almost entirely of facts and figures. The thrust of the piece was how much he thought (or had been told) I was to receive during the course of my contract.

When I checked in at my hotel one of the first people I was introduced to was Mr Gardner. I told him that I had read his piece and that I wasn't at all happy about its content. Had the figures he quoted been accurate then I would have been in no position to criticise.

When I took over at Maine Road, I knew that I would need to make changes, not only on the playing side, but also on the business side, the administration side, if you like. There were certain aspects of the way in which the club was being run which I was not happy about. In all my years as a manager I have never allowed journalists to travel on the team coach when a senior fixture is involved. In the past, I have allowed reporters to travel with the players during pre-season trips abroad but that is a completely different matter. As far as I am concerned, the team bus is an extension of the dressing-room. It is somewhere where players must feel relaxed and totally at their ease. It is vitally important that they are able to shed their inhibitions and talk freely and frankly about whatever they want without having to watch their manners and their language. Football is a man's game and if players want to use industrial language to ram home a point or two, I will not stand in their way just so long as they are keeping their own company.

Peter had always travelled with the first-team to away matches, irrespective of who was the manager. I told him that, in future, he would have to make his own travel arrangements. I stressed that I wasn't taking this action because of what he had written about me on that first day but that this was just my way of doing things. I pointed out that just as he was trying to be professional in his job, I was trying to be professional in mine. I told him that I wasn't anti-Peter Gardner, but that I was a firm believer in giving players absolute privacy before and after matches. I didn't want to upset, or alienate, him because a manager's relationship with his local press is possibly far more important than is his relationship with the national press.

I know for a fact that Peter was very, very annoyed by my decision and, sadly, I have to say that I believe his discontent began to show through in some of the match reports he served up to the Manchester public. That is only my personal opinion, but I stand by it. At one point it was getting really embarrassing because no matter how well we played, we were criticised, if not for our results, then for our style of football. We were steadily climbing up the table but nothing, it seemed, could please or satisfy Peter Gardner.

As I have said before, I think that sports writers can be powerful and influential people. I thought many of the things which Peter wrote to be unfair and unnecessary. I don't think he was reflecting public opinion, I think he was trying to shape it.

His attacks on my team were so swingeing that I felt I had to leap to the defence of my players. I did that by devoting my column in the City programme to the vexed question of the coverage the club was receiving in the local press. I didn't go so far as to actually name Peter because I didn't have to.

I have always respected the right of sports journalists to give their honest opinions about what they have seen during the course of matches but when report after report is written from a seemingly negative standpoint, it is very hard to stomach. All I was asking for was a fair deal. I didn't want him to try and mislead the public by saying we had played well when we hadn't, I just wanted credit where credit was due.

It is quite amazing how many supporters are influenced by the written word. Many will leave a ground believing that their team has played well only to undergo a dramatic change of heart when they read the sports pages, either that night or the following morning. It is as if some people really do believe that journalists are better qualified than anyone else to discuss the merits of a team's performance. Several of the journalists I know, I would classify as friends but to suggest that their understanding of football is any more expansive than that of the average supporter is utter rubbish.

Peter's personal crusade against what he obviously deemed to be English football's least attractive team went on for so long that I began to find his reports hilarious. Whether everything stemmed from my decision to stop him travelling on the team bus or not, I just don't know.

It is ironic because, as a person, I don't mind Peter Gardner at all. I wouldn't go so far as to say that he is a permanent fixture on my Christmas card list but he's an OK sort of a bloke.

In the end I had to accept that there was no way the two of us were ever going to forge a reasonable understanding. We were still at loggerheads when I left City to rejoin Everton in November 1990. I suspect that the news of my departure from Maine Road must have delighted him. However, life is far too short to harbour grudges and Peter can buy me a drink anytime he wants.

The bad press we received during those first few months certainly didn't help my players one little bit. When the problem of dismissive reporting was added to the bad feeling which had been brought about by the sale of Bishop and the purchase of four ex-Everton players it made for an unhealthy, and quite unnecessary problem.

I am often asked what I think about the supporters of Manchester City. It is a very difficult question to answer because, during my spell at the club, I experienced their good side and their bad side. I felt they never fully accepted me. I am sure that some of them don't like me one little bit. In some respects, I suppose that the die was cast on that Sunday at Goodison Park when I omitted Bishop from my starting line-up. The signings of Reid, Harper, Heath etc simply served to rub salt into a wound which would not heal.

The only time I felt as though as I was on the verge of some sort of breakthrough with the supporters was on the final day of the season when we played against Crystal Palace at Selhurst Park. For once, their team was going into a final fixture which was, in effect, totally meaningless. We had guaranteed our First Division future and the thousands of supporters who travelled down to London were in jubilant mood. There was a real carnival atmosphere and, for once, they actually looked as if they were enjoying what they were seeing.

I am certain that even my sternest critics would agree that my decision to bring Niall Quinn to Maine Road was the right one. I'm not looking for people to go down on bended knees to thank me for bringing Niall to City but sometimes I just wish that my critics at Maine Road would look carefully at those players I introduced and study the contribution they have made and the contribution they continue to make. I bought Niall because I felt we needed another dimension to our play when we were attacking. We had pace, aggression and will to win but we were lacking a genuine target man.

I went down to watch him play for Arsenal reserves and then made a lot of enquiries about him. Everyone said the same thing— he was a good player with a great first touch and was a lovely lad. He was so commanding in the air that I couldn't see any defender beating him to crosses if they were accurate. I paid £700,000 down for Niall with a further £100,000 placed on ice until after he had made a specified number of first-team appearances.

If City hadn't been struggling in the bottom half of the table, I don't think that I would have got him because George Graham rated him highly and would have been loathe to sell him to a club which was in with even half a chance of winning the Championship. I say that with some assurance because Aston Villa had tried, but failed, to sign him probably because they were enjoying a very successful League campaign.

Niall's had a wonderful time since joining City and I couldn't be more pleased for him. After he had established himself in my first team and was playing well, people within the game kept asking me how I had managed to get so much out of him. The truth is that I didn't have to do very much at all. He already had the skill and the enthusiasm, all I did was add a dash of confidence. Once Niall realised that he was a regular, first-choice player, all his inhibitions disappeared and he began to flourish. If his team-mates play to his particular strengths, Niall is one of the best one-touch finishers I have seen in a very long time.

We finished the season in 14th place, which was very pleasing bearing in mind the desperate position we had been in just four months earlier.

We had finished so strongly that I was very optimistic about our chances of making a real impression the following season. I knew that I would have to strengthen certain areas but, overall, I felt that we were on the right lines.

During the summer I negotiated new five-year contracts for David White and Paul Lake because they were both quality players and I wanted to make sure that they spent their most productive years at Manchester City. In many ways, the fact that I persuaded those two players to pledge their future to City is my answer to those people who do not believe that I was working for the club. If I had thought I was going to leave City, I wouldn't have drawn up contracts of that length. I would have told them to stick around Maine Road for a while and then join up with me later, after I had moved to another club.

Perhaps I was again flirting with controversy in July when I arranged a deal which took Andy Hinchcliffe to Everton and brought Neil Pointon to City but by this stage, I was almost impervious to the criticism; it had become a way of life, in some respects.

The signing of yet another player with Everton connections was the signal for more murmurings of discontent but that was the first—and only—direct transaction I was involved in with my former club. The reason I let Andy go to Goodison Park in a deal which netted City a top-quality defender and £600,000 in cash was that I had decided we needed a new goalkeeper. Andy Dibble is a very good goalkeeper but I have always believed that if you are going to win the major honours it is vitally important that you have a truly exceptional man between the posts. In fact, to sustain a genuine challenge for the biggest prize of all, the League Championship, you must have two top 'keepers.

The first man I tried to get was Neville Southall. It was only natural that I should enquire about him first because he is, quite simply, the best in the world. I rang Colin Harvey but he was having none of it. I am sure that there wouldn't have been too many City supporters complaining had I succeeded in bringing that particular Everton player to the club!

Having scrubbed Neville's name off my provisional list, I was left with three men: Chris Woods of Glasgow Rangers, Andy Goram of Hibernian and Tony Coton of Watford. After thinking the matter over very carefully, I decided to try for Coton. The only problem was that Watford, having placed a £900,000 price tag on Tony, were in a totally inflexible mood. They were not interested in anything other than a straight cash deal and the fee was non-negotiable.

Although I did not have that sort of money available to me, I know that it would have been provided had I asked my Chairman. However, I didn't really want to spend money which had been earmarked for other purposes so I looked around for an alternative. I knew that Everton were very keen on Andy so I arranged the transfer to help finance the Coton deal. I think it was a piece of good business because I got a top-class goalkeeper and a versatile defender for an outlay of only £350,000.

I knew that the deal would upset some people because Andy was a successful product of City's magnificent youth programme but, again, I was thinking long-term and building for the future.

The manner in which City has brought so many young players up through the ranks in recent years is the envy of practically every other club in the Football League. Having said that, I think some of them were pushed into the first-team far too early. Players like Redmond, Lake, White and Hinchcliffe were asked to do too much too soon. Had it been possible, and had circumstances not dictated otherwise, they should have been used more sparingly in their early, formative years to help their education. When I arrived at City, people kept referring to those four players as "kids" but as they had already amassed something like 500 senior games between them, I felt that was a ridiculous thing to say.

Five days after signing Coton, I paid Middlesborough £350,000 for Mark Brennan, a player I had admired for many years. I had first tried to sign him as a schoolboy when I was at Blackburn but he eventually opted to join Ipswich Town. Mark is not a big-name player but he has a very useful left foot and is adaptable.

My main priority as I worked towards reshaping my side in readiness for the new season was to find the best position for Paul Lake. I had used him as a sweeper, as a right full-back and in the centre of midfield but I still wasn't convinced that I had unearthed his natural footballing role.

Most people regard Paul as a midfield player but I don't think he is. When I used him in that position he made plenty of runs forward but I felt he was slightly lacking in vision when in possession. I spent the whole of the pre-season period settling Paul into a position at the heart of our defence. He really looked the part with his great pace and natural heading ability. The only thing which he lacked was experience and know-how but I knew that would come with time. Sadly, Paul sustained a serious injury in only our third game of the season—a bitter blow.

Paul is a marvellous footballer and his standing in the game is such that every time I approached another club to enquire about the availability of a player, I was asked whether I would consider including him in part-exchange. The answer was always no.

CHAPTER TWENTY

The Ties that Bind

I was in very optimistic mood as we started the 1990–91 season and was so convinced that the squad which I had assembled was well-balanced and competent that I did not feel over-ambitious in setting my sights firmly on a place in the top six. I knew that, barring a real disaster, we would not be faced by a prolonged struggle at the wrong end of the table; that if my team played to its true potential there was no question of that happening.

Although my relationship with the City supporters was still far from perfect, I think they realised that they had little option but to accept what had transpired in the eight months since I had arrived at the club and throw their weight behind their team.

This reduction in hostilities did not, however, stem the flow of jokes which had started to circulate around the Manchester area within days of my succeeding Mel Machin. My personal favourite was the one which suggested that David Bowie's summer concert at Maine Road was on the verge of being cancelled because someone had found out he'd never played for Everton. Dry. Very dry.

We lost our opening League game against Tottenham Hotspur at White Hart Lane, which was disappointing but not too surprising bearing in mind the circumstances. Fate often deals football teams an unfair blow and that was one such occasion because the ground was awash with emotion as the local supporters turned out in force to welcome home Paul Gascoigne and Gary Lineker after their World Cup exploits. We were in the wrong place at the wrong time.

Winning away from home was still proving to be something of a problem (we recorded five consecutive 1–1 draws on our travels in the League after that defeat at Spurs) but our form at Maine Road was so consistent that we found ourselves up with the early pacemakers.

Even though things were going well, I still found myself on the end of some stinging criticism after we had shared six goals with our neighbours, Manchester United, at Maine Road on 27 October. We were leading 3-1 with about ten minutes remaining so I decided to pull off Peter Reid who, typically, had run himself to a virtual standstill. In layman's terms, the man was knackered. Within a matter of a few minutes of Peter withdrawing from the action, United had scored twice to draw level. Inevitably, I was blamed for the loss of two points—and local pride. I felt the criticism to be unduly harsh because while it was true that United's revival had coincided with my decision to substitute Peter, the goals they scored were down to basic, juvenile defensive errors.

On 30 October, at the same time as we were losing to Arsenal in a Rumbelows Cup third-round tie, Everton were also going out of the competition against Sheffield United at Bramall Lane. As I sat in my office at Maine Road on that night, I had no idea at all that within a matter of six days, I would be clearing out my desk drawers in readiness for a move back to Goodison Park.

I suppose that in all the controversy which surrounded my impromptu departure from Manchester City, it was inevitable that some people should think that the whole thing had been set up weeks in advance. Believe me, it wasn't.

As a sport, football is notorious for springing "shocks" which have a distinctly prearranged look to them. It is hardly surprising that supporters, journalists, players—in fact, anyone outside of clubs' corridors of power—become highly suspicious in the immediate aftermath of a manager's dismissal.

It is often the case that a club which has sacked its manager is in a position to publicly announce a successor within a matter of hours. I would agree with those people who say that, sometimes, this is all a little bit too convenient. Because football is now big business, it goes without saying that some clubs will actively seek to line up a new manager before they part company with the man who is currently in charge of team affairs. This ploy—or sensible, forward planning as many would label it—is hardly unique to football because I am certain it goes on in many walks of commercial and business life. It is inconceivable that, say, a large building society or bank would dismiss its managing director without first giving serious consideration to who is to assume command.

Yes, this sort of thing does go on but I must stress that this was *NOT* the case when I resigned from City to return to Everton.

Like Manchester City, Everton is a club which has always believed in the virtues of honesty, sincerity and fair-play. It is a club which refuses to employ underhand methods when conducting business deals. I can place my hand on my heart and state, quite categorically, that there was no contact at all between myself and anyone connected with Everton Football Club before Colin Harvey's dismissal. I had absolutely no idea at all that Colin was going to be dismissed the day after his team had slipped to defeat in South Yorkshire. I was at Maine Road when a friend telephoned me with the news. He didn't simply say that Colin had been sacked, he said: "Colin has got a taxi home"—an infamous phrase which is very much a part of Everton folklore. It was a reference to the incident in 1961 when John Moores, now Sir John, the Everton Chairman, told Johnny Carey that he was being dismissed as the two sat in the back of a taxi.

I was very, very disappointed when I heard what had happened because I knew just how much the job meant to Colin. Everton had been his life for so long and he was forever telling me that all he wanted to do was win something for those supporters who had been so good to him down the years. He is one of my best mates so I was really choked for him. I didn't ring him straight away because no matter how close you are to someone, words don't come easily at a time like that.

My sense of shock was such that I never gave any consideration to the question of whom the Everton board would seek to appoint as Colin's successor. When my thoughts did turn in that direction, I just didn't have a clue. My response to those who still believe that I had come to some sort of verbal agreement with Everton before Colin was sacked is simple—do you really think that I would not only go behind the back of one of my closest friends but plunge a knife between his shoulder blades? Of course I wouldn't.

I had no idea at all who was going to be invited to manage Everton. It never even crossed my mind that they would want to take me back to Goodison Park. I can honestly say that not once in the 48 hours between Colin's sacking and my being approached for the first time, did I give any thought to leaving City and rejoining Everton. It wasn't a case of thinking, "Colin's gone, so I'm going back." It was something I never thought would happen in a million years.

The day after Colin's reign had been ended, the papers were full of stories linking Joe Royle with the vacancy. That was only natural after the great success he had enjoyed at Boundary Park. If there was a logical choice then, I suppose, it was Joe.

When a go-between rang me and asked me if I would be interested in going back to Everton, I was absolutely dumbstruck. I just couldn't believe it.

My initial reaction after hearing the question was: "Oh, no!" Although it was only a preliminary enquiry, I knew full well that if I was not facing a major dilemma at that precise moment, I would be in the not too distant future. I don't know whether I made my mind up there and then, on the spot, but the germ of an idea had been planted in my brain. It was decision time.

I needed time to think things over very carefully so I told the go-between that because the offer had come right out of the blue, and was so totally unexpected, I couldn't really say yes or no. Obviously, it was a predicament which I had not expected to find myself in. My mind was racing as I thought positively, firstly about staying with Manchester City and then about moving to Everton. I had to work out, and then examine, the pros and cons of both situations. It wasn't easy; in fact, it was one of the most difficult, and demanding, things I have ever had to do in my professional career.

However, the longer I thought about it, the more the idea of going back to Everton appealed to me. In my eyes they were still the best and, perhaps more importantly, I still regarded them as *MY* club. I kept on thinking about it; kept on exploring the implications of first one decision and then another and the more I did this, the more times I found myself saying, Everton. In the end, it didn't matter how many obstacles I mentally placed in my path, it was still Everton. I reached the stage where if I asked myself what the answer to the dilemma was, the answer was automatically Everton. The club's magnetic pull was just too strong for me to resist.

All along, the question had been, do I stay or do I go? I had asked that question of myself a thousand times. Did I want to accept the challenge of trying to transform Everton's fortunes for a second time? Deep down, inside, I knew that I did. I wanted to go back and make the club great once again.

It was a big decision but it was a big decision which had been made slightly easier because I knew that I would not be walking forward into the unknown. I was going back to a club which I knew inside out, and one which was in my blood.

Even now, I still find it a little difficult to explain why I decided to leave Manchester City at a time when the club was beginning to

blossom. I know that people say it was all down to my poor relationship with the club's supporters but I do not want to point the finger
at those supporters because they are fully entitled to their opinions.
Would I have remained had I struck up a better rapport with the
fans on the terrace? I just don't know.

Journalists often refuse to take things on face value. After I had
left they were not happy with the explanation I had given so they
put two and two together and insisted that I had been driven out by
the attitude of the City supporters. It is totally wrong to suggest
that because I will never be driven away from any job by the attitude of the fans on the terraces.

I read a lot of hurtful—and untrue—things in the weeks after my
departure; things which I hadn't said but which were nonetheless
attributed to me. It is true that I didn't always see eye to eye with
the supporters but I don't think I was at Maine Road long enough
to win them over. If I had stayed longer, and if City had gone on to
be successful, I am sure that we would have found a common
ground.

I had only spent 11 months at Maine Road and it had been a very
traumatic period, full of changes, uncertainty and, yes, controversy.
The City fans must have looked back over those 11 months and
thought I had done nothing more than arrived, ripped the club to
pieces in an attempt to find a winning formula and then left.
Perhaps now that the dust has settled a little, I can understand
why so many people were ultra-critical of what I did and of the
seemingly drastic methods I employed.

I was a little surprised that the news of my departure sparked
such fury in Manchester. To me, it seemed ironic that those people
who were constantly moaning about the way I was doing the job
should complain when they heard that I was leaving. You can't
have it both ways.

If every person who told me that you should never retrace your
steps in life had give me a pound at the end of their speech, I
wouldn't need Everton—or any other club—because I would now
be rich beyond my wildest dreams. "Never go back" became a sort
of catch-phrase in the days after the news of my departure was
announced. Friends said it, fans said it, reporters said it . . . the list
was endless.

Every time I feel in need of a little motivation, I whisper those
words to myself. If I can ridicule that phrase in the years ahead, I
will be a very happy man.

CHAPTER TWENTY-ONE

Passion Is No Ordinary Word

If a vacant managerial post at one of this country's leading clubs is not filled immediately, the gap between the departure of one man and the installation of his successor is somehow elongated by the enormous amount of speculation and media coverage. On this occasion, the dismissal of Colin and the appointment of myself was separated by just six days but so much happened in between those two events that there seemed to be an interminable delay before I was in a position to walk out from behind a screen in the Goodison Lounge on 6 November to face a battery of cameras and a host of incredulous reporters.

The upheaval in my life which followed after Everton's invitation to return to the club was such that many of my thoughts and actions have already been lost in the mists of time but I think I am right in saying that my decision to leave Manchester City was taken on, or about, 3 November—72 hours after Colin's departure. I had considered things so carefully, and at such length, that I could see no point at all in delaying what was by that point the inevitable. I knew that I would start to feel a whole lot better once I had nailed my colours to the mast so I telephoned Everton and told them that I wished to return.

As I have said before, I have great respect for the deductive and investigative powers of the media but for once they all got it wrong. It is difficult—very difficult—to keep anything of major importance quiet in football. Stories are usually leaked, not by those people with malice or mischief in their hearts, but by those who are unable to contain their excitement at having been entrusted with highly confidential information. This time there was to be no leak. The whole affair was submerged beneath a cloak of secrecy with Everton refusing even to hint at who was to succeed Colin and City telling no-one that I was to leave.

Although practically everyone assumed that the job was to be offered to Joe Royle, various other names were bandied about including Jack Charlton, Bobby Robson and Arthur Cox. It was strange to sit at home and read these stories knowing that, for once, my friends in the media were using the pretence of inside information to shield the fact that they did not have a clue what was going on. Not one story linked me with the Everton job—well, not one story which made it to print.

About a week after I had returned to Everton, I was told that the chief sports writer of a popular national tabloid had become so tired of trotting out the same list of potential candidates that he sat down and wrote a lengthy piece which exclusively revealed that I was to quit City and go back to Everton. It was pure guesswork, of course, but it was correct. When the writer presented his piece to his sports editor, he was told that there was no way such a stupid and ridiculous story could be used. We all make mistakes, don't we!

Telling Everton that I wanted to return was easy; telling Manchester City that I wanted to leave was unbelievably difficult.

The prospect of having to walk into Maine Road and inform my Chairman that I was going to quit after just 11 months in the job was unpleasant to say the very least. Although I had only been at the club for a relatively short period of time, I had built up a great affection for City. Because I always give 100 per cent to every job I tackle, it had become *MY* club.

Everton's determination to ensure that everything was conducted in a right and proper manner resulted in Philip Carter telephoning his opposite number, Peter Swales, to seek permission to approach me with a view to discussing the vacancy at Goodison Park. Under the terms of my contract, I was free to meet any club which was interested in offering me a job providing they understood that substantial compensation was payable should I ultimately decide to leave Maine Road. Mr Swales immediately informed me of the contact between the two clubs, saying that Everton had expressed a desire to speak to me about the possibility of my returning to Merseyside to take over from Colin. A couple of days later, Mr Swales said that he had done this purely as a matter of courtesy and that he never thought for one minute that I would show any interest in Everton's offer.

When he told me about Mr Carter's phone call I simply said: "I would like to go and speak to them." I think that he was very shocked by my response—he was certainly very disappointed.

I have great respect for Peter Swales and having to stand in front of him and say those words was very hard for me because I think he knew, straight away, that he was going to lose his manager. Even though I felt the club to be back on the right lines, the 11 months I had spent at City had been traumatic for many people, especially Mr Swales because, as Chairman, it was he who had sanctioned my appointment in the first place. I knew that my decision was going to disappoint him because after all the problems we had faced, and overcome together, the future was looking bright. I know just how much Manchester City means to Peter Swales and it hurt me to stand in front of him and virtually inform him that I had decided to leave. When you can see disappointment written large across someone's face, it is impossible not to feel pain yourself.

Things moved very quickly after that. Everton agreed to pay, in full, the compensation and City turned their attentions to the question of finding another manager—not that they had to look very far.

After so many years in football management, I have developed a thick skin when it comes to criticism. In my line of work you have to accept that accusations will be levelled at you and that ill-founded rumours will not only be circulated, but embraced by those who steadfastly refuse to let the facts get in the way of a good story. I knew that my motives for walking out on City would be

6 November 1990. Back home, rejoining Everton as manager

6 November 1990. I'm back—and so is Colin Harvey

Colin Harvey and myself back in the old routine

repeatedly called into question in the days and weeks after my departure. I was expecting all sorts of stories to surface and I was not to be disappointed.

I was not unduly concerned about most of the stuff which was written and said—even if it was lacking in substance and corroboration—but I was furious and upset by the suggestion that my decision to return to Everton was financially motivated.

Six days after I had moved back to Everton, a leading Sunday newspaper devoted most of its back page to a story which claimed

6 November 1990 and I'm back at Everton explaining to the world's press why I decided to leave Manchester City

that I had picked up—or was going to pick up—a fortune in wages during the course of my contract. The suggestion was that the Livepool-based Littlewoods Organisation had helped to put together a massive financial package to help lure me back to Goodison Park.

That was one of the most hurtful things which has ever been said about me during my entire career. The suggestion that I left Manchester City because Everton offered me more money caused me a great deal of pain. Money had absolutely nothing at all to do with my decision and it is nonsense to suggest otherwise.

When I joined Manchester City, the contract which I signed was identical to the one which had been offered to me by Everton before I left to join Athletic Bilbao in the summer of 1987. When Everton asked me to go back to Goodison Park, I just showed them my contract with City and said that if they changed the name of the club at the top of the document they would have a new manager. It was the same deal which I had been offered more than three years earlier; it wasn't improved or updated—it was the same.

I find it amazing that sometimes people simply refuse to believe that you are telling anything other than lies. I was so upset by these wild allegations that I immediately took legal action against the Sunday newspaper in question. The matter was settled out of court and it gave me great pleasure to divide the sum I received in compensation between two hospitals, one in Manchester and one in Liverpool.

I did not move for the money. In fact, if anyone would like to take me to court in an attempt to prove otherwise, then please feel free. If anyone does not believe that the basic salary I received at Manchester City and the one I now receive at Everton are identical, then let them sue me. If you think that you can prove me a liar, don't send anonymous letters, don't call me Judas, try and sue me. I'll win every time.

One of the first things Everton told me when they learned of my decision was that they had decided to make sweeping changes at management level. It was clear that the board was anxious to start afresh with a new team, which sadly meant the end of the line for four men who had served the club well—Mike Lyons, Terry Darracott, Graham Smith and Paul Power. I insisted it should be me who told four employees whom I regarded as mates that their services were no longer required. Having to tell them that they had lost their jobs was one of the most painful tasks I have ever performed in my life. It was distressing but, as the manager, I felt it only right and proper that I pass on the bad news.

The one thing which I was free to do was appoint my own assistant. I didn't have to give the matter any thought at all because there was only one candidate in my mind and that was Colin Harvey. I told my Chairman that I wanted Colin at my side as I began the task of steering Everton forward into a new era and he was totally supportive, as I knew he would be. The board not only gave their blessing to my proposal but they seemed genuinely delighted at the prospect of Colin returning to the club.

Their attitude towards what, I suppose, could have been a rather embarrassing situation said a great deal about their respect for Colin. Four days after sacking him, they were preparing to welcome the man back into the fold. What's more, they seemed really pleased to do so.

After I had decided to leave City, but before the official announcement, I had met up with Colin to ask him if he would be interested in making a swift return to Everton as my number two. He thought it over very carefully (it took about five seconds!) before saying he'd love to join up with me again. It must have been very confusing for him because he had spent the previous two days bidding a fond farewell to all his colleagues. I think it was a really brave thing for Colin to do because it can't have been easy for him to go back to Goodison Park and face those people who had just sacked him. It speaks volumes for his character.

When I heard that Colin had been sacked, I couldn't help but wonder why it is that English football has a propensity for cutting off its nose to spite its face. The manner in which clubs in this country discard men who still have so much to offer verges on the masochistic. Why is it that those individuals who have been in the manager's chair but who still have a great deal to offer are so swiftly shown the door? I know for a fact that this illogical practice is frowned upon on the continent.

A near-perfect example of what I am talking about is Alan Kelly, who was the manager of Preston North End between 1983 and 1985. After his career as a top-class goalkeeper came to an end, Alan moved on to the coaching staff at Deepdale and worked his way up to become the first-team trainer after spells with the youth and reserve sides. Because of circumstances he eventually found himself in the manager's seat, which was quite possibly a job he wasn't particularly keen on having in the first place. Two years later, after a poor run of form, he was sacked.

From my point of view that was a crazy situation. Alan was a Preston man, through and through, but because he had not been successful as a manager, his experience and enthusiasm was lost to the club he loved.

When I went to Spain, I replaced Iribar as the first-team coach but because Athletic Bilbao had great respect for his abilities, he wasn't sacked, he was placed in charge of the second team. It didn't work out for him at that level either so he is now the club's goalkeeping technician. The important thing is that he wasn't lost to the club. He was too valuable to let go so they found him another role.

The problem with English football is that as soon as you are appointed manager, there are only two ways you can go—forward to success or out of the front door. It just seems ridiculous to me that a man like Colin Harvey, who has spent all but two of his 28 years in professional football at Goodison Park, was almost lost to Everton. Bringing Colin back to the club resulted in just one problem. For the first few weeks, when a player shouted "Boss", we would both turn around.

At the risk of further upsetting the supporters of Manchester City, I must admit that had Colin declined my invitation, I would almost certainly have tried to persuade Peter Reid to join me at Everton.

Bearing in mind that Peter was contracted to City both as a player and as a coach and that he was the frontrunner to succeed me as manager, it would have been difficult to get him, but I would have tried. I did mention the possibility to him before I left Maine Road while lightheartedly pointing out that he wouldn't get in my team at Everton. He just smiled and said that he was going to stay because he was guaranteed a place in the City team if he got the manager's job.

To be honest, although Peter would have been the obvious choice had Colin decided against returning to Everton, I would have been loathe to try and take him away from City because to have done that would have caused even more disruption at Maine Road and that was something which I wanted to avoid at all costs.

Everton's success in keeping quiet the news of my appointment was hailed as something of a masterstroke in terms of subterfuge but, if I am honest, a very difficult and traumatic period in my life would have been made a good deal easier had the story been leaked to the media.

Because my resignation from City came as such a shock to everybody outside of the club itself, the resentment and disappointment which people felt was substantially increased. If my name had been linked with the job immediately after Colin's dismissal then people would possibly have been more prepared for what was going to happen. I can fully understand why it was that Everton were so determined to keep the whole affair under wraps because they wanted to make a big impact when the announcement was made. But looking back on things now, it would have been better for me if the suspicion of the Manchester City supporters had been raised at a very early stage.

I knew that a backlash was inevitable when the news of my departure was made public but when it materialised, even I was surprised by its ferocity and its longevity. It didn't take the minority within the club's support long to make their point because after meeting the press at Maine Road to explain my decision, I returned to my car to find that two of my tyres had been damaged.

After that came the hate mail. I received some very hurtful letters in the days after I had agreed to go back to Everton; a lot of hurtful letters. Receiving abusive letters is one thing but receiving anonymous, abusive letters is another. If people feel so strongly about something, why is it that they do not have the courage to put their names at the bottom of the page?

I must point out that several of the letters which I received were of a friendly and complimentary nature. Some supporters wrote to thank me for my efforts and to wish me every success in the future. It was a most welcome touch of sanity amid a maelstrom of unrest and gross indignation.

It was ironic that on 6 November as I made my way to Goodison Park to be unveiled as the new manager of Everton, the Manchester City reserve team was also making its way to the same venue to play a Central League fixture. As I stood in front of the world's media, some of those players I had decided to leave behind were beating, 2-0, some of those players I was inheriting.

Although I spent only 11 months at Manchester City, I shall always remember my time there with great fondness. There are a lot of dedicated, hardworking people striving tirelessly within Maine Road to build a better future for what is a magnificent footballing institution. I do not regret, for one moment, taking the manager's job there and when I walked out of the club's main entrance for the final time, I did so with a completely clear conscience. During my time at City, I worked 100 per cent for the club cause right up to the day I left, and I believe the club to be in a far healthier state now than it was when I arrived.

I am convinced that City can go on to win major honours in the not too distant future but when they do, you won't find me gloating and saying things like: "I told you, I was right." It is all down to Peter Reid now and when the success comes, he is the one who should be praised. I could not have left that club in better hands because Peter is a man in a million.

So, would I like the City fans to remember me for anything? It would be nice to think that they believe that I helped to lay the foundations for a great future. Obviously, they'll need some good luck along the way but I think they'll make it. I think the days of Manchester City constantly living in fear of relegation have been banished and that pleases me enormously.

There is a very healthy blend of youth and experience within the City dressing-room at the moment and although Peter will, I am sure, be seeking to make several additions to his pool in the months and years ahead, his senior squad has a sturdy backbone to it.

The platform which City now has available to it to build upon was provided, not just by those players I brought to the club, but by the exuberant, young talent which was available to me when I arrived. All I had to do was provide the framework upon which this talent could be draped. When youngsters are surrounded by seasoned professionals who talk casually about their past Cup and Championship glories, there is quite often an astonishing galvanizing effect within the dressing-room.

I suppose that, in the final count, I shall not be remembered as the man who bought people like Reid and Quinn and who worked hard to try and save the club's First Division status, but as the man who sold Ian Bishop and Trevor Morley. I find that very, very unfortunate.

CHAPTER TWENTY-TWO

No Regrets

Even if I was to achieve nothing else in football management, I shall at least be able to tell my grandchildren that I was once on the short-list for the most coveted job in domestic football—England manager.

After a representative of the Football Association had made contact with me during my time in Spain, I knew that I was one of the men under consideration as the game's governing body began to ready itself for the departure of Bobby Robson after the 1990 World Cup finals in Italy.

At the time, I gave little—or no—thought to the possibility of my succeeding Bobby simply because football is such an unpredictable game that there is absolutely no point at all in building up your hopes. To be honest, I wasn't even sure that I wanted the job. Had the FA rung me up and told me that it was mine for the taking I really don't know what I would have said. It would have needed much careful thought and consideration.

Although Bobby did not officially announce that he was to quit as England manager until 24 May it was by that point common knowledge that he had accepted an invitation to join PSV Eindhoven as coach. A few days before he convened a press conference to confirm that the rumour was indeed fact, it became clear to me that my name had been mentioned by those members of the FA charged with the responsibility for finding a man deemed to be suitable to fill the vacancy.

Peter Swales was the man who told me one morning at Maine Road. It can't have been an easy situation for him because he was not only my club Chairman but also the Chairman of the FA's International Selection Committee, the body which picks and shepherds the England manager.

Mr Swales walked up to me and said: "You don't want the England job, do you, Howard?"

I asked him what he meant and he said: "Well, you don't want it, do you?" I said that I was happy as the manager of Manchester City but I did go so far as to ask him if there had been an official approach. He told me that a short-list had been drawn up and that I was on it.

We went into his office to discuss the matter further and during the course of our conversation he said that the short-list contained just three names. He said that myself and Graham Taylor were included but before he could reveal the third name, I jumped in and said: "Terry Venables?" He shook his head and said that I would probably be surprised by the final name on the list. I don't think that I am breaking anyone's confidence by saying that the third man was Oldham's Joe Royle.

Obviously, I was delighted to learn that I was in the frame but why on earth Terry Venables wasn't one of those managers under consideration is totally beyond me.

I shall explain shortly why I disliked the idea of a short-list but if that was the way in which things were going to be done then Terry's name should definitely have been on it—of that there is no doubt. Terry had not only worked abroad but had been hugely successful abroad and, in my opinion, that is a real advantage when you are talking in terms of an international manager. I know that Terry does not have the best of records in English football but I was surprised—very surprised—that he was not considered by the men who mattered. To me, he was an obvious choice.

Don't get me wrong, I am not saying that the FA made a mistake in appointing Graham Taylor. I am not saying that at all, but what I am saying is that they should have examined Terry's credentials. He is a big-time manager with all the right qualities. The dignified manner in which he handled the massive problems at Tottenham Hotspur during the 1990–91 season was a lesson to us all.

Although I suspect that Mr Swales was hoping that I would rule myself out of contention on the spot, I said that I would need some time to think about it. It was a tremendous honour even to be considered and I thought it only fair that I take my time before reaching a decision.

I was interested in the England job (who wouldn't be!) but I wasn't sure if it was right for me at that particular time. I had been away from the English game for two-and-a-half years and I was still relatively young. On top of that, I was really enjoying the many challenges of managing Manchester City. I was very happy with life at Maine Road.

As our brief meeting drew to a close, Mr Swales said: "So, I can tell them that you are not interested?" I told him not to do that because I still wasn't sure what I was going to do.

I felt a little sorry for him because he was sitting in front of me having to wear two hats. On the one hand he had been a part of the committee which had placed my name on the short-list while, on the other, he was a club Chairman who was fearful of losing his manager. That was a conflict of interests which I firmly believe has no place at all in modern-day football. Not only was it farcical in a purely business sense, it was very unfair on the man.

I think that it is time a dividing line was drawn between football's clubs and football's administrative bodies. At present we have a situation where a man can be Chairman of the Football League and also the Chairman of a League club. That invariably leads to problems because the decisions taken by the Football League are not always in the best interests of some clubs. Surely, it has got to be separated. The man at the top has got to be a supremo with no vested interests outside of the Football League itself. It seems only logical to me; perhaps too logical.

Anyway, Mr Swales told me that the FA wanted me to travel down to London for an interview. I couldn't believe that. It really confused me because surely the FA knew what I had done and what I was capable of. I told him that I did not like that idea one little bit. Shortly afterwards, after thinking about things, I told him that I had no intention at all of going for an interview.

Although I was fully aware that Graham Taylor was the favourite to get the job, it was not the fear of failure which prompted me to turn my back on a chance which I fully appreciate may never come along again. People suggested that I ruled myself out of contention because to have gone down for an interview, to have even expressed an interest, would have further undermined my already fragile relationship with the supporters of Manchester City. That is not true because had I gone, and had I been given the job, I think they would have understood. Leaving a club to take charge of another club is one thing, leaving to take the job of England manager is the proverbial different kettle of fish. If I had walked out on City to succeed Bobby Robson, I don't think there would have been too many dissenting voices.

I have to say that if things had been handled in a different way, there may have been a different outcome. The word "may" is the key one in that statement.

The more I thought about the whole idea of a short-list and of interviews, the more ridiculous it seemed. In my opinion, the FA's International Selection Committee should have got together and decided exactly who it was they wanted as the new manager of England. They should have reached a unanimous verdict and then approached the man in question.

By all means then interview the choice of the committee and then if he is found to be unsuitable, talk again and pick someone else. That is a perfectly reasonable process but to have three men lining up outside an office is totally crazy. They shouldn't need to be persuaded, they should already *KNOW* who the right man is.

For a job of that size, of that immense stature, you shouldn't have to rely on a person's ability to make an impression during the course of what could be a brief interview. Some people are very adept at self-promotion, some are not. Surely, what you have achieved in the past and how you are performing at present is of far more importance than is the ability to provide suitable answers to surprise questions.

If the FA had decided that Graham Taylor was the right man, then why wasn't he offered the job straight away? If they hadn't reached a unanimous decision, then they should have talked things over until they did reach such a decision. To draw up a short-list of three was an awful way of going about things; it really was.

Because Mr Swales had a foot in both camps, there was no need for me to contact the FA directly to inform them that I did not wish to be considered, he simply made a quick phone call. It was a verbal response to a verbal invitation.

It would be unfair to say that I had myself struck off the short-list simply because of my dissatisfaction with the selection procedure because there was more to it than that. Managing England is a great, great honour but the job is completely different to the one which I am used to at club level. I am an impatient man. If my team plays badly and loses a game, I can't wait for the next game and a near-instant opportunity to put things right. That is something which you just cannot do at international level. If England lose a fixture, the manager may have to wait two or three months before he can try and erase an unpleasant memory. Now, I am sure that is something which all international managers learn to accept in time but I don't know whether it would have suited me.

Because I like to keep myself busy, I don't know whether I could have coped with only meeting my players every seven or eight weeks. After spending so long working with players on a daily basis, I think I would have struggled to adapt. Twenty-four hours may be a long time in politics but, to me, it is an eternity in football.

At the time of writing this book, it is far too early to say whether or not Graham Taylor will make a good England manager although, it has to be said, he has made an excellent start. In that job you must assess how a man has fared over a matter of a few years and not a few months. I wish him well.

Different managers have different opinions as to how the game of football should be played. I think that it is fair to say that when Graham was given the England job, many people feared that he would introduce the long-ball game which he himself had pioneered during his days at Watford. Again, it is still too early to say whether those fears will be realised or whether they were totally groundless. The early indications are that Taylor's England will seek to blend differing styles.

I am not a fan of this route-one style of play but, it has to be said, it does have its positive, as well as its negative, aspects. If you can combine the more traditional style of play with this direct and uncompromising approach then success can be achieved.

One of the problems with the long-ball game is that it is totally unacceptable at those clubs which have achieved success by using style rather than muscle; those clubs who like to play through a talented midfield section.

Howard Wilkinson showed what could be achieved by direct football but he also exposed its many limitations. Having used it to good effect at Notts County he did the same at Sheffield Wednesday. The problem was that he took Wednesday so far and then realised that he could take them no further without modifying his team's style of play. That proved to be very difficult and I think he realised that if he wanted to change his own approach to the game, he either had to change clubs or change his players.

Once you have convinced players that a particular style is the best way to help guarantee success it is very, very hard to get them to accept a change in system. If they have spent several years lofting the ball into their opponents' half of the field at the earliest opportunity, they are going to want to know why it is they should suddenly start using their midfield. That is perfectly understandable.

It is often the case that teams which have been built to use the direct system are simply not equipped to play in any other way. If a change of style or emphasis is forced upon them, their form disintegrates.

Howard Wilkinson has done very well at Leeds United by using a combination of the orthodox and the unorthodox.

The route-one style may get limited results at club level but I don't think it will ever prove to be successful at international level, where it is not only frowned upon but positively ridiculed in some quarters.

Shortly after I had joined Manchester City, I invited a friend of mine from Athletic Bilbao to watch our game against Wimbledon at Plough Lane. The first thing he said to me afterwards was: "That was not football—that was rugby." I tried to expain to him that Wimbledon had won the FA Cup by playing that way but nothing I said could reduce his sense of amazement and outrage.

Even the people who run those clubs who adopt this most basic of techniques seem envious of the football which is played by their more puritanical rivals. Whenever I meet the Wimbledon Chairman, Stan Reed, he always talks about the day his team was outplayed at Goodison Park.

He remembers that day so well not just because the quality of Everton's football was exceptionally high but because it is very, very rare that Wimbledon are taken to the cleaners by anyone. The direct approach may be unattractive to many people but it is sometimes hard to decry a system which is very difficult to stop.

A couple of years ago I was genuinely concerned about the future of English football at international level because I feared that the route-one system was going to become common practice at junior level. I remember going down to the national training centre at Lilleshall one summer for a sort of summit meeting of managers and coaches. The manner in which theories and techniques are promoted at Lilleshall is very persuasive; people are given the impression that whatever system is under discussion is going to prove to be successful.

We sat and watched various videos which seemed to show that the direct approach was definitely the way forward for the English game.

One of those attending the meeting was Ritchie Barker, the Sheffield Wednesday coach and a man for whom I have the very highest regard.

Ritchie, who was then the manager of Stoke City, had recently paid out a lot of money for three orthodox midfield players, Mickey Thomas, Robbie James and Sammy McIlroy, but that did not stop him returning to the Victoria Ground and trying to put into practice what had been preached at Lilleshall.

I am not criticising Ritchie in any way because he was simply using the information which he had gathered in an attempt to unearth a winning formula.

One of the biggest problems with football in this country is that youngsters are taught, from a very early age, that winning is all that matters. I am not saying that youth and schoolboy teams on the continent don't want to win tournaments and cups because they do—but not as desperately as we do here. Whereas we want to succeed at all costs, our European rivals look upon junior level football as a learning process; a natural progression. In Spain, for example, it is the performance rather than the end result which really matters.

I would much rather see our youngsters learn and lose than win and make only minimal progress. Surely, the important thing is that our kids are enjoying their sport and I seriously doubt whether that is possible if nine- and ten-year-olds are put under pressure to produce results.

Schoolteachers and parents are a big problem for me in English football because it is they who demand so much of children who, I suspect, would be far happier just playing the game for fun. We can't afford to have a situation where winning is everything when some of the players involved are still not old enough to tie up their own bootlaces; that is totally ridiculous.

Obviously, I wouldn't want to see the competitive edge phased out of football at any level in this country because that is one of the English game's greatest strengths, but I would like to see the players of the future encouraged to develop their natural talent within a less rigid and less disciplined framework.

Some people have suggested that there should be no medals or cups on offer to any player below the age of 15 or 16 and while I can't agree with that, I do believe that the whole system of rewarding success should be carefully looked at.

As part of my job, I attend numerous prize-giving ceremonies and it would seem to me that kids are given medals for everything these days—best player, best penalty-taker, best attendance record, top scorer, cleanest kit. At any level of football you have to deserve your trophy or your medal; you have to have worked hard for it and you have to have earned it.

The difference between youth football here in England and over in Spain is quite astonishing. During my time at Athletic Bilbao, I returned home one weekend and watched my son, Simon, play for his local side. I just couldn't believe the aggression and the language of those parents who were standing on the touch-line. It was a real culture shock.

I am certain that if this overwhelming desire to win at all costs was removed from our game at the very lowest level, we would start producing better, more talented, footballers. They would also be a good deal more relaxed and that is absolutely vital.

No-one was happier than I was when Bobby Robson found himself in a position to step down as the manager of England with his head held high. After all the abuse and criticism the man had been forced to contend with during the course of his reign, I was absolutely delighted that he was hailed as something of a national hero when he stepped off the plane which carried the England squad home from the 1990 World Cup finals in Italy.

In my opinion, Bobby did an excellent job and I thought that it was only right and proper that he should depart for Holland to take over at PSV Eindhoven with his pride restored and with people full of respect for the manner in which he had undertaken one of the most demanding—and thankless—tasks in world football.

To say that Bobby was hounded by the press during his time in charge would be an understatement of monumental proportions because he was subjected to one of the most vicious campaigns I can ever remember. Not only was it vicious, it was totally unnecessary. Why is it that the English media swop their pens for knives when discussing the words and deeds of the England manager? Why is it that, irrespective of results and progress, their actions always seem to be destructive rather than constructive?

This sort of character assassination certainly doesn't happen in other countries so why on earth does it go on here? I may be tempting fate by suggesting that it is highly unlikely that any of Bobby Robson's successors will be subjected to such an unpleasant, orchestrated and thoroughly nasty propaganda campaign.

I am full of admiration for the way in which Bobby handled himself during his time as manager. He faced an, at times, simply appalling situation with great dignity and immense courage. Believe me, there was not one man in this country who has been employed as a football manager at one time or another who did not feel desperately sorry for him during that period in his career when he was being subjected to the most fearful criticism. My goodness, he soaked up that pressure well.

The ironic thing is that after all the stick he took, he very nearly ended up emulating Sir Alf Ramsey and winning the World Cup.

Quite what his tormentors would have made of that, I just don't know.

Looking back now, I believe England's final position of fourth to have been just about right. Having said that, had England managed to overcome West Germany in the lottery of a penalty shoot-out at the end of their semi-final, I believe they would have lifted the famous trophy because Argentina were certainly the poorest side—and arguably the luckiest—ever to win through to the competition's final.

I have to admit that I was surprised that we managed to reach the last four because, once again, we started a major tournament so very slowly and only managed to get out of first gear when the prospect of elimination became a distinct possibility. We are not alone in this apparent inability to muster a full head of steam from the word go because other big sides, like West Germany and Italy, are often similarly guilty of initial hesitancy. That may not be such a bad thing, however, because some countries, notably Brazil, have developed the annoying habit of starting brightly and then fading.

England could be rightly proud of finishing fourth and even more satisfied at winning the fair play award which was very, very important and very significant. The fact that England had the best disciplinary record in Italy is a great tribute to Bobby.

After we had been beaten by the Germans on penalties there was much discussion about the selection of those players who stepped forward to take our spot-kicks. Many people thought it was rather strange that Chris Waddle—who missed our final kick—should later reveal that he had never taken a penalty at senior level before.

From a managerial point of view, picking five men to take part in a penalty shoot-out is very difficult. The problem is that the dressing-room is invariably split into three quite distinct sections. There are those players who do not wish to be considered, those who are fully confident and willing to have a go and those people who aren't confident but who say they are because they do not want their team-mates to think they are scared.

So what do you do? All you can do is fall back on your knowledge of the individuals concerned, back your judgement and select the five who believe themselves to be capable of finding the target. Sometimes it works, sometimes it doesn't.

Penalty-taking is an art; a job for a real specialist. Some players don't want anything to do with them if they miss one while some players, Alan Ball for example, will willingly go on taking them even if they have failed with their previous three attempts.

The strange thing about Italy was that Bobby Robson only found the successful blend which he had been looking for after deciding to make dramatic changes once the tournament had actually got underway. I say strange, because the same thing happened in 1966.

In Italy, Bobby opted to play with three centre-backs, so abandoning the more traditional English defensive system which he had employed during the previous three or four years. It was radical, totally unexpected—and hugely successful. Twenty-four years earlier Sir Alf began our assault on the World Cup by using orthodox wingers, only to modify the system when it became clear that it was proving to be unproductive. He brought in players like Ball, Martin Peters and Roger Hunt and went on to win the Cup with a team which was promptly labelled "the wingless wonders".

I suppose that it would be fair to say that our success (or relative success) in the Mexico finals of 1986 only came about after a major shake-up in terms of personnel. However, on that occasion, the introduction of players like Peter Reid, Steve Hodge and Trevor Steven was down to circumstances as Bobby had lost Bryan Robson through injury and Ray Wilkins because of suspension.

Overall, I think Bobby Robson did an exceptional job, both on and off the field of play. The manager of England has to be as adept at ambassadorial duties as at picking the right team and Bobby approached both roles with professionalism and honesty. Certainly, had he been as bad at his job as some newspapers would have had us believe, he wouldn't have lasted anything like as long as he did.

As I said, the job of England manager is a thankless task and that is a rather sad reflection on the divisions which still exist within our game. If you are in a top footballing job in this country people seem to think they have a license to say whatever they like about you; they seem to think that you are there to be shot at and that you will willingly accept unjustified criticism.

Graham Taylor may not have been the manager of England for very long but he will have already sampled what lies in store for him in the years ahead irrespective of whether his team wins, loses or draws. There just doesn't seem to be any middle ground in English football whether it be at club or international level. Everything is cut and dried, black and white. If you win you are the hero, if you lose you are the villain.

I just couldn't believe what happened after England had won a crucial European Championship qualifying game in Turkey in May 1991. Despite negotiating a far from simple task, the England team was insulted, Graham was heavily criticised and some of the supporters who were at the match were chanting for the return of Bobby Robson!

I believe half the problem to be that those two or three thousand supporters who regularly follow England abroad are not united as are the supporters of other countries. The banners which we see draped around foreign stadia do not usually say "England", they say "Millwall" or "Leeds United" or "Chelsea". Perhaps that is something to do with the fact that all England games are played at Wembley Stadium; perhaps the rest of the country somehow regard England as a London side.

The argument against moving internationals outside of the capital, into the provinces, is that it would prove to be financially unviable. I don't think that particular argument holds up because simply by moving the games around, a novelty value could be created. England's friendly game against the Soviet Union in the summer of 1991 attracted a crowd of less than 30,000. I am convinced that had that game been staged at Old Trafford or Goodison Park, the attendance would have been considerably higher.

In an attempt to smash this "them and us" situation why not experiment and give the fans in the Midlands and the North the opportunity to see top-class international fixtures? If the experiment fails then, fair enough, go back to Wembley. It is a case of nothing ventured, nothing gained as far as I am concerned.

In an ideal world, I would like to see a massive, national stadium in the Midlands, say Birmingham. That would encourage far more supporters from the North and the far North to attend matches which may be of little significance. I agree that Wembley has that special, unique magic but I can see no reason why the occasional friendly game should not be farmed out to regions of the country which are every bit as patriotic and fanatical as the South.

I am still asked at regular intervals why it was I had my name removed from the Football Association's short-list and whether I would like to be considered for the job of England manager in the future.

It is a difficult question to answer because I honestly believe that I am still too young to undertake that role. With the greatest of respect to Graham Taylor, I think it is a job best suited to someone who is older and more experienced.

It was a great honour to be linked with the job in the days after Bobby Robson announced that he was to step down and my sense of pride would not be diminished if the same thing was to happen when Graham decides to call it a day, although I think we may have to wait many years before that occurs.

As a club manager, I shall give Graham all the support I can—should he ever ask for it. If he carries on the solid work which was started by his predecessor, I don't think he'll go far wrong.

The only thing which I would take issue with Graham on is his plan to visit the leading clubs and take charge of the odd training session. When I was at Manchester City my Chairman told me about the idea but I said I didn't feel it was right. What I did say was that he was more than welcome to come along to Maine Road and watch those players who were on the verge of full and Under-21 international honours.

I don't think that I blotted my copy-book in any way by ruling myself out of contention the last time because I believe that the members of the International Selection Committee fully understood the reasons behind my decision.

The chance may come along again, who knows? If it does, it does—if it doesn't, it doesn't. I have never looked any further than the job I am in at the present and I do not intend to start now.

I am very optimistic about the future of English football at international level, even if we still have a tendency to be lulled into a false sense of security by results immediately prior to a major tournament.

CHAPTER TWENTY-THREE

Remake, Remodel

I knew full well that resuming control at Everton was not going to be easy because, contrary to popular belief, football managers do not pack a magic wand along with their training kit when they leave for work in the morning.

The first thing I had to do was impress upon my players that relegation was not something that only happened to lesser clubs; that it was a genuine threat and something which had to be faced as a matter of some urgency. It is absolutely ludicrous to believe that any club is too big to drop down into the Second Division. It is also ludicrous for any club to believe itself to be safe until relegation is mathematically impossible.

It was somewhat ironic that after achieving so much success between 1984 and 1987, I should be faced with the task of trying to safeguard a major club's First Division status for the second time in less than 12 months. I had done it at Manchester City and I was reasonably confident that I could do it again at Everton.

To be fair to the senior squad which I inherited, I believed they were good enough to move away from the danger area; I felt there to be enough talent and ability. It was a slightly different problem to the one which I had faced at Maine Road because on that occasion there was a definite need for major surgery.

Although I was convinced that our League position would gradually show signs of improvement, I knew that changes would have to be made, if not immediately, then in the future. From the moment I walked back into Goodison Park, I was thinking in terms of winning the League Championship. Sure, the problem of avoiding relegation was the pressing issue but that was only the first stage. I was already looking ahead—not just weeks and months ahead, but years ahead. I was looking at my players during training and on match days and saying to myself: "Is he good enough to be a member of a side with designs on the title?" I hadn't been invited back to the club to preside over a team with limited ambition; I had been invited back to restore Everton's position as England's leading side.

When I was involved in discussions with Philip Carter shortly before I announced my decision to quit City, he said that my only priority was to move the club away from the relegation trap-door. That was something which impressed me rather than surprised me because it meant that Everton were looking at the situation realistically. There was no feeling of false security within the boardroom—the club was in trouble and everyone was pulling together to try and rectify the situation. It would have been so easy for Mr Carter to have started talking about titles and cups but he didn't; he spoke honestly about a situation which he had carefully analysed.

It was a sharp contrast to the attitude I encountered at Crystal Palace when I was interviewed about their managerial vacancy shortly before I succeeded Gordon Lee in 1981. They dismissed the looming threat of relegation and insisted that they were definitely going to be *THE* team of the Eighties. I turned the job down and a few months later they were relegated. You always have to be realistic in football. To do anything else is to tempt fate.

When I took over on 6 November 1990, Everton were in 17th place in Division One. It goes without saying that morale within the dressing-room was very low indeed. One of the problems was that the senior squad could be split into two quite distinct groups. On the one hand you had players who had known the good times (Southall, Ratcliffe, Sheedy etc) while on the other you had the "new boys" who had spent two or three years at the club without tasting any success at all. It would be totally wrong to suggest that there was a sort of "them and us" situation because there wasn't (Colin Harvey wouldn't have allowed that to happen!) but there definitely was a division, a mental barrier.

Any squad which seriously expects to be successful must be fully integrated so my first job was to try and provide a feeling of collective unity. I think perhaps those players who had been at Goodison Park for many years were looking at their new team-mates and wondering why it was they were not realising their full potential. Then again, it is highly likely that those recent arrivals were looking at the older, established players and wondering why it was they were not performing as they had between '84 and '87. It is sometimes hard for footballers to readily acknowledge that it is they who are at fault. They have a great deal of pride and it is far easier—and far more acceptable—to identify the shortcomings of those around you.

I don't care who is in my side, when things are not going well the finger can be pointed at everybody. In fact, the finger must be pointed at everybody. Only by being hypercritical can you hope to put right the wrongs.

This lack of unity and confidence had obviously been reflected in Everton's early season results. After losing their opening two League games, against Leeds United at Goodison and Coventry City at Highfield Road, they played against my City side at Maine Road. Although Colin was later to tell me that his team's performance during the course of a 1–0 defeat was one of the poorest he had witnessed during his time as manager, I must say that Everton were a pretty sorry sight on that afternoon. The passion and commitment which I had always associated with the club was missing and, even at that early stage, there seemed to be a feeling of despondency. I knew they were capable of much, much more.

Because we needed to pick up as many points as was possible in as short a time span as was possible, I had no hesitation at all in chopping and changing my starting line-up and altering, significantly, our tactics. Everton is a club which has always tried to do things in style but, for once, results were of far more importance than performances.

What I was desperate to avoid was a situation where we would enter the final two weeks of the season requiring a certain number of points to stay in the First Division. Those teams whose struggle against the drop is of a perennial nature are more than adept at last-ditch dog-fights but I knew that the players I had at my disposal would not relish the pressure of such a situation.

I knew that if we could achieve safety, my job of assessing the strengths and weaknesses of my players would be made a good deal easier because they would be free to perform in a more relaxed manner.

I think that it quickly became clear to all the Everton supporters that I was going to give every member of the senior squad a chance to impress. I didn't want anyone coming to me at the end of the season and complaining about lack of opportunity.

Once we had picked up sufficient points to banish the threat of relegation, I was afforded the luxury of being able to sit back and closely study exactly what my players had to offer. I suppose that I was doing nothing more than putting my players on trial. I sat in the dug-out waiting for people to impress me.

This explains why several of the line-ups I selected towards the

My first game back in charge against Sheffield United at Bramall Lane on 10 November 1990

end of the season were a little on the radical side. I didn't always pick what many people would possibly regard as my best team because I felt that I needed to experiment in order to discover the true capabilities of all my senior players.

Although we only managed to secure a goalless draw in my first game against Sheffield United at Bramall Lane, I felt it to be a good result under the circumstances. The fact that we didn't go there and win handsomely served to underline my claim that there is no such thing as a miracle-worker in modern sport.

By the time we played my former club, Manchester City, at Goodison on 13 January, we had risen to mid-table and that most priceless of commodities, confidence, was slowly beginning to return. We beat City 2–0 on that day but the afternoon was soured by the reaction of the City supporters when I took my place on the touch-line shortly before kick-off.

Some people now refer to that fixture as the "Judas" game because that short, but hurtful, word was scrawled across numerous banners and flags at the City end of the ground. Actually, this particular form of Kendall-baiting was first used on 11 November during City's first game after I had left the club, against Leeds United at Maine Road.

Maybe I was being naïve but I honestly did not expect such a vicious backlash from the supporters of my former club. I knew they wouldn't be rolling out the red carpet for me but I thought that I had made clear my reasons for leaving. Obviously the message hadn't got through. It upset me a lot to read those banners and to hear the abusive chants drifting down the length of Goodison Park. I wasn't anticipating that kind of reception at all. Naturally, I was overjoyed with our performance, particularly as the game was broadcast live on television.

Having moved into the last 16 of the FA Cup by defeating Charlton Athletic and Woking Town, I was not exactly ecstatic to learn that we had been paired with Liverpool, at Anfield, in the fifth round. Bearing in mind our problems on the League front, I was looking upon the FA Cup as something of a bonus. I wanted us to do well in the competition as a way of thanking the club's supporters for their loyalty during a very difficult period.

By chance, we were due to play at Anfield in a League game just eight days before the Cup-tie, which gave me the perfect opportunity to assess the challenge we would be facing. Although we lost the game 3–1, we played exceptionally well and were perhaps a little unfortunate not to take something away from the match.

273

The result was disappointing but the important thing was that I had learned a great deal, not only about Liverpool but also about Everton.

Everyone was optimistic about going back there the following weekend—the players, the fans, the coaching staff, everyone. Defeats in derby matches are usually followed by a slight depression but that just wasn't the case this time. I sensed that my players really did believe that they could cause a major upset.

I changed things around for the Cup-tie, leaving out Milligan and Beagrie and opting to play with three centre-backs. A hard-fought and hugely entertaining game ended goalless but I still believe we should have been awarded a penalty when Gary Ablett brought down Pat Nevin. It looked clear-cut to me and to thousands of other people.

The replay at Goodison three days later was a quite astonishing game, one which is already being hailed as possibly the greatest FA Cup tie of all time. Magnificent spectacle though that 4–4 draw may have been, it still does not rank as the finest game I have ever been involved in for that particular slot is filled by the European Cup Winners' Cup semi-final tie against Bayern Munich at Goodison in 1985—probably because we won that one.

Things happened during the course of that replay which no-one had any right to expect. It had everything—magnificent goals, passion, commitment, great goalkeeping, mistakes. It was breathtaking.

The suggestion afterwards was that I must have learned a great deal about my team on that night as they fought back, four times, to draw level. I did learn a great deal—I learned that we still weren't good enough. That might sound harsh bearing in mind the excitement which was generated by a very special occasion but it was clear to me that there was still room for improvement.

My telephone was red-hot in the days after that game as the calls flooded in from old friends and colleagues in Spain. Although the game had been shown on television over there, they all wanted video recordings to watch at their leisure.

The second replay constituted our fourth game against Liverpool in a little over a fortnight. We won a much tighter contest courtesy of a Dave Watson goal, to inflict a defeat on our neighbours which only served to compound the misery they felt at losing Kenny Dalglish, who had announced his retirement from professional football five days earlier.

Having moved through into the quarter-finals by eliminating the competition's favourites, most of our supporters possibly felt that a return to Wembley was something of a formality. I knew that we had a very good chance of reaching the final but my optimism was undermined a little, not so much by the sixth-round draw itself, but by the timing of the game.

West Ham United at Upton Park was never going to be easy but the task became even more difficult once British Sky Broadcasting had announced that they wanted the game moved to a Monday night to accommodate a live screening.

Some football grounds seem almost designed for night matches and, unfortunately, Upton Park is one of them. The atmosphere was such that any neutral who had wandered into the ground to complain about the noise would have thought we were involved in a replay. That is exactly what it felt like—a replay.

I felt we did quite well on the night but the one thing we failed to do was deal with Stuart Slater, who orchestrated his side brilliantly. Although I felt we just about deserved a draw, he was clearly the difference between the two sides. That defeat ruined the rest of the season for our supporters which explains why the attendances at Goodison for our five remaining League games were well below average. It was perfectly understandable that our fans should decide to save their money. I wouldn't criticise them for that at all.

Forty-eight hours after the defeat by West Ham, my team showed its real character by defeating Barnsley, at Oakwell, in the Northern Area semi-final of the Zenith Data Systems Cup. That was a game I really wanted to win because the prize on offer was a two-legged Area final against Leeds United. After drawing 3-3 in the first leg at Elland Road, we booked a trip to Wembley by winning the return leg 3-1 at Goodison. The ZDS Cup has its detractors but the look of disappointment on the faces of the Leeds players after that game said it all. They were absolutely desperate to reach the final.

The final against Crystal Palace brought disappointment for me and cuts and bruises for several of my players; it was a no-holds-barred sort of a game which would probably be X-rated if it was ever to be released on video. We lost 4–1 after extra-time but I took solace from the fact that over the course of the opening 90 minutes we had more than matched a side which was to finish third in the First Division. That performance proved that some of my players were nothing like as bad as people had been insisting.

We finished the season in ninth place and bearing in mind the position the club was in when I arrived, I was quite pleased with the progress we had made. What delighted me was the improvement in our record away from Goodison Park because while we threw away leads at Aston Villa and Tottenham Hotspur, we played with great spirit on our travels.

The only new player I introduced during that period when we were fighting to improve our League standing was Robert Warzycha, the Polish international midfielder who joined us from Gornik Zabrze. It was somewhat ironic that he should be my only purchase because I have always been against bringing in foreign players.

Although I had a very large first-team squad available to me, I knew that I needed to improve the quality in certain departments. I also knew that wasn't going to be easy because I was working within a tight financial framework. When Robert was first drawn to my attention, I did not show a great deal of enthusiasm because, these days, a First Division manager needs an assistant just to deal with agents recommending players from overseas.

The reason I finally decided to take a look at what Robert had to offer was because the man who was insistent that he had what it takes to make the grade in this country was Frank McLintock, the erudite former Arsenal star who knows a good player when he sees one.

Frank said that he would send me several video recordings of Robert in action but I told him that wasn't good enough—I wanted to see him in the flesh. Because he had already won 27 full international caps, I didn't want the lad coming over here thinking that he was on trial. All I wanted was for him to have a look at us and vice versa.

Despite the obvious communication problems, Robert really impressed me during a brief spell training with the senior squad; he looked a very good player. I obtained permission for him to play in a reserve fixture against Sunderland at Roker Park and although the match was a real ding-dong affair, he did exceptionally well. I still had my reservations about his ability to settle in this country but I decided to press ahead with the deal and Robert signed for Everton after he had played for Poland against Northern Ireland in Belfast.

Robert made his senior debut in the first leg of the Northern Area ZDS final against Leeds United at Elland Road. He scored one, made one and was an instant hit with those supporters who had travelled across the Pennines.

Few players could have handled such a traumatic change in lifestyle better than did Robert and I would like to think that he has now settled in at Everton. If he picks up the language side of the things as swiftly as he has the football side, he'll encounter very few problems in the years ahead.

The big danger with foreign players is that the English game could well find itself flooded with individuals of dubious quality simply because they are on offer at what, at first glance, would appear to be bargain prices. The important thing to remember is that the fee has to be smaller because whenever a manager in this country signs a player from abroad, he is taking a calculated gamble which could backfire on him at any moment.

The quality of some of those foreigners currently on offer is indisputable but it is impossible to say whether or not they will adapt to a totally alien environment. I paid £450,000 for Robert and although his natural ability would suggest that he is worth considerably more, I believe that figure to be just about right. I hope he turns out to be a bargain.

I have always considered myself to be somewhat fortunate when chasing new players because, in the past, I have usually succeeded in getting my man. Unfortunately, that was not the case in the summer of 1991 when my attempts to persuade Derby County's Dean Saunders to move to Goodison Park proved to be unsuccessful. I was bitterly disappointed not to secure the services of a player I have long admired, particularly as the negotiations seemed to drag on for an eternity.

Because most of the people connected with County were preoccupied with the sale of the club, it was difficult to lodge—and have accepted—a formal bid. When we were eventually asked to submit written bids, I even went so far as to drive down to the Baseball Ground to hand in my sealed envelope. It was just a little touch which I hoped would help underline my desire to bring Dean to Everton. We had agreed to meet Derby's asking price of £2.9 million, an enormous sum of money which, I admit, was considerably more than I wanted to pay. However, I didn't baulk at the price, or consider withdrawing my interest, because I had decided that Dean was the player I wanted; in my eyes he was the right choice.

Even though I kept reading in the press that the whole thing was cut and dried and that Dean would definitely be playing for Everton Football Club the following season, I never once felt totally confident that I would manage to get his name on a contract. It would have been stupid (and naïve) for me to have believed that he was Goodison-bound because he is a top quality footballer and when a man of his stature becomes available for transfer demand will always outstrip supply. It was inevitable that several of the leading clubs would be interested in buying Dean—whether they were prepared to admit it or not.

As soon as I opened negotiations with Dean himself it became crystal clear that his biggest concern was whom exactly he would be partnering in the Everton attack. I told him that he would have to leave that to me while pointing out that he was not the final piece in the jigsaw. Although I sensed that Dean was very interested in joining Everton I always got the feeling that he had a burning desire to play alongside Ian Rush for his club just as he does for his country. I could offer him many, many things but, sadly, I couldn't offer him that.

If it had been a straight fight between ourselves, Leeds United and Nottingham Forest, I would have backed us to win the day but, in the final count, the pull of Rush was always going to be the decisive factor if Liverpool decided to come in with an eleventh hour bid. I really didn't know whether or not Graeme Souness was preparing a late offer but I knew that if he was, I would face real problems.

I was in Switzerland, on our pre-season tour, when I heard the news that Dean had decided to join Liverpool. I was disappointed but, bearing in mind the fact that Dean's father had played for Liverpool back in the Fifties, I wasn't over-surprised. In 1987, when I signed Ian Snodin from Leeds United, I had beaten Liverpool to the punch; this time they had beaten me. In football it is always a case of you win some, you lose some. The lad made his decision and I wish him well—but not too well.

With the new season fast approaching, I had to put my disappointment behind me and look elsewhere. I desperately wanted a quality player and when it became clear that Peter Beardsley's future at Anfield was in some considerable doubt, I made my move.

I spoke to Graeme Souness about Peter's availability but, to be honest, I really thought that any proposed deal had died a death when it was announced that Ian Rush had sustained an achilles tendon injury and would be sidelined for several weeks. Although Graeme had bought Dean, I just couldn't see him sanctioning the sale of a top forward while his senior squad was below full-strength.

However, with our neighbours having pushed out the boat to sign Dean and Mark Wright it quickly became clear that they would accept the right sort of offer whether it came from Newcastle United, Leeds United . . . or Everton. I had no hesitation at all in meeting Liverpool's asking price of around £1 million because I had been a Peter Beardsley fan for a number of years. Peter is what I would label a young 30-year-old and if he manages to steer clear of serious injury there is no reason at all why he shouldn't still be performing at the very highest level in three or four years time.

Shortly after landing Peter, I bought Mark Ward and Alan Harper from Manchester City, so signing the former for the second time in his career and the latter for a third time. It is always nice to know what you are getting. I know both men so well that there was never any question of an unknown quantity.

The deal was all about timing because although Peter Reid was reluctant to sell the two lads he was in the process of preparing a big bid for Wimbledon's Keith Curle. I was looking to spend some of the money which had been made available to me, Peter was looking to bank as much cash as he could—so the deal went through.

Shortly before the 1991–92 season got underway it was announced that my Chairman, Sir Philip Carter, was to stand down after more than 13 years at the helm. I have the utmost respect for Sir Philip and the biggest compliment which I can pay him is to say that I will always remember him as the Chairman who gave his manager a public vote of confidence and actually meant it. He stuck by me when the going got tough and we both emerged to share some very good times together.

CHAPTER TWENTY-FOUR

Farewell, Kenny

When told that Kenny Dalglish had announced he was to retire from football, I was as shocked and surprised as the next man. Although Kenny and myself had been friendly for so many years, I had no inkling at all that he was ready to call it a day and so close one of the most memorable chapters in Liverpool's recent history. It was a real bombshell and one whose shock value even managed to eclipse the news that I was to leave Manchester City and return to Everton.

The departure of Kenny from Anfield would have been front page news irrespective of its timing but the fact that he chose to go at a point when his team's defence of the League Championship was nearing its climax and the all-Mersey FA Cup, fifth-round tie still had to be resolved served to add yet more intrigue to a sensational story.

Because Kenny announced his decision less than 48 hours after Everton and Liverpool had shared eight goals in an epic replay, people seemed to assume that I knew what was about to happen. Believe me, I didn't.

After that astonishing game at Goodison Park, Kenny gave no hints at all that it was to be his last game in charge. He was, perhaps, a little more subdued than usual but as his team had surrendered the lead on four occasions, I didn't find that surprising in the least. If my team had been in front four times on the ground of our most fierce rivals and still failed to secure victory, I would have been subdued too!

I still don't know why Kenny decided that he had had enough—I don't need to know the reasons behind his decision because whatever they may be, they were good enough for him so they should be good enough for everybody else. For 14 years, Kenny Dalglish gave his body and soul to Liverpool Football Club; he lived and breathed the place. His contribution to the club has been so immense that I don't believe anyone has the right to question his motives. Those people who felt moved to criticise his decision should be ashamed of themselves. Instead of asking, "Why?", they should have been saying, "Thank you for everything."

At the press conference which was called to break the news of Kenny's retirement, he said that he simply felt the time to be right to break away from professional football; for once, he was placing his own interests before that of the club which he had served so magnificently.

In the two weeks which followed, the newspapers were full of articles which sought to unearth the story behind the story. No-one seemed to be satisfied with Kenny's explanation or the reasons which he had given. Theories ranging from the bizarre to the quite ridiculous were bandied about and the man's integrity was called into question time and time again. I just couldn't believe some of the things I was reading and hearing. Why was it that no-one seemed to believe him? After being respected and idolised for so many years, Kenny was suddenly being painted as someone who had a terrible secret to hide. Almost overnight his reputation was blackened.

If Kenny had left Liverpool and then, a few weeks later, accepted the job of manager at another leading club, I would have understood the criticism which was directed at him, but he didn't do that.

The main bone of contention seemed to be the timing of his retirement coming as it did so near to the end of the season. The timing may have seemed odd to many people but obviously not to Kenny himself.

I do not believe for one second that Kenny decided to go on the spur of the moment. It must have been a very difficult decision and one which was reached only after a great deal of careful thought and soul-searching. You don't leave a job like that simply because your team has failed to win one game. It was obviously something which he had been thinking about for several weeks.

Aren't football managers allowed to be a little selfish once in a while? Why shouldn't he place his family and his own well-being and peace of mind above his job? I can see absolutely nothing wrong with that at all. I can fully understand why it was he felt he needed a break from football. The job of a football manager has undergone a subtle change in recent years. The suggestion is that there is a great deal more pressure on the man at the top but that is a word I don't like to use when discussing my profession. There is more hype about the job these days and that is something which many managers feel very uncomfortable about.

I don't know whether Kenny will ever return to football management or whether he will miss the daily involvement with the game—only time will tell. I do know that many, many people suspected that he would take a short break and then make a swift return. At the time of writing these words, that has not happened so who knows what the future will hold for him?

I think the acid test came in the summer of 1991 when the job of Celtic manager was up for grabs following the departure of Billy McNeill. I believe that if Kenny had wanted to take an extended holiday and then go back into management, he would have shown an interest in that vacant post. If any club could have tempted him to come out of retirement, it would have been Celtic.

Four months after he left Anfield for the last time, there was much speculation that Kenny was to take over at Marseille but as that particular story was sustained by rumours rather than facts, I feel it would be unfair to discuss it.

I have only spoken to Kenny once since he retired from the game and that was after the pair of us had played in a testimonial game for Roly Howard, the long-serving manager of Merseyside club, Marine. We exchanged a few pleasantries but I did not march up to him and ask whether he was missing football or whether he regretted his decision. With the greatest of respect that is something which will be asked by those Liverpool supporters he will meet in the months ahead and not a topic which should be raised by a fellow professional.

While I fully respect Kenny's decision to put football behind him, I have to say that it will be a terrible loss if he does ultimately decide that his future lies elsewhere. The game lost George Best and the biggest compliment which I can pay Kenny is to say that I hope it doesn't lose him. It is vitally important that those players who have graced the sport with dignity and style maintain at least some level of contact with football. Men like Bobby Charlton, Denis Law, Johann Cruyff, Franz Beckenbauer and Jimmy Greaves are still involved with the game in one capacity or another and it can only be to the benefit of the game that these elder statesmen continue to pass on their immense knowledge.

It may well be that Kenny will decide he wishes to return in another role, perhaps in a job which is of a less intense nature. Let's hope so. I think the important thing is that everyone should accept

Kenny's reasons for quitting Liverpool, leave him alone, and give him the breathing space which he so obviously requires.

I don't know why it is that people expected Kenny to carry on forever at Anfield. The history books show that Liverpool not only produce highly successful managers but that they also change them, for one reason or another, at regular intervals. During my first spell in charge at Everton between 1981 and 1987, I found myself in direct competition with three different men—Bob Paisley, Joe Fagan and then Kenny.

If Kenny Dalglish does not return to football it will be a disappointment but nothing should be allowed to detract from his achievements—both on and off the field of play. He was one of the greatest players this country has ever seen, or is ever likely to see. He was an unbelievably talented footballer who scored some great goals and who made some great goals. His partnership with Ian Rush was priceless to Liverpool and was very, very special indeed. He had many of the attributes of those players who are now regarded as the all-time greats (Best, Pele, Cruyff etc) and it is to his eternal credit that he managed to sustain his brilliance for so many years.

To be honest, I must admit that I was surprised when he was appointed as Liverpool manager in the wake of the Heysel Stadium tragedy in 1985. I hadn't really considered him as managerial material and, like most people, I thought that the task of following Joe Fagan would probably be handed to either Phil Neal or Roy Evans. Like his departure, his appointment came right out of the blue.

In many respects, I suppose that he had a head start because he was not only inheriting a great side but was still playing in a great side. On top of that, he had the support of an established and totally professional back-room staff, not only at dressing-room level but also at administrative level. I have always felt fortunate to have Jim Greenwood behind me at Everton and I am sure that Kenny felt the same way about Peter Robinson. It is absolutely essential that a manager has a close working relationship with "the man upstairs" and I count myself fortunate to have forged an alliance with some of the best in the business. Jim at Goodison, John Howarth at Blackburn Rovers, Fernando Ochoa at Athletic Bilbao and Bernard Halford at Manchester City are not only astute businessmen but also great footballing enthusiasts.

Bearing in mind that Kenny was taking control of England's best side, I don't suppose he suffered from not having served a managerial apprenticeship at a smaller club beforehand. I was not surprised that he proved to be a successful manager because it never surprises me to see the managers of that club winning trophies. I am not saying that anyone could walk in off the streets, assume command and be successful because that would be ridiculous but the continuity at Liverpool is such that the new man at the helm usually finds that he has little to do in terms of building up a suitable squad.

But for the canny, perceptive judgement of Bob Paisley, Kenny would never have been a Liverpool player in the first place. Shortly after Kevin Keegan had left Anfield for Hamburg, at a time when I was playing for Birmingham City, I bumped into Bob in Malton, Yorkshire. He said that two players were under consideration as a replacement for Keegan—Kenny and Trevor Francis, who was a team-mate of mine at St Andrews. I told him that Trevor was one of the most gifted players I had ever seen. He took no notice and promptly signed Kenny which, bearing in mind the injury problems which plagued Trevor throughout his career, was obviously a very good, and astute decision.

Kenny's departure was so sudden that it was inevitable Liverpool would have to appoint a caretaker manager while they searched for a full-time successor. Ronnie Moran was the obvious choice but, my word, he took over at a bad time in terms of Liverpool's immediate programme. His opening eight days in charge could not have been any more demanding, with games against Luton Town on Kenilworth Road's infamous plastic surface, Everton at Goodison in an FA Cup second replay and then Arsenal at Anfield. As fate would have it, Liverpool lost all three fixtures.

It quickly became apparent that Ronnie did not want the job on a permanent basis, which gave rise to speculation that John Toshack was to return home from Spain to rejoin the club where he made his name as a prolific striker. It is still rather unclear as to whether Liverpool did officially approach John but if they did, I wasn't too surprised that he decided to remain in San Sebastian. I think John realises that when he does decide to return to England, it will take some time to readjust because he has been away for a long time now.

Traditionally, when a manager of Liverpool steps down, there is no period of transition following the appointment of a successor because the new man is simply told to carry on the good work. I think it could be a little different this time because, while the present Liverpool side is still very formidable, there is some rebuilding and restructuring to be done.

Everyone knows that Liverpool have always gone out and bought the best players but this changing of personnel has tended to be a gradual, rather than a dramatic, process; big-name players have arrived at the rate of about one or two per season. At the moment, several of the members of the club's recognised senior side are reaching—how shall I put it?—maturity. I'm thinking of men like Rush, Whelan and Grobbelaar. It is difficult to replace one famous name, let alone two or three.

Liverpool are one of the wealthiest clubs in the Football League but even they are not in a position to go out and buy four new players at a cost of nine or ten million pounds. Even they must work within a sensible financial framework. Having said that, you are better off placing your trust in a very good 30-year-old player than in a youngster who is not up to scratch.

Liverpool must have been absolutely delighted to have persuaded Graeme Souness to leave Glasgow Rangers for Anfield. They were obviously looking for someone who had been successful at a big club and who had had strong Liverpool connections—he fits that bill perfectly.

Another thing which, I am sure, would have been uppermost in the minds of the Liverpool directors was the need to find a man who would prove to be a popular choice with the supporters. It was never going to be easy replacing a legend like Kenny Dalglish but they have done well to find a natural leader and a born winner.

Graeme was a tremendous player and he has carried forward into management the uncompromising attitude he always displayed out on the field of play. I wish him well and I hope he succeeds in picking up the trophies which Everton miss out on!

The arrival of another top-class manager at Liverpool doesn't make my job at Everton any more difficult. When I joined the club from Blackburn Rovers in 1981, Liverpool were the team to beat. A decade later nothing at all has changed. As I said, I think Graeme faces a tricky task in getting together a squad with which he will feel totally happy. Like every manager of a leading club, he may find it rather difficult to move on those players he feels are surplus to requirements.

Despite the fact that Graeme, like myself, has much hard work ahead of him, I believe Liverpool to be once again in very good hands.

CHAPTER TWENTY-FIVE

Nil Satis Nisi Optimum

It will surprise no-one to learn that as I sit here in the summer of 1991, I am optimistic about the immediate future of Everton Football Club.

As I said earlier, the fact that so many people told me that I was wrong to leave Manchester City and return to Goodison Park has only served to double my determination to work tirelessly in an attempt to put the club back where it belongs—at the very summit of English, and hopefully European, football. I don't need to be told that it won't be easy, because to achieve my ambitious target I know full well that I must overcome many problems. It is a very big challenge, but one I relish.

The supporters, players and directors have tasted success in recent years and I know how desperate they are to see a repeat performance in the seasons ahead. Once a football club has been universally acclaimed as the best, it is very difficult, if not impossible, to settle for second-best. I don't want to be anything other than a winner.

When I took over at Everton in 1981, the supporters displayed great patience. Because of the success which the club enjoyed in the mid-Eighties, I do not expect them to be as patient this time around. I know that I am working on a much shorter time-scale and that progress must be seen to have been achieved, if not overnight, then very quickly. I don't mind that; supporters have every right to be impatient.

During my first spell in charge it took me three years to turn the tide—hopefully it won't take that long this time. It is always foolish to make promises in football so all I can say is that I shall give it my best shot. We had so many special moments between 1983 and 1987 and I want to experience those moments again.

One of my favourite (and most accurate) sayings over the past decade has been that any side which finishes above Liverpool in the First Division will stand a very, very good chance of winning the

League Championship. While I do still believe that to be true, there are now perhaps two sides any would-be title-winners must overhaul—Liverpool *AND* Arsenal.

I do actually believe that things may become a lot tighter over the next few seasons and that clubs like Leeds United and Manchester City may well come into the reckoning. If that does happen, it can only be good for English football.

Arsenal may still have their critics but, make no mistake, they are a very fine and competent footballing unit. To go through an entire League programme and lose just one game, as they did during the 1990–91 season, is quite remarkable. Arsenal may be more efficient than they are attractive but they are so well organised that it is no wonder they have done so well over the past three years.

Even so, I still have this sneaking suspicion that Liverpool will still be *THE* team to beat over the next two or three years. Graeme Souness has much rebuilding to do at Anfield but the club's backbone is so strong that I am sure they will continue to pose a major threat. Try as I might, I just can't look any further than Liverpool despite Arsenal's tremendous progress.

Like Everton, Liverpool will be very annoyed that they didn't win anything at all last season. It is very rare that the two Merseyside clubs have nothing but footballs to display on their traditional pre-season team photographs. The absence of silverware on both photos will be a painful reminder of a campaign which promised so much yet yielded so little.

By inviting me back to the club, the Everton directors have placed an enormous amount of faith in me and I don't want to let them down in any way at all. Those people who were bold enough to appoint me for a second time know me as a man and they know me as a manager; they know how I work.

They want a job doing and they want it doing quickly. If the money I feel I need is made available to me and I am able to bring to the club the players I think we need, then I feel we will have a fairly good chance of achieving success.

However, if my judgement proves to be faulty and things do not go well, no-one will need to tell me when it is time to go because I will know.